Italy Under Victor Emmanuel
by Carlo Arrivabene

Address:
HardPress
8345 NW 66TH ST #2561
MIAMI FL 33166-2626
USA
Email: info@hardpress.net

Ital.

$19 \frac{5}{12}$

Anwaben.

ITALY

UNDER

VICTOR EMMANUEL.

VOL. II.

ITALY

UNDER

VICTOR EMMANUEL.

A PERSONAL NARRATIVE.

BY

COUNT CHARLES ARRIBAVENE.

IN TWO VOLUMES.
VOL. II.

LONDON:
HURST AND BLACKETT, PUBLISHERS,
SUCCESSORS TO HENRY COLBURN,
13, GREAT MARLBOROUGH STREET.
1862.

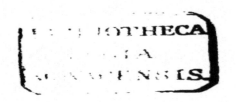

LONDON:
SAVILL AND EDWARDS, PRINTERS, CHANDOS STREET,
COVENT GARDEN.

CONTENTS

OF

VOLUME THE SECOND.

CHAPTER I.

PIEDMONT.

CHAPTER II.

THE LIBERATION OF SICILY.

CHAPTER III.

PALERMO AND MESSINA.

CHAPTER IV.

THE LANDING IN CALABRIA.

CHAPTER V.

CALABRIA.

CHAPTER VI.

GARIBALDI'S MARCH THROUGH CALABRIA AND BASILICATA.

CHAPTER VII.

THE LAST HALT IN GARIBALDI'S MARCH.

CHAPTER VIII

NAPLES UNDER GARIBALDI.

CHAPTER IX.

THE TWO ARMIES.

CHAPTER X.

MY IMPRISONMENT.

CHAPTER XI.

NAPLES UNDER THE NEW RULE.

CHAPTER XII.

NAPLES IN 1860.

CHAPTER XIII.

TRAITS OF NEAPOLITAN LIFE.

CHAPTER XIV.

THE FUTURE OF ITALY.

CHARTS.

ITALY

UNDER

VICTOR EMMANUEL.

CHAPTER I.

PIEDMONT.

Papal Excommunication—Opinion of a young Priest on the subject
—Opening of the Sardinian Parliament in 1860—The Royal
Speech—Cavour's Return to Power—Great Effects from little
Causes—Parliamentary Discussions on the Cession of Savoy
and Nice—Attacks of the Opposition on Cavour—A Conversa-
tion with Cavour at the Marchioness Rorà's—Explanation of
an apparent Contradiction—Social Habits of Italian Deputies
and Senators—Cavour's Parliamentary Ability—Society at
Turin—Victor Emmanuel at Home—Etiquette of the Sardi-
nian Court in former Times—The Ribands of a Russian "Am-
bassadress"—Journey of Victor Emmanuel through Central
Italy—Victor Emmanuel and his Suite on board the "Maria
Adelaide"—Count Cavour's opinion on Orders of Knighthood
—Rejoicings in the Towns and Villages of Central Italy—Preparations for Garibaldi's Expedition to Sicily—Cavour's Policy
—Departure of Garibaldi—His Letter to Victor Emmanuel.

WHILST the Bull of Excommunication against the
Italians who had either directly or indirectly taken
part in the regeneration of the Papal States, was
posted up in Rome at Campo di Fiori and at Monte

Citorio, Victor Emmanuel for the first time addressed the representatives of 12,000,000 of people from the hall of the Palazzo Madama. The King had not been much affected by the threats fulminated from the Vatican. Following the example of his ancestor, Amadeus II., who disputed for thirty years with Rome, and conquered in the end, he wisely adopted that line of policy which alone could secure the happiness of the Italian nation. On the 2nd of April, 1860, therefore, two hundred and seventy deputies, and as many senators, were present at the opening of the Sardinian Parliament, in spite of the spiritual weapons of the Holy Father. The news that a Bull of Excommunication had been issued from the Roman Cancellaria reached Bologna on the previous day, while I was leaving that city for Turin. To say the truth, the effect produced by its publication was far from being alarming to the friends of the Italian cause. Every person to whom I spoke on the subject was actuated by one sole sentiment—a feeling of pity for the poor old man whose power of punishing fell so short of his inclination. The time has gone by in which spiritual arms carried terror into the palaces and camps of the proudest princes, as well as amongst the masses of the people.

"What do you think of the excommunication?" asked Marquis Pepoli of a young priest who entered at the Parma station the railway carriage in which I was seated.

"I think," answered the priest, " that the Pope has been very wrong; for there is no divine law which prevents people getting rid of governments they do not like.   Moreover, religion has everything to gain in going back to its former simplicity.   St. Peter, and many of the Vicars of Christ who came after him, as you know, had no temporal power to exercise."

"Well," interposed I, "but do you believe that there are many of the Italian clergy who share your opinions?"

"Yes, I do," answered the priest; "not, of course, amongst the older of my colleagues; but priests of my age are by no means opposed to the regeneration of our country, nor are they inclined to support the pretensions of the Roman Court, as far as the temporal power is concerned."

On my arrival at Turin, I found that the opinion of the young priest was shared by the majority of the people I met.   Everybody was abusing the Cardinals and Bishops, and many had even made up their minds to dispense with the Holy Communion and confession, should the clergy follow the strict injunctions of the Papal Bull.   Although Piedmont is a Catholic country, ten years of liberal institutions had borne their fruit, and the benefit of this good example had already begun to show itself in the other parts of Italy.   It may seem an exaggeration, but the Bull of Excommunication was perhaps the very thing which gave the last shock to the influence of the Pope-King.   From that day, every intelligent and unbigoted Italian, though remaining a Catholic, ceased to be a partisan of the temporal power.

The opening of the Sardinian Parliament was, indeed, a national solemnity.   During the previous week, the railroads had brought to Turin thousands of people, and the crowd of visitors was so great that to find a room was next to impossible. Had it not been for the kindness of a friend, I should have had to spend the night *sub Jove,* or at best under a portico. On that day, the streets of Turin, as always is the case during popular festivals, were elegantly decorated with numberless banners, pennons, festoons of flowers, and similar ornaments. All the main streets were full of people with joyful faces, hastening to the Piazza Castello, and all animated by the thought of greeting the *Re galantuomo.* As eleven o'clock struck, Victor Emmanuel, followed by a brilliant Staff, alighted, and ascended the grand staircase of the Palazzo Madama, where the deputies, senators, and about a thousand other persons, who, like myself, had been fortunate enough to get cards of admission, were waiting for him.

A tremendous cheer outside made us aware that the King had entered the lobby of the Palace. Victor Emmanuel is not handsome, but there is something in his soldier-like face, in his air of frankness and his martial bearing, which secures at once the sympathy of those who look on him. He entered the great hall with a firm step, and ascended the throne, bowing right and left, amidst shouts of "*Evviva il Re!*" The cheering of the house was instantly echoed by the shouts of the crowd outside.

When silence had been restored, Farini, who had been appointed Minister of the Interior, called on the new deputies to take the oaths of allegiance according to the constitutional laws of the country. This being done, the King began to read the Royal Speech. It was a noble and dignified oration, calculated to assure the Italians that both he and his Government were prepared to meet whatever events the future might have in store to secure the political unity of the country. No pen can describe the thrill of enthusiasm which ran through the audience when Victor Emmanuel, in firm, distinct, and ringing tones, pronounced the famous words—

"True to the creed of my fathers, and, like them, constant in my homage to the Supreme Head of the Church, whenever it may happen that the ecclesiastical authority employs spiritual arms in support of temporal interests, I shall find in my steadfast conscience and in the very traditions of my ancestors the power to maintain civil liberty in its integrity, and with it my own authority—that authority for which I hold myself accountable to God and my people only."

These words, and the end of the speech, in which the King said that Italy was thenceforth to be for the Italians, were the two passages most applauded by the audience. The outburst was one both of gratitude and hope—gratitude for what had been achieved, hope for what was still to be done.

In these enthusiastic manifestations Cavour had his share; for the Italians had not forgotten how much they owed to him. Towards the end of January, 1860, Rattazzi and his colleagues had resigned, and Cavour had been charged by the King to form a new Administration. Within the short period of two months, the Count saw the annexation of Central

Italy accomplished, and was now able to open Parliament, increased by the representatives of the newly-annexed provinces. A curious circumstance hastened the downfall of Rattazzi's Ministry. It will be remembered that at the beginning of 1860 the European Powers proposed to have the Italian question decided by a Congress. It appears that the English Cabinet expressed its wish that Sardinia should be represented at the diplomatic meeting by Count Cavour. The Count was still at his country house of Leri, when a Piedmontese General was sent by Rattazzi to see whether he was inclined to accept the mission. Although at one time great friends, Rattazzi and Cavour were not then on the best terms, and disagreed in their politics, especially on the question of annexation. The appeal made by Commendatore Rattazzi to his former colleague, however, was not rejected, and the Count answered, that on certain conditions he was ready to accept. The most important of those conditions was, that the dictatorial power which had been conferred by the Chambers upon the Executive, at the breaking out of the war in April, 1859, should cease, and that Parliament should be convoked within a week.

Having sent this message to Rattazzi, Cavour went to Turin, in order to see the Ministers in case his proposal should be accepted by them. For many years he had been on terms of intimate friendship with the representative of a foreign Power which, without being actuated by selfish motives, was, and still is, the constant friend of Italy. This diplomatist Count Cavour went to consult on his arrival from Leri, and sent word to the General to join him there as soon as he had obtained Rattazzi's answer. The messenger returned, but the answer was not altogether satisfactory. Rattazzi said he would convoke Parliament, but declined to fix the day. Count Cavour was not the man to yield on such a question, and he therefore made up his mind to break off the negotiation. He was urged, however, by the foreign Minister to put his precise conditions on paper, that the officer might take them to Rattazzi, and avoid any further misunderstanding. Cavour, however, not wishing that any document in his handwriting should be laid before the Cabinet, requested the General to write from his dictation; but from some cause or other he declined. The Ambassador himself then volunteered to become the secretary of the Count on that occasion; and the ultimatum of Cavour having been written, it was conveyed to Rattazzi, who was then discussing with his colleagues the conditions insisted upon by the great Italian statesman. He at once recognised the handwriting of the diplomatist who had written it. An uproar ensued in the Council chamber, the Ministers observing that, had they accepted the ultimatum of Cavour, they would have yielded to foreign pressure, and that it was a contrivance for forcing them out of power. It was in vain for the General to explain the imbroglio : they refused to listen to the explanation, and decided to resign. The King, who was convinced that Cavour was the only statesman who could satisfactorily solve the question of Central Italy, accepted the resignation of Rattazzi's and La Marmora's Ministry on the 19th

of January, charging, as I have already stated, Count
Cavour to form a new Cabinet.

That Victor Emmanuel was not mistaken, was fully
proved by the result of the vote in the Æmilian
provinces. In Tuscany, the same enthusiasm prevailed; for, out of a population of 1,806,940, as many
as 386,445 voted for the Annexation; while only
14,925 threw in their suffrages for a separate State.
To the policy of Cavour, therefore, must in the main
be attributed the formation of the newly-enlarged
kingdom, and the presence of the Deputies of Central
Italy in its Parliament—a result in itself sufficient to
immortalize him.

The triumph of the Sardinian Premier, however,
was obtained at a great national sacrifice. Shortly
after the Deputies had left Palazzo Madama, and
assembled at the place of their usual meeting, they
were made aware that Savoy and Nice were to be
ceded to France. This sad fact had been already
anticipated by some Italian politicians; for it was
known that when, two months before, General
Dabormida, the Minister for Foreign Affairs during
Rattazzi's Administration, went to Paris to settle the
war expenses claimed by France, a hint was thrown
out that, if those two provinces were made over to
her, the sum would not be asked for. Cavour was
subsequently induced to consent to the sacrifice
as the only means of removing the opposition of
Louis Napoleon to the annexation of Central
Italy.

The first discussion on the famous treaty of cession
arose on the 19th of April from Garibaldi's question

with respect to Nice. At one o'clock, the galleries of the Chamber were crammed with people ; for it was known that Garibaldi intended to attack the advisers of the Crown for having betrayed the interests of the nation in consenting to the cession. The scene I witnessed that day will never be effaced from my memory. There was something very affecting when the great Italian General rose, and in a stern voice began to read the fifth article of the Constitution, by which no sale or barter can be made of any part of the State without the sanction of Parliament. " The vote which has now been put to the populations of Savoy and Nice," pursued Garibaldi, " is neither legal nor valid without the sanction of the Chambers. Nice came into the power of the House of Savoy in 1388, and in 1391 a compact was made with Count Amadeus VII., in virtue of which the Count could not part with either the city or any portion of the territory or people ; but, in the event of his releasing his Nizzards from their vote of allegiance, the latter were free in their choice of a new Sovereign, without being therefore amenable to the charge of rebellion. The treaty of the 24th of March, by which Nice is ceded to France, is not only an infraction of the old charter of Nice, but also a violation of the right of nationality. We are told that the exchange of two small Transalpine provinces against Æmilia and Tus- cany is a desirable bargain ; but the sale of a people is always a deplorable transaction, and the Italians of the Centre have a poor earnest of the estimation in which the rights and wishes of the people are held. If the Government reckons on the vote of the populations, why should the vote of Nice be appointed for the 15th, while that of Savoy is to come off on the 22nd? The moral pressure now exercised upon Nice by the French police renders an appeal to universal suffrage a mere mockery." Other representatives of the provinces which were about to be transferred to a foreign Power also spoke of the intrigues of the French police, and of Luboni's manifesto, published at Nice; but their indignant protests were of no avail. This first parliamentary struggle on the cession of Nice ended in a majority against Garibaldi and the Opposition; and the treaty itself, having been discussed by the Deputies on the 26th of May, was passed by a great majority.

It was in this legislative contest that Cavour displayed all the resources of his oratory. To Guerrazzi, who had endeavoured to establish a comparison between him (Cavour) and the Earl of Clarendon, when the latter sold Dunkirk, the Sardinian Premier replied with all that readiness which was one of the characteristics of his genius, and said :—" The Honourable Guerrazzi read me an historical lecture, and reminded me of Lord Clarendon, who, on account of the sale of Dunkirk, was impeached by the Commons and banished by the King. I must, in my turn, remind him that, if Clarendon had added new shires to the Crown of England, he would not have been so ill-requited either by King Charles II. or by his Parliament. Clarendon fell; but Signor Guerrazzi ought to remember who were the men by whom his ruin was compassed. They were the men of that famous clique which bore the name of 'Cabal'—unprincipled, selfish, inconsistent men, who played the tribune in the street and the flatterer at court. Those were the men who ousted Clarendon — the Cliffords, Ashleys, Buckinghams, Arlingtons, and Lauderdales." Alluding to the pathetic lamentations of Deputy Bertani, Cavour confessed that he fully sympathized with the speaker's grief, but that the interests of Italy required the sanction of the treaty. Rattazzi, and other more or less eminent Opposition orators, took part in that solemn discussion; but Count Cavour sat on the Ministerial bench with a mournful expression of countenance, cold as an image of destiny, and stern as a reason of state. The *consummatum est* had been pronounced; and nothing remained but to bow the head, and accept with resignation the sacrifice which had been imposed on Italy. This was what the majority of the Sardinian Chambers did, with a heavy heart.

The vote was strongly urged as an imperative political necessity, and as such it was carried. As for Victor Emmanuel, it is stated that when he heard that the cradle of his ancestors was asked for by his powerful ally, tears came into his eyes. No doubt he was prepared for the sacrifice, for he well knew of the arrangements of Plombières; but, as the peace left Venetia to Austria, he had hoped that the sacrifice would be spared.

Amongst the various biographies of Count Cavour recently published, one appeared in the *Quarterly Review* of 1861, which I consider by far the best that has yet been written. The author of that remarkable article, in vindicating the memory of the

Italian Premier as regards this question—which has
been either imperfectly understood or purposely dis-
torted by his political adversaries—states that Count
Cavour "had a settled conviction that Italy would one
day regain her lost provinces." This statement is entirely correct. A few days before the debate on Garibaldi's motion, I was invited to dine at the Marchioness
Rorà's. Cavour was one of the party, and, although
he knew the storm that was about to burst over his
head, he observed, in speaking of the cession of Nice
and Savoy, that he was convinced he had fulfilled
his duty, for to have refused the demand of the French
Emperor would have been tantamount to renouncing,
perhaps for ever, the unity of Italy. Though the
great statesman never reverted to that sad event without a pang, I ventured to ask him, when dinner was
over, some questions upon the matter. Taking me
apart, Cavour entered into some of the details of
the question. "How can England complain," said
he, "when M. de Persigny actually informed the
Queen's Government that, in case of Piedmont increasing its territory, the security of France would
require the annexation of Savoy and Nice, should
the majority of their population vote for the annexation? When I assured Sir James Hudson that
the cession of those two provinces would not take
place, I spoke in good faith; but matters have since
changed."

After thus explaining the position in which the
Government of Victor Emmanuel had been placed by
the course of events in Central Italy, he suddenly put
a stop to our conversation by a phrase which distinctly

implied that at least Nice might one day or other be restored to Italy.

Much was said at the time about the apparent discrepancy between the facts of the case and the answer made by the Marquis Serra (the Governor of Chambéry) to the Savoy deputation, as well as the assurance subsequently given by Count Cavour to Sir James Hudson, to the effect that there was no engagement whatever between France and Sardinia respecting the annexation of Savoy, and that it was not the intention of the King of Sardinia to yield, sell, or exchange that province. Those who wish to depreciate the memory of the great statesman say, "How could Cavour direct the Marquis Serra to deny on the 29th of January, and on the 7th of February deny himself, the existing treaty, whilst at the meeting held at Geneva on the 3rd, M. Fazy announced that the treaty of cession had been signed at Paris on the 27th of the previous month?" Now, any conscientious man who will take the trouble to examine the facts will doubtless come to a contrary conclusion. Cavour reassumed power on the 21st of January, 1860. It was therefore reasonable to suppose that the conversation he had with the English Minister at Turin on the subject did not take place until some days afterwards. The convention for the cession of those two provinces, moreover, could not have been concluded without long discussions; and it is impossible to believe that the French Government asked the price of its tacit assent to the annexation of Central Italy so soon after Cavour came into power. I think it is more in accordance with the natural

course of political affairs to assume that Cavour, on
again accepting office, examined the real state of the
question, and afterwards acquired the melancholy
conviction that without the sacrifice of Savoy and
Nice the annexation of Æmilia and Tuscany could
not be effected. The apparent contradiction is in this
way explained. At the beginning of February, the
Sardinian Premier believed himself to be in a position
to carry out his plan without any territorial sacrifice ;
but, being subsequently convinced of the impossibility
of doing so, he felt obliged to yield to the Imperial
demand. The alleged assertion of M. Fazy, that the
convention was signed on the 27th of January, is ma-
nifestly based on an error; for the treaty bears date
the 24th of March.

I have no doubt that when the history of this transaction is unreservedly brought before Europe, the
memory of the Italian Minister will be fully vindi-
cated. At any rate, there are but few politicians in
Italy, or perhaps in Europe, who would deny that, in
ceding Savoy and Nice to France, Count Cavour acted
upon sound principles of policy. Without that sacrifice,
the unity of the country, now almost accomplished,
would probably have been indefinitely postponed.

Although the parliamentary session of 1860 may
almost be considered a new one, owing to the number of members returned by the annexed provinces,
the Sardinian Chamber of Deputies did not look like
an assembly of inexperienced politicians. The greater
number of its members were the old deputies of the
Subalpine Parliament, already trained to political life,
and able to set a good example to their new compa-

nions. Most of the latter were known to the former, as some had spent the years of their exile at Turin, and had co-operated with Piedmontese patriots in the triumph of the national cause. The most courteous and friendly spirit, therefore, animated the daily intercourse of the deputies. In the Italian Chambers, many members who widely differ in their political opinions are nevertheless personal friends. When the sitting is over, they meet and talk in the lobbies, the news-room, or the library, without caring whether they belong to the Left or to the Right, or, according to the phraseology of the English House of Commons, whether they are Opposition or Ministerial members. Of course there were, and still are, some rabid politicians, who look with animosity upon their political opponents; there are also a few conceited fellows, who think themselves great authorities because they were so regarded in the discussions of the apothecary's shop or café of their village, and who believe they were returned to Parliament to read a heavy speech once a-year, and to be silent during the rest of the session. But these are the exceptions. The majority of the Italian deputies are young and active men, animated by mutual goodwill, and well-informed, both on the questions which belong exclusively to their country, and on those which affect Europe generally.

As the town of Turin affords scarcely any good society, the deputies and senators pass their evenings at the café or under the porticoes. It is there that the subject which stands for discussion in Parliament next day is examined and canvassed, as in London it would be at the Reform Club or the Carlton. The

chances of the ensuing vote are talked over at Fiorio's
or at the Nazionale Café, with that quickness and
natural intelligence which belong to most Italians.
With the exception of some solemn individuals, who
deliver their harangues in a style more like that of
bad actors than of cultivated statesmen, the speeches
one hears at the Carignano Palace are uttered in an
unpretending manner, especially by the members belonging to the Northern provinces.   This simplicity
has been a little spoiled of late by the deputies from
the South ; but it is to be hoped that the latter will
shortly learn that clear and simple manner of speaking
without which there is no true eloquence.   Even on
this ground, the death of Cavour has been a great
calamity.   No one of the members of the Italian Parliament had a more perfect standard of practical rhe-
toric.   His speeches, though not always elegant in a
literary point of view, were invariably concise and
luminous, and never failed to go straight to the essential
point of the question.   On hearing him, no matter on
what subject, the comprehensiveness of his mind
made itself felt amidst the quick and fluent forms of
his oratory.   Rattazzi, Farini, Minghetti, Mellana,
Mancini, Chiaves, and Tecchio, were perhaps, after
him, the most able orators of the Sardinian Parliament
in the year 1860.   Avvocato Brofferio and Professor
Ferrari are undoubtedly more brilliant ; but their eloquence speaks to the imagination rather than to the
reason.

As I have already stated, social life in Piedmont is
far from being pleasant.   Turinese ladies are generally
imperfectly educated, and they husband their scanty

income by practising strict economy, which does not allow of their drawing-rooms being often opened to visitors. The proud aristocracy of the Piedmontese capital, far from mixing with the commonalty, as in other Italian towns, does not associate or marry with any lower class. A Turinese or Genoese nobleman would think himself humiliated were his daughter to marry a gentleman without title. With a few exceptions, the nobility of Turin are very bigoted, and therefore completely under the influence of that section of the priesthood belonging to the Ultramontanist party. Marchionesses and Countesses pass their lives at the fireside with two or three priests and a few *Codini*, whose business it is to abuse the Liberal Government and the institutions of the country, and to pray that God may, as they say, touch the heart of the King, and lead him into the path of salvation. There are now and then official receptions of Ministers and diplomatists; but there are very few ladies at Turin who can be said to receive. Before 1848, the political *salons* were more flourishing than they are now. The Palaces of the Duchess St. Clement—an aunt of Cavour—those of the Countesses Sclopis and Valperga di Masino, as well as that of Count Balbo, and many others, were then regularly opened either to the political or literary society of the Piedmontese capital. But, strange to say, since liberal institutions have developed both the moral and material resources of the country, the social intercourse of high-minded people, instead of increasing, has rather diminished. Indeed, the only *salons* worthy of notice are those of the Countess Alfieri ; of the Marchionesses Rorà, Arconati, D'Adda,

and Doria; of Madame Peruzzi and Madame Cornero.
At the house of the Countess Alfieri, a niece of Cavour,
the most enlightened society of Turin may be met. It
is said that the Countess's illustrious uncle did not disdain to talk with her on the most important political
questions, and had a great esteem for her opinion. The
salon of the Marchioness Rorà—a half-sister of the well-
known authoress, Princess Christiana Belgiojoso-Tri-
vulzio, and the wife of one of the most distinguished
men of the Turinese aristocracy—is a sort of neutral
ground, where people of different opinions meet in
friendly communion. That of the Marchioness Arco-
nati-Visconti is much frequented by the moderate
Liberal party. You meet there Massimo D'Azeglio,
Manzoni, Count John Arrivabene, Cibrario, the Marquis Alfieri-Sostegno, Massari, and others. The receptions of Madame Peruzzi and Madame Cornero are
likewise almost exclusively political, and are attended
by deputies, men of letters, and journalists.

It will be seen from this that Turin is not the most
pleasant city to live in. There are no public pro-
menades worth speaking of; for the Piazza d'Armi,
though enjoying the splendid scenery of Old Monte
Rosa, is only frequented by a few equipages during
the summer season. A club and several theatres, however, are to be found at Turin. The club is exceedingly good—so well regulated, indeed, that (though
on a smaller scale) it may match the best in Pall Mall
or St. James's-street. As for the theatres, they are
not very remarkable, although the Government allowance for singers and actors reaches a considerable
sum. But this deficiency in native dramatic per-

formances is explained by the fact that the Turinese are fonder of French than of Italian plays. And they are not altogether wrong; for, excepting the productions of Giacometti and D'Aste, and two or three of Fortio's, dramatic art in Italy has gradually fallen into decay.

The want of court patronage is another cause of this decline in the theatres of Turin from the brilliant position they occupied a few years ago. The Duchess of Genoa lives a retired life, and the King is fonder of military occupations and of country life than of operas and comedies. It can hardly be said that Victor Emmanuel lives at Turin at all. As soon as he can get rid of the cares of State, his Majesty goes to the Veneria, or to some other Royal villa, for the purpose of hunting or shooting with a few intimate friends. The habits of the King are in truth rather those of a country squire than of a sovereign. If any stranger were to meet him at the Veneria, he would scarcely believe that the man dressed in a velvet suit with a " wide-awake" on his head is the chief of the State. When in the country, Victor Emmanuel rises at four o'clock in the morning, and goes to the mountains with the few friends who always accompany him.

His three sons, Princes Umberto, Amadeo, and Otone, have been brought up in the same simple habits. The first is fond of military life, and has shown so much skill as a marksman as to have been appointed President of the National Rifle Association ; but he is said to have made great progress in his more scholastic studies, which begin at six in the morning, and last eight hours. The second son, although only sixteen, has devoted himself to scientific inquiries, with an earnestness rarely seen in youths belonging to princely houses. The youngest son was born a cripple; but he was so well nurtured in childhood that he is now quite straight, and is being educated for the navy, where his pleasant manners are already making him very popular. Victor Emmanuel takes great care of the education of his sons, whom he loves tenderly. Even when he is obliged to leave Piedmont, he receives almost daily the reports of their tutors.

" Mind," he said to Commendatore Buoncompagni, who had been appointed teacher of constitutional laws, " what I want from you above all else is, that you should make good citizens of my children."

The Sardinian Court, in matters of etiquette, has always been considered one of the strictest in Europe; but it has been greatly modified by recent events. There was a time—and by no means long ago—in which no one would have been admitted to the balls of the Court, had he not been able to show at least two centuries of nobility. Even foreign ladies were obliged to submit in the minutest particulars to the strict rules of the Court. There are many people at Turin who still remember the exchange of diplomatic notes between the Sardinian Minister of Foreign Affairs and Count Nesselrode about the dress of the Countess Obrescoff, the wife of the Russian Minister at Charles Albert's Court. The Countess was the handsomest lady in Turinese society, and therefore the most envied. According to the fashion of her country, she was in the habit of wearing a sort of half Circassian costume, requiring the introduction of long ribands which descended from the head down to the lower part of the dress.   I do not know why, but it appears that these ribands were not in accordance with the etiquette of the Sardinian Court.   The Countess Obrescoff was therefore officially desired not to appear at Court with the obnoxious ornaments. Her husband, however, declined to yield to this order, and referred the matter to the Russian Cabinet.   The Emperor Nicholas not only backed his representative by approving of his resistance, but positively ordered that the Countess should appear at the Sardinian Court with the ribands, or not at all.   I do not remember how the squabble ended; but I know that half-a-dozen notes were exchanged on the important subject.

Matters, however, have now undergone considerable modification.   Victor Emmanuel, when his mind is not engrossed with state affairs, is an exceedingly good-humoured man, very well disposed to get rid of the tiresome formalities considered indispensable by the Grand Master of the Ceremonies.

I had myself an opportunity of seeing how unpretending are the manners of Victor Emmanuel, whilst I followed him on his journey through Central Italy in the month of April, 1860.   Count Cavour had had the kindness to propose that I should accompany the Royal suite as temporary secretary to Commendatore Buoncompagni, the excellent patriot who has always sacrificed his personal interests to the welfare of Italy.   I accepted without hesitation, and at the beginning of April started for Leghorn on board the *Maria Ade-*

laide, a fine frigate under the command of Admiral Persano.

Belonging thus to the Royal suite, I saw the King, as one might say, perfectly at home. We started from Genoa at ten o'clock at night; so that his Majesty was obliged to take his supper and to sleep on board. Accommodation had been provided to this end; but the *Maria Adelaide*, though a fine frigate, could not afford room for all the gentlemen of the Royal household, who were not less than a hundred in number. The King's supper was served in the officers' cabin; but there was scarcely space enough for the Ministers, aides-de-camp, and orderly officers of the court. Accordingly, Count Maffei and Cavaliere Arton—the two secretaries of Count Cavour —waited on deck, together with myself, until the Royal party should break up, and permit us to take its place at the table. We waited more than an hour, and yet no supper was forthcoming. "No doubt, secretaries do not stand high in the estimation of navy officers," observed Count Maffei; "for, although the Royal supper is over, there is no sign that our turn is about to come." We were thus grumbling and yawning, as men with empty stomachs do, when the King made his appearance on deck. The night was clear enough for him to distinguish our faces, and to detect the not very satisfied expression they bore; for we heard him observing to Admiral Persano :—

"Admiral, it seems that you have forgotten the *avvocati*. I see three of them, who I am certain would not disdain a good supper." The reason why the King designated us by the appellation of *avvocati* was because we were the only persons of the Royal suite who were not in uniform, but, on the contrary, wore plain evening dress.

The hint thus given by the sovereign soon produced its effect. Supper was provided, and even a mattress to lie upon during the night.

Our beds, however, were not so snug as to allow us to indulge in long or sound sleep. As soon, therefore, as the sun had risen into the pure sky of the Mediterranean sea, we went on deck to ascertain if Leghorn was in sight. The King and Count Cavour were already there, smoking their cigars. The three *avvocati*, therefore, withdrew into a corner, and talked over the incidents of the night, which, if wanting in sleep, had not been without merriment. Among other things, Cavaliere Arton began to speak of medals and decorations.

"I do not like all those medals which the officers of our army wear on their breasts," said he to me, pointing out a brave Colonel who had half-a-dozen of them.

"Why?" asked I. "When they are gained on the field of battle, I do not see any reason against their being worn."

"Oh, you do not understand me," rejoined the Cavaliere. "I mean that I would suppress all medals given by the different National Governments of Italy, and have one struck instead, which should be bestowed upon all who have worked for the triumph of our cause."

While engaged in this discussion, Count Cavour came up, and asked what was the subject which so interested us. I informed him; whereupon he turned to Arton, and said :—" How can you lose your time in such a discussion? Do you not know that in thirty years all these baubles" (pointing to the stars which adorned his uniform) "will have disappeared utterly, and will only be found on the breasts of actors who play the parts of Generals and Ministers on the stage?" I give this anecdote as illustrating the opinion of Cavour, that Europe is marching steadily towards more democratic institutions.

The journey of the King through Central Italy was one unbroken triumphal march from Leghorn to Piacenza. I shall not, however, describe the feasts of Florence, nor the illuminations of Pisa, nor the mediæval display of Siena. I shall not speak of the performances at the theatre of Bologna, in which more than a hundred ladies of rank sang the National Anthem, nor of the pageants at Modena, at Reggio, and at Parma. In every town and every village, arches, towers, churches, the whole extent of streets and piazzas, were adorned with flowers, with coloured lights, and with rich hangings of every sort. The poorer dwellings made a tasteful appearance by the side of their wealthier neighbours. Here and there, Justice poised her balance, or Force grasped his club, leaning upon his faithful lion. Victory and other goddesses of Olympus were also represented; and flags were waving by thousands. The waters of the Arno, of the Reno, and of the Parma reflected myriads of lights, and the tribunes were thronged with applauding ladies,

Whose bright eyes
Rain'd influence, and judg'd the prize.

It was in fact a succession of feasts, all animated with

that popular enthusiasm which speaks, more than any other display, to the heart of an honest and patriotic sovereign. Even *Te Deums* and high masses were not wanting; for in every city there were liberal-minded priests, who sang them in spite of excommunications and interdictions.

Following the triumphal march of the King, I arrived at Bologna on the 1st of May. In the evening, a Bolognese friend entered my room, and told me that news had been received from Genoa that Garibaldi intended to sail for Sicily. Although neither of the two secretaries of Count Cavour who were my companions had uttered a word upon this subject, I had guessed that something important was then brooding on the political horizon; for I observed that the Premier was exceedingly preoccupied. He had besides abruptly left the King at Pisa, taking with him Count Maffei. Putting together all these circumstances, and reading certain facts in the newspapers, I came to the conclusion that the party of action was meditating some bold movement. The news given me by my friend, therefore, did not take me by surprise, but confirmed my previous opinion. Arriving at Modena on the 5th of May, I found that Cavour had come back from Turin, and that he had had a long interview with Victor Emmanuel. On the morning of the 6th, I heard that Garibaldi had started upon his daring expedition.

Judging by what I saw and heard at the time from the officers of the King's suite, both at Modena and at Piacenza, I have reason to believe that Count Cavour, far from having encouraged the project of

Garibaldi, tried all he could to prevent it. A practical man, as Cavour was, could not have great faith
in the result of an expedition which everybody thought
at the time to be mere madness. He knew besides—
and subsequent events have proved that he was not
altogether mistaken—that, even on the supposition of
success, the annexation of the Neapolitan provinces
would rather weaken than strengthen the newly-
enlarged Kingdom of Sardinia.. "Let us organize ourselves—let us have a strong army at our command—
and then we can turn our eyes towards Venetia and
the South, and Rome will follow," was the opinion
that Cavour constantly expressed when he was required to speak upon the subject of Italian Unity.
But, when once Garibaldi had embarked on his heroic
enterprise, he did not dream of abandoning him.
He was too great a patriot to do so ; his mind was
too deeply penetrated with the principles of the revolution to abjure them when a handful of heroes were
risking their lives to secure the triumph of the Italian
cause. Indeed, had he even so wished, he had not
the power to carry such an intention into execution ;
for the whole of Italy was in too great a state of
excitement to allow of it. Had Cavour ordered the
Sardinian squadron to stop and bring back Garibaldi,
he would have risked the crown of his Sovereign.
Victor Emmanuel himself, moreover, was so ardent an
admirer of Garibaldi that he would not have consented
to sacrifice him to the demands of foreign diplomacy.
He had done all he could to persuade the General to
give up his plans ; but his exertions had failed, and
he now accepted the results as inevitable. To his

various remonstrances he had received the following respectful answer :—

"SIRE,—The cry for help which reaches me from Sicily has touched my heart, and the hearts of some hundreds of my old soldiers. I have not advised the insurrectionary movement of my Sicilian brethren ; but, as they have risen in the name of Italian Unity, personified in that of your Majesty, against the most disgraceful tyranny of·our age, I did not hesitate to take the lead of the expedition. I know that I am going to embark on a dangerous undertaking; but I trust in God, and in the courage and devotion of my companions. Our war cry will always be 'Long live the Unity of Italy! Long live Victor Emmanuel, its first and bravest soldier!' Should we fall in the enterprise we have undertaken, I trust that Italy and liberal Europe will not forget that it has been determined by the most unselfish sentiments of patriotism. Should we succeed, I shall be proud to adorn the crown of your Majesty with a new, and perhaps its brightest, jewel, on the sole condition that you will prevent your advisers from handing it over to foreigners, as has been done with my native country. I have not communicated my project to your Majesty, for I feared that the great devotion I feel for you would have succeeded in persuading me to abandon it.

"Your Majesty's most affectionate subject,

"G. GARIBALDI."

After this letter, there was nothing to be done but to wish God-speed to the thousand heroes and their illustrious leader.

CHAPTER II.

THE LIBERATION OF SICILY.

A Wonder for Posterity—Two opposite political Systems—Political
Condition of Sicily in 1860—Preparations for a Revolution in
Sicily—A Monk acting as a Spy—The Convent of La Gancia
—Two brave Patriots—Preparations for Garibaldi's Expedi-
tion—The Thousand start from Genoa—Order of the Day—The
Commanders of the Companies—Talamone—Conversation at
Sea—The Alarm—A threatened Danger—The Landing at Mar-
sala—The first Victory—March on Palermo—Palermo taken
—Rear-Admiral Mundy—Cruelties of the Neapolitan Troops
—Medici's Expedition—Contradictions of American Statesmen
concerning International Law—Garibaldi's forward March—
Preparations for the Battle of Melazzo—Heroism of Captain
Missori—The Neapolitans capitulate—Loss of the Garibaldians
—Colonel Bosco humiliated—The Convention of Messina.

IN Roman history we are told of the wonderful deeds
of Octavius at Actium; and the Greek historians
record with pride the valorous achievements of a band
of Hellenic heroes in the defiles of Thessaly. But
neither by ancient nor modern historians has it been
related that a General who sailed with an expedition
of 1000 men conquered a kingdom within the period
of one hundred and twenty-two days. Such, however, is the fact; this is what Garibaldi performed.
In reading the narrative of those wonderful events,
posterity will be at first inclined to regard the

expedition to Sicily, and the victories of the liberating force, rather as a splendid fiction than as an
historical reality.   In distant ages, people will perhaps ask if there has not been some mistake about
numbers and dates, as often occurs in the manuscripts
of ancient Arabian writers, or in the chronicles of the
Middle Ages.   We, however, have witnessed these
grand deeds ; we have followed them with anxious expectation, and have been bewildered and amazed by
the success of the great Italian leader.   For us, therefore, doubt does not exist.   The English public are
already familiar with the main course of events, and
all I have got to do is to trace them in their interesting details.

The reader who has followed the first chapter of this
work will have discovered that since the beginning of
the war in 1859 there existed no sympathy between
Garibaldi and Cavour.   The former had unlimited confidence in the popular element of Italy ; he wanted his
country to be freed *by* the Italians, and *for* the Italians.
The latter—although his recently published letters
prove that he was by no means an anti-revolutionary
politician—trusted more in diplomacy and in dynastic
connections.   Which of the two systems was the best,
or whether, indeed, the one could have succeeded without the other, the future must decide.   To this diver-
gency of opinion, which could not fail to separate
these two illustrious men from the beginning of the
national war, other causes were subsequently added,
which embittered still more their mutual antipathy.
Garibaldi thought that his volunteers had been badly
treated in Lombardy ; he conceived that he himself

was wronged by Farini in the Æmilia, by Ricasoli in Tuscany, and by General Fanti in both these provinces. The responsibility of all these misdeeds, or presumed misdeeds, Garibaldi threw upon Cavour, thinking that the others were but secondary agents of the Count. To render still more decisive the split caused by the events of Central Italy, and to render the antagonism between Garibaldi and Cavour insurmountable, came the cession of Savoy and Nice. This was the last blow ; thenceforth, dislike deepened into open hostility. From that moment, Garibaldi and the leaders of the party of action decided upon seizing the first opportunity to snatch from the grasp of Cavour, and of the moderate party, the initiative of the Italian movement, and to establish the supremacy of the popular or revolutionary element.

Sicily was the field chosen by them for the first trial of their plans, that being a country in which both the upper classes and the people were actuated by a deep-rooted hatred of the Bourbon Government. Since the restoration of Ferdinand II. in 1848, and even before, the Sicilians had been ruled with a brutal tyranny only equalled in the darkest epochs of the Middle Ages. Exile, hard labour for life, and torture, were not spared them by Miniscalco, Pontillo, Simone, Carega, and other agents of the Bourbonic despotism. At the beginning of 1860, the political persecutions had been carried to such an extent that the worthiest citizens were either imprisoned or obliged to seek safety in exile. Two of these last—Mario Palizzalo and Enrico Amato—arrived at Genoa. The news they brought from Sicily was at once heartrend-

ing and full of hope : heartrending, because of the sad
condition of their countrymen ; full of hope, inasmuch
as the temper of the Sicilians seemed to prove that
they were ready to rise. Mazzini and his party at
once decided for action. Nicola Fabrizzi was sent to
the island to bring instructions for the secret committees ; arms were smuggled into Palermo by con-
cealing them in timber imported into the island, and
everything was prepared by the patriots for an out-
break. Their meetings at Palermo were held in the
convent of La Gancia, and it was decided that the
revolution should begin on the morning of the 4th of
April. The monks were almost all in the conspiracy,
and were the most ardent supporters of the movement.
A traitor, however, was amongst them. On the evening of the 3rd, the Director of Police, Miniscalco, was
in his office, when a monk of sinister appearance was
ushered into his presence.

"What is the matter, Father Michele ?" asked
Miniscalco.

"I have come to warn you," replied the monk,
"that at dawn to-morrow a revolution will break out
in this city, and in other parts of the island."

"Who is the chief of the conspiracy?" asked Miniscalco.

"Francesco Riso, the fountain manufacturer," was
the answer of the friar.

"And where are the conspirators to meet?"

"At the convent of La Gancia."

"Thanks, Father Michele. I will give my orders
accordingly."

Next morning the bells of La Gancia tolled out

the signal, and the fight began. In a few hours, however, the convent was stormed by the Royal troops, and the brutality of the Neapolitan soldiery appeared in all its horror. Men, women, and monks were indiscriminately killed or imprisoned, and a few days afterwards Riso's father was shot without trial, together with twelve of his companions. The chief conspirator could not be executed, for, having been mortally wounded during the fight, he died at the hospital.

Although this first attempt of the Sicilian patriots was fruitless, it had the effect of rekindling throughout the island the flames of revolution. The Neapolitan troops would perhaps have succeeded in extinguishing the new conflagration, had it not been kept alive by the words of encouragement which came from the Sicilian exiles in Piedmont. On the evening of the 10th of April, a fishing-boat entered a creek not far from Messina, and landed two Sicilian exiles : that boat carried with her the firebrand of the revolution. The two exiles had sailed from Genoa to take the lead of the revolutionary bands scattered about the island, to increase them, and to spread the insurrection far and wide. One of the two was a brave patriot, and an old friend of Mazzini, named Rosolino Pilo, son of Prince Capece ; the other was Giovanni Corrao. On their arrival, they set to work, roused the hopes of their countrymen, and told them that help would soon come from the north of Italy.

In spite of the great force possessed by the Bourbonic Government in Sicily, the noble exertions of Rosolino Pilo and his friends succeeded in maintaining the focus of the national movement until the end of

April.   In the meanwhile, the friends of Mazzini and other Sicilian exiles had established a committee at Genoa, which (aided to a certain extent by La Farina, the secretary of the National Society) took the initiative in preparing an expedition.   Garibaldi, to whom this project was communicated, at once accepted the command.   Men, arms, ammunition, and an American clipper were already provided, and placed at the disposal of the General.   But only a few days before the time fixed for the departure of the expedition, a despatch was sent from Malta to Crispi—a Sicilian exile of great influence—in which it was announced that the Sicilian movement had failed, and that there were but a few *squadrè* which still held their ground. This unexpected news seemed to cut short the hopes of the patriots : the expedition was thought useless, and was abandoned.   The project, however, was soon revived, and on the evening of the 30th of April, La Masa and Bixio went to see Garibaldi, who was then living near Genoa, at the Villa Spinola, belonging to an intimate friend of his, Colonel Vecchi.   The plan was discussed anew ; and Bixio, who is one of those determined men whom no difficulty can daunt, spoke with such eloquence, and depicted the sufferings of the Sicilians in such vivid colours, that the heart of Garibaldi was touched.

" Enough, Bixio," said he ; " let us go, even with twenty men, provided we go at once."

In five days, two merchant steamers—the *Lombardo* and the *Piemonte*—were hired, and one thousand and sixty-seven volunteers were ready to embark.   On the morning of the 5th of May, Bixio organized the naval

service of the two steamers, and was appointed by
Garibaldi commander of the *Lombardo*, while Garibaldi
himself was to take the command of the *Piemonte*.
At dawn next morning, everything was ready, and the
expedition sailed from a spot a little to the south-east
of Genoa, the *Lombardo* taking the lead.   The gallant
band, carrying with them the fortunes of Southern
Italy, and trusting in God and the righteousness of
their cause, were soon well out to sea.   The waves were
calm, the night brilliant, and a gentle breeze, blowing
from the north, seemed as if sent on purpose to expe-
dite the voyage of the heroes.

At seven o'clock the following morning, the two
steamers entered the harbour of Talamone, on the
Tuscan coast.   It was the intention of Garibaldi to
organize his troops, and provide some guns and ammunition, of which they were in want.   Having,
therefore, landed his men, he issued the following
order of the day :—

"On board the *Piemonte*, May 7th, 1860.

"CORPS OF THE CACCIATORI DELLE ALPI ! — Your
mission will be, as it always has been, based upon complete self-denial, for the regeneration of the common
country.   The brave Cacciatori have served, and will
serve, their country with the devotion and discipline
of the best military corps, without any other hope,
without any other pretension, than that of a stainless
conscience.

"No rank, no honour, no recompence is held out
to my brave companions : when the danger is past,
they will return to a quiet domestic life ; but, now

that the hour of battle has struck, Italy sees them again in the front rank, cheerfully volunteering to shed their blood for her. The war-cry of the Cacciatori delle Alpi is the same that resounded a year since on the banks of the Ticino—' Italy and Victor Emmanuel!'—and this cry will strike terror into the hearts of the enemies of Italy.

"ORGANIZATION OF THE CORPS.

" Giuseppe Sirtori, Chief of the Staff. Staff Officers : Crispi, Manin, Calvino, Majocchi, Graziotti, Borchetta, Bruzzesi. Türr, First Aid-de-Camp of the General. Orderly officers : Cenni, Montanari, Bandi, Stagnetti. Orsini, Commander of the Artillery.

"COMMANDERS OF COMPANIES.

" Nino Bixio, Commander of the 1st company ; Antonio Forni, 2nd ; Stocco, 3rd ; La Masa, 4th ; Anfossi, 5th ; Carini, 6th ; Cairoli, 7th.

" COMMISSARIAT.

" Acerbi, Bovi, Maestri, Rodi.
" Ripari, Chief of the Medical Staff.
" This organization is the same as that of the Italian army to which we belong ; and the rank, given to merit rather than to interest, is that already achieved on other battle-fields.

." G. GARIBALDI."

Let us see, now, who were the officers chosen by Garibaldi to command the various companies. Sirtori, a Lombard priest, was appointed Chief of the Staff, more for the courage and patriotism he had shown in the defence of Venice in 1848-9 than for any knowledge of the science of war. Crispi was a Sicilian exile, who had played an important part in the national movement of 1848 ; a man, brave, intelligent, and highly experienced as an administrator. Basso, the private secretary of Garibaldi, was a warm patriot from Nice. The name of Türr is already familiar to the reader of this book. Nino Bixio, also a native of Genoa, was, and still is, most popular in Italy. He was wounded at Rome in 1849, by the side of his friend, Mamelli, and joined the Cacciatori delle Alpi in 1859. Used to the ocean, like Garibaldi (for he had served as a sea-captain), he was the fittest man of the expedition to be at the same time a naval commander and a leader of soldiers. Forni, who had superseded Orsini in the command of the 2nd company, was a Sicilian, very much esteemed in his country, where he exercised considerable influence. Baron Stocco, a Calabrese, served as a lieutenant in 1848, in the insurrection of Calabria, and gave especial proof of his bravery and skill on the 27th of June in that year, during a combat, at long odds, at a spot between Angitola and Maida, in which from four to five hundred Calabrians fought against a brigade commanded by General Nunziante. La Masa was one of the leaders of the Sicilian movement in the same year, and had worked unceasingly for the national cause during the ten years of exile he had passed in Piedmont. Anfossi was a distinguished officer of the old Sardinian army, who had proved, by a long exile, his love of liberty. Carini had had the command of a cavalry regiment at Palermo during the revolution of 1848; and even after the Italian cause had broken down, he continued to serve it by his *Courrier Franco-Italien*, a French paper published in Paris until the beginning of 1859. The reader is already acquainted with the name of Cairoli, which has been mentioned in the Garibaldian campaign of Lombardy. He was the brother of the young man who was killed at Varese. As soon as he heard of Garibaldi's plan, he hastened to Genoa with his mother, who, still in mourning for her son, presented him to the General, and, as if she had not yet done enough, offered to Garibaldi a sum of thirty thousand francs for the expedition to Sicily. Orsini, the commander of the artillery which had yet to be obtained, was one of the principal defenders of Messina in 1848. Compelled to fly, he took service in Turkey, with the rank of Colonel of Artillery; but at the first cry from Sicily he hastened to Genoa, where he became one of the most active members of the Sicilian committee.

Not far from Talamone is situated the small fort of Orbitello, which Garibaldi knew was well provided with ammunition and guns. As soon as he had landed, he said to Türr, " Colonel, are you the man to go to Orbitello, and obtain from the commander of the fort all the guns and powder he can spare?"

" Well, General," answered Türr, " I will go and try; but save for the interference of the English Government, the Austrian General Coronini would have shot me at Bucharest during the Crimean war. I hope the Piedmontese officer who commands the fort will be a little more amiable."

Türr went, and in a few hours brought with him

the commander of the fort, who was not very well
disposed to grant the demand.   Garibaldi is remarkable for the way in which he overcomes difficulties.
On the present occasion, he put on his uniform of a
Piedmontese General, and received the commander
with such an air of superiority that the latter forgot
the strict duty of a military consignee, and willingly
gave all he had been asked for.

Thus furnished, Garibaldi detached one hundred
men from the expedition, and placing them under the
command of Colonel Zambianchi, marched them off
with instructions to invade the Roman States, and stir
up a revolution in those dissatisfied provinces.   Zambianchi, whom Garibaldi was possibly anxious to get
rid of (at least, such is the impression I have derived
from facts communicated to me), was directed to spread
the subjoined proclamation as soon as he had entered
the Papal States :—

“ April 30.

“ ROMANS !—To-morrow you will hear the priests
of Lamoricière say that some Mussulmans have invaded your territory.   Well, these Mussulmans are
the same who fought for Italy at Monte Video, at
Rome, and in Lombardy ; the same whom you will
mention to your children with pride when the day shall
come which, by emancipating you from the tyranny of
the stranger and the priest, will leave you free to
enjoy recollections ; the same who for a moment
yielded to the numerous and warlike soldiers of Buona-
parte, but who yielded only with their brows turned
towards the enemy, and pledging themselves to return
to the fight, and not to leave their children any other

legacy than that of hatred to oppressors.   Yes, these companions of mine fought outside your walls, by the side of Manara, Melana, Masina, Mameli, Daverio, Peralla, Panizzi, Remorino, Daniell, Montaldi, and so many other brave Romans who now sleep near your catacombs, and whom you buried yourselves, because *wounded in front.*   Our enemies are both astute and powerful; but we tread the land of the Scævolas, the Horatii, and the Ferruccios : our cause is the cause of all Italians.   Our war-cry is the same which was heard at Varese and Como—' Italy and Victor Emmanuel!'—and you know that with us, whether defeated or victorious, Italian honour is safe.

" G. GARIBALDI,

" General of the Romans, by a Government
elected by Universal Suffrage."

It would seem by this document that Garibaldi's first intention was to commence operations in the Papal States.   But whether the expedition was a mere pretext, or whether it really formed part of Garibaldi's insurrectionary plan, matters little; for Zambianchi and his followers were beaten by General Pimodan, at Valentino, on the 10th of May.

The two vessels have steamed out of Talamone harbour, and have turned their bows towards the Island of Maretimo.   May they safely reach the land they have sworn to free from the tyranny of the oppressor !   May God be propitious to their cause !   But, alas ! the wind, only a few hours before so calm, on a sudden begins to blow.   Grey clouds are rolling down towards the far east ; the sea becomes rough, the night dark. The gallant band may fall into the hands of the Neapolitan cruisers ; there is no chance of seeing and avoiding them if they are on their way. Both vessels labour heavily through the waves of the Mediterranean ; but, in spite of dangers, the valiant Cacciatori are laughing, joking, and singing songs of liberty. Two men, however, are engaged in close consultation in the fore-cabin of the *Piemonte.* From time to time they point out, on the large map spread before them, one or other of the numerous bays and gulfs which indent the Sicilian coast. These two, whose conversation not one of the officers dare disturb, are Garibaldi and Castiglia, and they are both occupied in determining the best place of landing.

"I think," suddenly broke out Garibaldi, in his ringing voice, "I think that we must make for Porto Palo. It is not far from Menfi, and I consider it a good place for landing. What is your opinion, Castiglia ?"

"I should agree with you," answered the commander, "were this map correct ; but from what I recollect, I am certain that the entrance to the small harbour of Palo is not deep enough to afford our steamers a secure landing. I should recommend Marsala."

Garibaldi, after remaining silent for a few minutes, said :——

"You are right, Castiglia. To get to Marsala, we must pass between the small islands of Maretimo and Favignana, which will afford an excellent shelter to our vessels. Were the Neapolitan ships to discover our expedition, we might easily escape by steaming either in the direction of Sardinia or towards Africa. This, however, I would never do, unless the enemy were in great force. Should we encounter only two frigates, our guns are ready ; and I will also show our Cacciatori how to board the enemy's vessels."

Garibaldi had scarcely done speaking when an alarm was raised on deck. The General rushed up to learn the cause; when, at the distance of a hundred yards, he perceived through the dim night a vessel steaming with all her power towards the *Piemonte*. There appeared to be no doubt that the expedition had been discovered by a Neapolitan cruiser. The order to clear the decks for action was given by Garibaldi, and in a few minutes every man was at his post. It was a solemn moment ; for the vessel might have been sunk, and the cherished hopes of Sicilian freedom would have foundered with it. Fortune, however, favoured the brave. The *Piemonte* having arrived within a few yards of the other vessel, a cry was heard of—" Stop her ! It is the *Lombardo !* it is the *Lombardo !*" And so it was. Owing to the darkness of the night, and the heavy sea with which he had to contend, Bixio had not been able to follow a straight line. He also had regarded the companion ship as a Neapolitan vessel, and believing it was too near to be avoided, had not hesitated to steam close up, and trust to the chances of a fight. Happily, however, the two steamers recognised each other before the collision occurred ; and they pursued their voyage in safety.

On the morning of the 11th of May, the expedition, having coasted the western cliff of the island of

Favignana, rounded Point Providenza. Though from
that moment the invasion was signalled by the telegraph of Colombara di Trapani to the Neapolitan
cruisers, the patriots were safe; for the distance from
Providenza Point to Marsala was scarcely twelve
Italian miles. Our brave volunteers were therefore
in high spirits; in a few hours they would certainly
reach their place of destination. But suddenly an
unfortunate discovery was made : two men-of-war
were lying in the harbour of Marsala, and were perhaps Neapolitans. An English schooner, passing
hard by, was hailed by Garibaldi, and her captain
removed all apprehension : the two vessels were British.
There was no time to be lost, however ; for the Neapolitan cruisers, which were away south towards Mazara,
had been summoned by the Colombara telegraph.
They had already turned their bows in the direction
of the expedition, and were coming with all the power
of steam from a distance of only twenty miles. With
that happy audacity which never fails him, Garibaldi
hastened the course of his two vessels, and at half-past
one o'clock in the afternoon ran straight from the
north-west into the harbour of Marsala.

The English men-of-war, *Argus* and *Intrepid*, were
anchored in the port, to protect the wine factories
belonging to British subjects. Some of their officers,
who were in the town of Marsala, saw two steamers
coming straight in from sea at full speed. They were
speculating on the nature and object of these two
vessels, when three Neapolitan ships were also seen to
come up towards Marsala. Both the *Lombardo* and the
Piemonte made direct for the mole, the smaller vessel

getting in safely, and the larger grounding about
a hundred yards short of the mole-head. The expedition, however, had reached the desired port, and the
Neapolitan ships, which by this time had caught
sight of the revolutionary vessels, could not get near
enough to open fire until at least two hours had
elapsed. There was accordingly time to land the men,
and clear the steamers of ammunition, guns, and stores.
By half-past three, this operation was successfully
accomplished, with the help of the town boatmen. In
the meanwhile, the Neapolitan steamers *Stromboli* and
Capri were coming as fast as they could, the frigate
Partenope following with every sail set, right before
a beautiful breeze. The Bourbonic steamers, on
arriving, drew up well within range, and cleared
for action. But instead of opening fire at once,
they backed and filled, now ahead, now astern, sig-
nalling all the time to the frigate, which was getting
close. At length, the first shot flew from the *Capri* ;
but it fell short. Then came another and another ;
but the Garibaldians were under cover of the wall,
and the round-shot passed over them. The *Partenope*
then came closer, shortened sail, and moved gently
along in a line with the mole. Passing abreast of the
Garibaldians, gun after gun was fired, and a whole
broadside of grape and canister was directed against
the patriots. The Garibaldians, however, were by
this time out of harm's way, having marched in good
order into the town; with very few of their men hit ;
and the Neapolitans could only give vent to their
wrath by bombarding the unprotected buildings of
Marsala.

Garibaldi, the moment he entered Marsala (where he was saluted as a liberator), issued the following proclamations :—

"SICILIANS !—I have brought you a body of brave men, who have hastened to reply to the heroic cry of Sicily. We, the remains of the battles of Lombardy, are with you : all we ask is the freedom of our land. United, the work will be easy and short. To arms, then! He who does not snatch up a weapon is a coward or a traitor to his country. Want of arms is no excuse. We shall get muskets, but for the present any weapon will do in the hands of a brave man. The municipalities will provide for the children, women, and old men deprived of their support. To arms, all of you! Sicily shall once more teach the world how a country can be freed from its oppressors by the powerful will of a united people.

"G. GARIBALDI."

"TO THE NEAPOLITAN ARMY.

"Foreign insolence reigns over Italian ground in consequence of Italian discord. But on the day that the sons of the Samnites and Martii, united with their brethren of Sicily, shall join the Italians of the North, on that day our nation, of which you are the finest part, shall resume its place, as in former times, among the first nations of Europe. I, an Italian soldier, only aspire to see you drawn up side by side with these soldiers of Varese and San Martino, in order jointly to fight against the enemies of Italy.

"G. GARIBALDI."

The march of the Italian leader from Marsala to

Salemi was a succession of enthusiastic receptions. Men, women, children, priests, and monks fraternized with the thousand heroes. Halting at Salemi on the 13th and 14th, to impart some organization to the *squadre*, or armed bands of Sicilian volunteers, who were pouring in from all parts of the country, Garibaldi, on the evening of the second day, sent Bixio to Vita on a reconnoitering expedition. The Neapolitan General Landi had in the meanwhile advanced from the mountain pass called Monte del Pianto dei Romani with four battalions, a squadron of cavalry, and four mountain howitzers, with intent to crush—as he announced in a pompous order of the day—the firebrand of Italy, the outlawed filibuster of South America. To this well equipped and organized force Garibaldi could only oppose 1005 Cacciatori delle Alpi, and 1200 Sicilian peasants, hastily organized by Crispi and La Masa.

It was at nine o'clock of the 15th that Garibaldi attacked the Neapolitan forces in their strong positions. His military genius and unequalled quickness in manœuvring staggered the Bourbonic General; while the bayonets of the Cacciatori and the fire of the *squadre* (who, directed by Garibaldi, had outflanked the enemy,) decided the first fight on Sicilian ground in favour of the soldiers of liberty. But the band of heroes paid dearly for the victory of Calatafimi. The battle lasted three hours. Garibaldi had two hundred men *hors de combat;* while his son Menotti, the son of the great Manin, and Baron Stocco were amongst the wounded.

From Calatafimi to Palermo the liberators marched

on, constantly fighting and conquering, and carrying
out, under the guidance of Garibaldi, the most admirable strategical plans.   The Cacciatori delle Alpi knew
not what flinching was ; the Sicilian *squadre* soon acquired a better organization, and became familiar with
the enemy's bullets.   Garibaldi's plan was to slip into
Palermo on its southern side, passing through the line
of ten thousand Neapolitans massed at Monreale and
Parco, the two points from which Palermo can be
easily defended.   To carry out his scheme, the General
menaced Parco at dawn on the 23rd of May.   He
had crossed the mountains by following the goat-
tracks (causing his guns to be carried on men's
shoulders), and had suddenly appeared with his troops
on the opposite slopes.   Surprised by this unexpected
movement, the Neapolitans fell back on to the plain ;
but being reinforced by Colonel Bosco's column on
the next morning, they reassumed the offensive.   It
was then that the military genius of the Italian leader
showed itself in all its splendour.   Foiled in his attempt
to advance, he feigned a hasty retreat on Corleone.
Leaving Colonel Carini with a small force on the road
which leads to that town, in order to make the
Neapolitans believe that he was still engaged in his
backward movement, he pushed across the mountains
in the direction of Milismeri, where he arrived on the
25th.

The Neapolitan Generals at Monreale and Parco
were so thoroughly deceived that they telegraphed to
General Lanza at Palermo that Garibaldi was in full
retreat, his troops being completely demoralized.   But
the Bourbons soon discovered their mistake.   Having

arrived at Milismeri, Garibaldi sent for La Masa, and ordered him to take all the Sicilian *squadre* which were concentrated at Gibilrossa, and proceed with them in all haste to the heights between Palermo and Parco. In the early morning of the 27th, Garibaldi brought his forces to the outskirts of Palermo. The troops of Rosolino Pilo (who had lost his life at the head of his men) and the *squadre* of La Masa had to fight on the heights against the Neapolitans. So far was General Lanza from imagining that the " filibuster " was close upon him, that the first intimation of the enemy's presence in the suburb of the city he received while in bed, dreaming, perhaps, of the total destruction of the national bands.

On hearing this astounding intelligence, he hastened to the Termini Gate, where the sharpshooters of Garibaldi had already taken up a position. The twelve thousand Neapolitans who defended the city, however, were in less than four hours dislodged from their positions of Sant' Antonio and Quattro Cantoni ; the houses of the suburb were carried, and Garibaldi, forcing his way through the Piazza Bologni, occupied the Piazza del Pretorio, where he established his head-quarters. Before night, his troops were in possession of the whole of the town with the exception of the Royal palace, its immediate vicinity, and the forts. This great success was achieved by the Italian Liberator under a shower of projectiles ; for, by the orders of General Salzano, the forts and the naval squadron hard by had opened fire upon the city, in spite of the energetic protest of the English Rear-Admiral Mundy.

After this triumph of Garibaldi, General Lanza had nothing better to do than to urge Admiral Mundy to negotiate a cessation of hostilities for twenty-four hours, in order that a conference between his Generals and Garibaldi might take place on board the English flag-ship *Hannibal*. The conference was held, and the armistice agreed upon on the 30th of May, on board the British Admiral's vessel, in the presence of the French, American, and Sardinian naval commanders. It was on this occasion that one of the two Neapolitan general officers, who had been sent by Lanza to negotiate the suspension of hostilities with Garibaldi, began to speak in a bombastic and haughty manner of himself.

"You must know," said he to Garibaldi, "that I am an old officer, that I have been through a great many campaigns, and that it has been the occupation of the greater part of my life to make war."

"If that be so, I congratulate you," answered Garibaldi, in a quiet and dignified manner. "For myself, I have only once seen military service in a regular army, and cannot therefore boast of possessing your experience in the art of making war."

The lesson was good enough ; but I am sure it was scarcely understood by the Neapolitan negotiator.

This first armistice was the forerunner of a second, and of the convention, signed on the 6th of June, by which the Neapolitans were to evacuate Palermo and the whole of Sicily, except Messina, Melazzo, and some other less important fortresses.

The diplomatic skill and humanity shown by the English Admiral during the whole of this difficult transaction cannot be sufficiently praised. When I arrived at Palermo, a few days after the liberation of the city, I was told by many of its inhabitants that, had it not been for the energy of that gallant officer, the town would have been almost entirely destroyed by the bombardment of the Neapolitans. Both Italy and civilized Europe owe Admiral Mundy a debt of gratitude—a debt which I am happy to acknowledge in these pages, and which will never be effaced from Italian hearts. The reader will better appreciate the noble conduct of the British commander when he has been made acquainted with the misfortunes which had already fallen on the town during the bombardment. A whole quarter of Palermo was in ashes; families had been burnt alive in their dwellings; and the atrocities perpetrated by the Bavarian and Neapolitan troops were frightful. In a house near the Royal Palace, an old man was burnt in his bed, not by accident, but deliberately. In another house, near the burning palace of Prince Carini, a whole family was bayoneted. Nuns, monks, and citizens were massacred without even the shadow of a pretext. In various parts of the city, convents, churches, and other edifices were demolished by the shells continually thrown into them from the forts and the Neapolitan ships of war. For many nights, the flames of the conflagration, mixed with clouds of grey smoke, rose upwards to the blue sky of that enchanting region. For many nights, a red glare was thrown upon the picturesque bay, colouring with its light the summits of the mountains, and touching even the distant waves of the sea as with golden threads.

Such were the useless cruelties which opened a gulf between the Sicilians and the Bourbons—a gulf which no subsequent events will ever be able to close.

On leaving Genoa, Garibaldi had given instructions to Dr. Bertani, the chief of the National Committee for the Sicilian Insurrection, to collect money, arms, and volunteers, for further expeditions, and to forward them as soon as possible. At the same time, he directed Colonel Medici to take the command of the next contingent, and to come to his help as soon as possible. Whilst Medici was at Genoa, occupied in the organization of the new forces, he sent to Garibaldi a small Genoese steamer, with a cargo of arms and ammunition, which, commanded by the Leghornese Captain, Lavarello, succeeded in running through the Neapolitan fleet, and in safely reaching Palermo. At the beginning of June, Medici was ready to sail with the second expedition, which he divided into two parties : one under the command of Major Corte, the other under his own orders. The first of these two columns, which mustered 900 men, sailed from Genoa on the evening of the 7th of June, on board the American clipper *Charles and Jane.* The second, which numbered about 1600 men, left Genoa on the following evening on board three merchant steamers. Both the expeditions were to meet at Cagliari, and thence proceed together to Palermo.

On arriving at the Corsican Cape, the contingent under the command of Major Corte was captured by the Neapolitan frigate *Fulminante,* which towed the rebel vessel into the bay of Gaeta under the batteries of the Neapolitan fortress. There the American clipper lay for twenty-two days, whilst Medici, who was more fortunate, reached the harbour of Palermo in safety. As regards the capture of the clipper *Charles and Jane*, the American Minister at Naples enforced a principle not strictly in accordance with the theories of international law recently put forward by some American writers in the case of the *Trent*. The clipper had on board armed Garibaldians, and there was no doubt that she intended to go to Sicily. The capture of the *Fulminante* was therefore a lawful act; for the King of Naples was not at war with America, and Garibaldi had not been recognised as a belligerent by the Cabinet of Washington. In spite of all this, however, the Government of Francis II. was compelled to bend before the threats of the American Minister. The captured clipper was given up; and Major Corte and his men were enabled to reach their destination.

Now that he was master of Palermo, Garibaldi did not rest idle. He increased his troops; he summoned all the resources Sicily could afford; he hired steamers, bought arms and ammunition, and made every preparation to resume the campaign. He appealed even to the patriotism and charity of the Palermitan ladies, and in so touching a proclamation that I cannot forbear transcribing it :—

"I present myself in confidence to you, noble ladies of Palermo, to confess an act of weakness. I, an old soldier of two worlds, shed tears, and am distressed in mind. I weep not at the sight of the misery and misfortunes to which this unhappy city has been condemned; not with indignation at the recent butchery, nor for bodies mutilated by the bombardment; but at the sight of victims and orphans exposed to die of hunger. At the Orphan Asylum, eighty per cent. of the inmates perish for want of nourishment; and yet a very little would suffice to feed these beings created in the image of God. But here I stop. I leave the rest to be understood by your generous hearts, already palpitating with emotion at the spectacle of such misfortunes."

Towards the middle of July, Garibaldi began his march to Messina, the stronghold of Bourbon despotism. Medici was ordered to occupy Barcelona and Miri, and Colonel Fabrizzi to obtain possession of the heights which overhang the road from Melazzo to Messina. Some companies of Cosenz's brigade were sent to support Medici, whilst the other companies of the same brigade were directed to march from Palermo to Barcelona.

Medici was attacked by the Neapolitans under the command of Colonel Bosco, at Archi, on the morning of the 17th of July. Fortunately enough, he had intercepted a letter addressed to the Neapolitan Colonel by General Clary, the commander of Messina, in which it was stated that in three or four days he would join Bosco with eight thousand men, and so crush the Garibaldians. Medici at once telegraphed the intelligence to Garibaldi at Palermo; and the Liberator, assembling all his available forces, which had been unexpectedly increased by the arrival from Gaeta of the nine hundred men commanded by Major Corte, sailed from Palermo on board the steamer *City of Aberdeen*, for Patti, on the evening of the 17th of July. It was

PLAN OF MELAZZO

AND

FIELD OF BATTLE.

20th July, 1860.

Scale of Miles

Bay of S. Antonio

Belvedere Pt.

Ponta Tower

Coles Tower

Fairino Pt.

Jonny Fishery

Castle

■ Neapolitan Position.

⚔ ,, Guns.

■ Garibaldini Position.

⚔ ,, Guns.

⚓ Veloce Steamer.

on that occasion that the sympathy already shown by the Sardinian Admiral Persano began to assume the character of unmistakeable support. A Piedmontese man-of-war for the first time escorted the Garibaldians, to prevent their being captured by the Neapolitans. At a point near the bay of Patti, the Sardinian frigate came so near the *City of Aberdeen*, that the shouts of "Long live the King of Italy!" "Long live Garibaldi!" from the men of the two vessels mingled in one cry. From that point are seen the three volcanoes of Southern Italy — Stromboli, Etna, and Vesuvius; and the pyramidal columns of smoke, rising into the air, might have seemed to an imaginative mind a prayer from earth to heaven for the success of freedom.

Landing at Patti during the night of the 18th, Garibaldi moved at once on Barcelona and Miri, and decided to attack the Neapolitans (who, under Colonel Bosco, occupied Melazzo) on the 20th.

The town of Melazzo is situated on a promontory forming a peninsula, which is joined to the Sicilian continent by a strip of land whereon many of the houses of the city are built. From the heights of the promontory, a strong castle, armed with powerful artillery, frowns upon the town. Colonel Bosco had placed his troops partly in the fort, partly about the gardens and farms which dot the country extending in the direction of Miri. This force consisted of four battalions of Rifles, the 15th regiment of the Line, two squadrons of Dragoons, and 500 Artillery; altogether 6500 men, and twelve field-pieces. To this well-organized and well-equipped force, Garibaldi could only oppose Medici's and Cosenz's divisions (3700 strong), and Malenchini's brigade of Tuscans, 700 in number; in all, 4400 men, and three guns—that is, if two old 12-pounder carronades, and a 6-pounder, cast seventy years ago, deserve such a name.

Garibaldi, having made up his mind to attack the enemy, placed at the extreme left of his line of battle, and towards the sea, Malenchini's battalions, which were in communication with the right by means of Simonetta's regiment. On the right itself—that is to say, along the high road of Miri to Melazzo—were placed Major Corte's battalion, and a few companies of Cosenz's division. The Sicilians, under the command of the English officer Dunne, as well as those belonging to Corrao's and Vacchieri's battalions, were kept in reserve in the centre and on the right. Having thus disposed his forces, Garibaldi at seven o'clock commenced the action along the whole of the line. The fight was sharp, the fire well maintained on both sides; and two hours elapsed without any marked result. The Neapolitan sharpshooters, being screened by the hedges and shrubs of the country, stood their ground without yielding an inch. It was ten o'clock when Garibaldi, having brought up all his reserves without obtaining any marked success, had recourse to one of those extraordinary expedients which he always has at command, and which invariably secure the result at which he is aiming. Taking with him two of his aides-de-camp (Captains Missori and Statella), with about fifty of Dunne's men, he turned the right of Bosco's line, passing along the road which skirts the sea in the direction of Messina. In this daring movement he succeeded, but at the risk of his own life. Indeed, he had hardly passed through the marsh bordering on the sea, when, at the turning of a garden wall, he met a troop of Neapolitan horsemen, who at once fell upon his small band. Garibaldi, who never loses his coolness, even in moments of extreme danger, drew his sword, and, seizing hold of the bridle of the Neapolitan officer in command, cried out, "Surrender yourself! I am Garibaldi!"

"It is for you to surrender," answered the Neapolitan officer, aiming a blow with his sabre at the General's head.

Garibaldi, however, had not lost sight of his adversary's movement, and, avoiding the blow, gave him a cut across the face, which made him fall from the saddle. But, at the same moment, two of the enemy's horsemen fell upon the General, who, no doubt, would have been a dead man, had not help been near at hand. Missori had also been surrounded by the Neapolitan horsemen, but, sabring right and left, had succeeded in extricating himself, when, turning suddenly, he saw the peril which threatened his chief. Drawing his revolver, he aimed so well at the two horsemen who were pressing Garibaldi, that he speedily laid them low. The rest, seeing their officer and some of their comrades dead, took to flight in the opposite direction.

In the meanwhile, Colonel Malenchini, whose troops, as I have said before, formed the extreme left, had suddenly fallen back towards Miri, leaving unprotected the left of Simonetta's regiment.   This mistaken and unnecessary movement would have had the most disastrous results, had not Medici seen the danger of the situation, and prevented its evil consequences.   Rallying the troops of Simonetta and Corte, he forced his way towards the isthmus which joins Melazzo to the main land, and got possession of it.   At the point where the isthmus begins, there is a bridge.   This was occupied by Medici, who was speedily joined by Garibaldi.   From that moment, the Neapolitan troops were in full retreat, and soon found themselves shut up within the town of Melazzo and its fort.   Judging at once the position of the enemy, Garibaldi ordered Medici to hold the bridge, whilst he himself, going on board the *Veloce*, a Neapolitan man-of-war which had passed over to the National cause, ordered the gunners to throw a few shells into the city of Melazzo and the fort.   The fire of the *Veloce* was so well directed, and its effect so powerful, that Bosco was compelled to retire into the fortress, where he capitulated the next day, his Swiss, Bavarian, and Neapolitan troops being totally demoralized.

The victory of Melazzo had the important result of securing to Garibaldi the possession of Sicily—a possession which was the first step to the conquest of the Neapolitan continent.   Both the Neapolitans and the Garibaldians fought gallantly ; but the heroism of the last knew no bounds, for there are perhaps few instances recorded in military history of an army having lost twenty-five per cent. of the men engaged.   Such, however, was the loss sustained by the liberating forces that day.   More than eight hundred of them were put *hors de combat ;* and among the wounded were Colonel Cosenz, Majors Brida, Corte, and Cattò. The brave Major Migliavacca was killed.

Two days after the battle of Melazzo, Bosco was allowed to embark with his troops for Naples, having given his word of honour not to take up arms against the national forces for three months. The man who had boasted to annihilate Garibaldi was seen, on the 22nd of July, walking through a double row of those ragged volunteers he had so often despised. Garibaldi was generous towards the vanquished : he said he did not want to humiliate his brethren. However, he was inflexible on one point, for Colonel Bosco was not allowed to take his charger with him.

Shortly after the Neapolitans had embarked, another letter, addressed by General Clary to Bosco, was intercepted. In this letter, the commander of Messina said that he had received orders from the Minister of War to send the greater part of his troops to Naples. The news was precious, and the occasion excellent to force Clary to come to terms. Garibaldi therefore gave orders to Medici to march from Gesso on Messina, as it was his intention to prevent the departure of the Neapolitan troops. General Clary was not the man to stand his ground against a victorious army ; and he hastened to come to terms. A convention was agreed upon between him and Medici, by which the fort of the Lighthouse, those of Gonzaga and San Salvatore, and the town of Messina, were given up to Garibaldi, the Neapolitans remaining, however, masters of the citadel. Messina and its harbour were to be respected, and no bombardment was to take place without provocation on the part of the Garibaldians. The towns of Syracuse and Augusta were also to be evacuated by the Royal troops. Such was the convention which enabled Garibaldi to prepare the means for his subsequent triumphs on the Neapolitan continent. Of materials for combustion there were plenty in Calabria and Basilicata, and the firebrand was very shortly to fall upon the powder.

CHAPTER III.

PALERMO AND MESSINA.

The Bay of Palermo—The City—Father Pantaleo—Nuns and
Nunneries—A Love Story—A hasty Survey of Palermo—Gari-
baldi's Intimation to General Lanza—A Visit to the Hospital
—Misdeeds of the Director of Police at Palermo—Arrival at
Melazzo—People of Melazzo—Father Gavazzi—Interview
with Garibaldi—Colonel Dunne—How to Storm a Garden
Wall—Letter of Victor Emmanuel to Garibaldi—Departure
for Messina—Faro Point—The Albion Club—Spada Fishing
—Messina—The Sindaco of Messina—How to procure Lodg-
ings—A witty Irishman—Life at Messina—Night Alarms—
Sicilian Boatmen—Original Letters of the Virgin Mary and of
San Diavolo.

I SHALL never forget the thrill of joy which I felt when,
a few days after the battle of Melazzo, our steamer
approached the famous Conca d'Oro—the Golden
Shell. I do not know why this name has been
bestowed on the western limit of the famous Bay
of Palermo; but I feel that the place fully deserves the appellation. The numberless tints which
colour on a summer day the sides of Monte Pellegrino,
the spire of the shrine of Santa Rosalia crowning the
cliff, the masts of the vessels in the anchorage hard
by, the picturesque town, the old Spanish palaces of
Maqueda and Toledo, and the ever-green groves of

the Marina—these multitudinous and vivid hues make the scenery appear as if it were covered with a golden and iridescent veil. It is a sort of mirage which even the pencil of Claude Lorraine or Turner would in vain have attempted to paint.

But let us land ; let us pass the troublesome Custom-house officers, who, in spite of the liberal institutions proclaimed by Garibaldi, could not all at once forget the habit of asking for a *buona mano*, or gratuity. Let us throw some coppers to the groups of dirty, half-naked children and women, shouting " We are starving ! Give us something for the love of Garibaldi !" Let us proceed through Toledo and Maqueda Streets, full of memories of ancient and modern tyrants, and of the wrath of that revengeful people.

The day I landed at Palermo I was in company, and in good company too. My companions were a host of Englishmen, and two or three vivacious Irishmen, one of whom, though an amusing fellow, seemed to have sworn never to pay his bill at the hotel, because, as he said, his " relieving officer," meaning his father, had taught him that the soldiers of liberty ought never to " stand Sam." All these gentlemen were bound on the same errand, their object being to join Garibaldi's army. To give variety to our party, even a diplomatist was not wanting. Count Giulio Litta Modignani, though sent on a very important mission (of which I shall by and by have occasion to say a few words), was extremely un-affected and good-humoured, and fond of England and Englishmen. In the society of these genial fellow-travellers, I proceeded through the crowded streets of Palermo. The people were full of merriment. The *canta storie*, or buffo singer, was there, reciting poetry, and playing national airs on the guitar. Girls were dancing round the fountains; gentlemen were smoking their cigars on the ground-floor halls of the *ridotti*; men and women were shouting their eternal " Long live Garibaldi ! Long live Victor Emmanuel !" The streets and piazzas were ornamented with myriads of tri-coloured flags, reminding one so closely of similar displays in Northern and Central Italy that I forbear to enter into details, lest I should weary the reader with unnecessary repetition. Nevertheless, the *couleur locale*, as a French writer would say, is not wanting. As we proceed, we meet with all sorts of uniforms, from the Piedmontese tunic to the fancy dress of some eccentric fellow, who, although clad in a half-mediæval costume, and armed to the teeth, seems to have kept out of harm's way. The red shirts are, of course, most numerous ; for that is the accepted garb of the Garibaldians, and it has become famous since Calatafimi, Palermo, and Melazzo. Here and there, monks and priests emerge from amongst the crowd ; and some of these, too, are armed. Their daring looks and powerful limbs show that there is in them the stuff out of which good soldiers might be made. One of the monks has in fact shortened his hooded gown, under which he wears the red shirt of the revolutionary bands. He carries about with him a perfect arsenal of arms, and from his belt, by the side of the pointed and shining dagger, hangs a long ivory crucifix. This monk is the famous Padre Pantaleo, the

chaplain of Garibaldi. May his Holiness be consoled
in knowing that the great Italian leader *had* a
chaplain! I do not wish to over-state the air of char-
latanism which Father Pantaleo has about him; but
I am bound to say that he possesses a great deal
of it. Let us, however, make due allowance for
exceptional times, and not be too severe; for, after
all, the father has bravely led the *squadre* at the
attack on Palermo, with a crucifix in one hand and a
sabre in the other, whilst the Neapolitan bullets were
whizzing around.

All is gaiety about us—all is smiling and beautiful. Even the convents—and God knows there
are many at Palermo—do not appear dismal, as in
other Italian cities. The nuns are peeping out from
the gratings of their windows, or from those of the
lobbies above. They look by no means as strangers
on the lively scene which the streets present; for they
answer the salutes of the passers-by, and from time to
time even venture to throw bunches of flowers to the
officers.

The reader will no doubt willingly dispense with sta-
tistics of the convents and monasteries of Sicily; but I
can assure him that there are plenty of them, and well
provided for. The annual income such corporations
enjoy amounts to no less than seven millions of francs.
There is no great harm in their being so rich; for
nuns and monks in Sicily are generally good and
generous, and the nuns in particular are far from being
bigoted or afraid of social intercourse. The majority
of the Sicilian nuns belong to the higher classes of
society—a circumstance which accounts for their rela-

tive freedom and liberality. There is scarcely a family of the nobility that has not a daughter in some convent. In this respect, the old Spanish fashions have not as yet been done away with, but are religiously followed. The taking of the veil is a ceremony of frequent occurrence among the young female aristocracy of Sicily; for a girl of high birth is almost certain to succeed to the place of abbess whenever the vacancy occurs. This dignity is, if not by the monastic laws, at least by consuetude, almost hereditary in patrician families. The abbesses and nuns are often young and pretty; always courteous, and fond of society. That they are not insensible, either, to tender emotions may be inferred from the story I am about to relate.

Convents in Sicily are almost always built close to churches, and indeed the churches have generally access to the cloisters. A few days before the battle of Melazzo, a company of Garibaldians were quartered in one of the churches of a town not far from Palermo. From the door of its sacristy the grounds of the convent could be entered. The Garibaldians had been there a few days, when one evening two of their officers, finding the door open, ventured to stray through the alleys of old sycamore trees which shaded the garden of the nuns. The stillness of approaching night prevailed all round, and no light appeared along the double row of the convent windows, except at one end, where a solitary lamp was burning in the private chapel of the abbess. The murmur of the sea gently bathing the terrace of the garden was the only sound perceptible through the

calmness of the southern night. The two officers
were absorbed in the contemplation of that beautiful
scene (for they were students of Pavia, and a little
given to poetry), when suddenly they heard the
rustle of gowns coming from the chapel. Turning in
the direction of the sound, they saw through the soft
moonlight two nuns walking slowly towards them.
Had not the officers been poets already, they would
assuredly have become so, for the sisters were not
only young, but of remarkable beauty. They approached the officers without any sign of alarm, and
one of them said—

"Are you enjoying the fresh air? What do you
think of our garden? Is not the evening magnificent?"

This was an overture which the officers were
not very likely to disregard. They began, therefore, to talk of moon and stars, as poets generally do
with handsome women. So long, indeed, was the
meeting in the garden protracted that, when morning
began to "stand tiptoe on the misty mountain tops,"
the four actors in that scene were still whispering to
one another. On the very day which was then breaking, however, an order came to the Garibaldians to
advance. The sisters went at the appointed hour
to the old sycamore alley, but it was deserted; the
students had departed for the field of battle. In
a few days, the officers returned to the town—one
with his arm in a sling, for he had been wounded at
Melazzo. His friend was unhurt; but the two comrades were inseparable, for the wounded man might
have been in need of assistance. The door of the

sacristy was of course not forgotten by them.   Sacristans of churches are fond of piastres, and when piastres are generously given, they are by no means intractable Cerberuses.   In short, the sacristan of that particular church was bribed, and a new meeting between the gallant officers and the fair sisters took place two nights after the return of the former to the town.

Next morning, the nuns went as usual to prayer; but two of the sisters were absent from the choir. The abbess sent to their cells, but they were not to be found.   Every part of the nunnery was diligently searched without success.   The sisters had disappeared, and, strange to say, the officers were seen no more in the town after that evening; they had joined their battalion at Messina, and, according to what was whispered in Garibaldi's camp, two pretty young women had volunteered to nurse the wounded of the National army.   I give this story as I heard it repeated at the time at Faro, where, the heroes having been pointed out to me, I could not help coming to the conclusion that the nuns were not, after all, to be blamed for leaving their monotonous life, and following such handsome companions.

The adventure of these ladies has led me astray from my friends.   Count Giulio Litta, being on a diplomatic mission, was a great personage, and we kept close to him.   All of us went together to the castle, where the Pro-Dictator, Depretis, and his Secretary-General, Crispi—two men who are kindness itself—gave us good rooms, an excellent dinner, and, what was still more important, a pass which threw open the doors of the prisons and forts we were desirous

to see. Forth we went, therefore, accompanied by
our English companions, and by Baron Gioachino
D'Ondes, who, although holding the important office
of a Governor of the Royal Castle, very courteously
volunteered to be our guide. We visited the different
places where the Garibaldians had to sustain the hottest fire. From Porta di Termini, we went through the
whole line of buildings, passing San Francesco di
Paola and the Quattroventi. We then halted at Sant'
Antonio, and proceeded to the Quattro Cantoni, sur-
veying with a feeling of increasing admiration the
field of battle of the 27th of May. On arriving
at the Piazza del Pretorio, Baron D'Ondes, pointing
out a stone bench, said to me, "Here is the place
where Garibaldi lay down to rest after he had entered
Palermo."

"Did the bombs of the Neapolitans reach so
far?" asked one of our Irish companions in broken
Italian.

"To be sure they did," answered the Baron. "Both
the General and his Staff, during the whole time the
bombardment lasted, were under a shower of shells
and round-shot. You have but to look round, and
you will see many traces of the enemy's projectiles."

And, indeed, such was the case; for there was not a
house in the piazza whose walls were not pierced by
round-shot, and whose roofs and windows were not
shattered by the explosion of the shells.

I asked our kind cicerone if he thought it was the
protest of the English Admiral and of the foreign
consuls that determined the Neapolitan Generals to
desist from their work of destruction.

"No doubt," answered he, "the protest of the Admiral had great influence; but I think the intimation sent by Garibaldi to Marshal Lanza had the greatest effect of all."

"I did not know," I said, "that Garibaldi had made any intimation. What was its purport?"

"He sent word (I think through Missori) to General Lanza, that, if the bombardment did not cease, and if the shedding of blood, then of no avail, were not put a stop to, he should feel himself obliged to make reprisals; that he had two hundred Neapolitan prisoners, and that he should order one to be shot for every shell fired into the town."

"Bravo!" exclaimed the Irishman. "The rascals had found their man. Hurrah for Garibaldi!" And Garibaldi had three thundering hurrahs from our company, to which the bystanders rejoined with hearty *evvivas*.

We were consulting where to direct our steps, when a Capuchin monk stepped out from the crowd with marked gesticulations, and said to me:—

"Do you wish to see the ward where poor Francesco Riso died of his wounds?"

The offer of the friar was accepted, and up we went to the hospital of the town. On entering the ward, which was clean and tidy, we saw at its northern end a bed, from which garlands of fresh flowers were hanging. A crucifix and a few burning tapers were placed upon a board over the head of the bed. It was here that Riso expired.

"You see," exclaimed the friar, "the place where one of the martyrs of our island gave his last thoughts

to Italy, his last breath to our Lord. You do not
know, however, all the anguish the poor man had to
endure before his departure from this world."

We all besought the monk to relate the particulars
of Riso's death ; and he did so, somewhat in these
words :—

" It is a sad story, which I shall never forget. Poor
Riso was almost dying, when one morning Miniscalco
made his appearance at the bedside of the sufferer.
He told him that it lay in his power to spare the life
of his father, for that, if he would consent to denounce
his accomplices, the old man should not be shot. Poor
Riso summoned up all his strength, and with the voice
of a dying man said to the Director of the Bourbonic
police, ' My accomplices, sir, are Italy and God.'   He
then turned on his side, and refused to answer any further questions. The poor man," added the monk, " thus
saved his honour, without the remorse of sacrificing
his father's life ; for, shortly before his death, he was
informed that, when Miniscalco urged him to speak,
the old man he loved so much had been already
shot."

This narrative was sad enough to justify the curses
on the King of Naples with which the monk concluded ; for it was hardly to be expected that any feeling of charity towards Miniscalco and his master
should animate one who had so recently witnessed the
devilish devices of their cruelty.

From the hospital our steps were directed to the
fortress, where a large number of Palermitans had been
imprisoned during the last month of the deposed
tyranny. To show the reader how indiscriminately

those arrests had been ordered by Miniscalco, it is enough to say that lads, old men, noblemen, and people belonging to all classes of society, were shut up and continually threatened with death, without being informed of the cause of their imprisonment. Amongst the more aristocratic prisoners were Prince Colonna (the present *attaché* to the Italian Legation in London), Don Lanza, uncle of the Prince Buttera, and Prince Giardini, who were all three manacled together wrist to wrist.

Our survey of Palermo being at an end, we prepared to depart for Melazzo. Count Litta was anxious to fulfil his mission, and our travelling companions and myself were not less desirous to join the head-quarters of Garibaldi. On that very evening, therefore, we bade farewell to Palermo, and steamed out of the bay towards Melazzo, where we arrived at daybreak next day.

My readers are already acquainted with the position of this town; so I need not again describe it. As soon as we had landed, we hastened to Garibaldi's head-quarters, which were established in a palace facing the sea. We passed through the crowded streets of the little town, deserted only a few days before by almost all its inhabitants, who did not like to find themselves amidst the storm of cannon-balls, or to hear too closely the rattle of musketry. Some of my readers will perhaps ask why the people of Melazzo left the town, instead of falling on the rear of its Neapolitan defenders. To say the truth, the Sicilians are not all courageous, and the smell of gun-powder seemed not to be very popular in that part of the island.   An honest citizen of Melazzo, to whom I addressed the same question which I have put into the reader's mouth, answered, " Courage is a gift of nature; and on this score nature has not been generous with the Melazzese." The remark was but too true. The people of this southern city like well enough to talk, scream, and gesticulate, with an accompaniment of juicy fruit and iced water; but they are not very fond of decisive action.   I do not wish to wrong the Sicilians, for they are in many respects a noble race; but the populations of Palermo, Messina, Partenico, and two or three minor towns are, I should say, the most warlike of the island : the rest will shrink from fighting until they are taught and trained.   In Sicily, as in the other Neapolitan provinces, ignorance and demoralization (purposely encouraged by the Bourbon Government) have spread their fatal influences; and from such influences courage does not spring.   With elements like these at work, no community, even were it of the old Roman or Hellenic stamp, could keep alive the warlike instinct of its nature.   Matters, however, are in a fair way of changing; for, since Sicily has been freed, it gives to the Italian army soldiers who are worthy comrades of those drawn from the provinces of Piedmont, Lombardy, Tuscany, and the Æmilia.

In the immediate vicinity of Garibaldi's head-quarters, I met two officers of my acquaintance.   One of these was Carissimi, whom, it will be remembered, I left simple sergeant during the Lombard campaign, but who was now captain of a small squadron of Hussars which he had organized.   The other was

Missori, the hero of Melazzo, who wore the insignia of a Major. These kind friends introduced us to Garibaldi's apartment. It was swarming with officers and private soldiers, busily at work, and talking with all the force of their lungs. Padre Gavazzi was also there. He had exchanged the gown of the Barnabite monks for the red shirt of the Garibaldians, and was to be the Peter the Hermit of the national crusade.

When we were ushered into the room of Garibaldi, he was writing despatches at a small table, for he intended to start in a few hours for Gesso, where Colonel Medici had preceded him. His manners were, as usual, very cordial and kind, and he said that he was most grateful to the English people for all they had done to help the cause.

" I am very proud," he proceeded, addressing Count Litta, " of having some English officers and soldiers amongst my troops. They represent that great nation which will always be the defender of freedom in Europe."

Colonels Peard and Dunne were present, and they naturally thanked the General.

" I am not flattering either your countrymen or you, gentlemen," said the Liberator, turning towards the two English officers. " I am satisfied with you and your companions ; and I mean exactly what I say."

I do not know whether the General had occasion to change his opinion on this subject when the battalion of British volunteers joined his camp before Capua. It may be so ; for, with the exception of their gallant Colonel, and a few officers like Lord

Seymour, they were assuredly not very manageable fellows.

Dunne, Peard, Windham, and two or three other of these English amateurs, had already shown at Melazzo that they could be most efficient officers. On my arrival at that town, the first-named of these gentlemen was very popular at Garibaldi's camp, owing to a curious trick he had played on some of his soldiers during the last battle. Colonel Dunne was in command of a regiment formed of " Picciotti." This was the name given to the riff-raff of the Sicilian volunteers, the organization of whom had been entrusted to the Colonel. They were not very pleasant fellows to deal with, and there had been no time to train them to military discipline. Having never been placed under fire before, it was hardly to be expected that they should at once prove steady soldiers; and the first impulse of many was certainly to run away. But Colonel Dunne would not allow such tricks to be played before him with impunity. He had a good sword in his hand, and he used it freely. Woe to the " Picciotto" who on that day flinched from his post! He was a dead man. A few minutes before the scuffle which, but for the interposition of Missori, would have cost Garibaldi his life, a battalion of Dunne's regiment had debouched on the high road of Melazzo, skirting the wall of a garden from which a company of Neapolitans was keeping up a brisk fire. Dunne directed one of his companies to escalade the wall, jump into the garden, and dislodge the enemy. The order, however, was not executed with the quickness which the Colonel desired. Seeing that his men were wavering, he resorted to the usual expedient of his sword, sabring his "Picciotti" right and left. But even in this way the Colonel could not get his orders executed. He therefore galloped amidst the files of his men, and grasping two of them by the shirt, threw them into the garden like puppets. This, repeated two or three times, had the desired effect. The Neapolitans, seeing the Garibaldians enter the garden as if they had descended from the sky, took to their heels, crying out, "A malora! volano, volano!" ("They fly, they fly!")

After having remained a quarter of an hour in Garibaldi's room, my companions and I left the ground to Count Litta, knowing that the General had something better to do than gossiping with fighting amateurs. I must now make more specific allusion than I have yet done to the errand on which the Count had been sent. Pressed by foreign diplomacy, the King had been obliged to exercise his influence, to induce the conqueror of Sicily to renounce his already too manifest project of crossing the Straits, and carrying on his work of national redemption throughout the whole of the Neapolitan kingdom. I think it not without interest to transcribe here the letter of which Count Giulio Litta was the bearer. It ran thus :—

" GENERAL,—You know that I did not approve of your expedition, and that I was entirely foreign to it ; but to-day the very grave circumstances in which Italy is placed make it a duty to enter into direct communication with you.

" In the event of the King of Naples consenting to

evacuate the whole of Sicily, voluntarily abandoning all sort of action, and formally pledging himself to exercise no pressure whatsoever upon the Sicilians, so that the latter may freely pronounce their will, and choose the mode of government which they may prefer, I believe it will be wise in you to renounce altogether any further enterprise against the kingdom of Naples. In the contrary event, I expressly reserve my entire liberty of action, and relieve myself from making any comment in regard to your projects.

" Your affectionate

" VICTOR EMMANUEL."

The result of this letter is well known. Full of respect and affection for his King, Garibaldi nevertheless declined to comply with the Royal request. His mission was too noble to be relinquished : he had sworn to Italy to accomplish it, and he kept his word.

The convention of Messina, of which mention was made at the end of the preceding chapter, freed that town from the despotism under which it had long suffered, and gave to Garibaldi a safe base of operations. Messina accordingly became the place of rendezvous of the Garibaldian army; and of idle adventurers of all sorts. My travelling companions and myself (to whom were added Major Corte and his wife) made up our minds to start also for Messina. After a great deal of trouble we procured a boat, not without some quarrelling with the rowers, who were lazy, and afraid of meeting the Neapolitan cruisers. There is not a more noisy set of men in the world than the Sicilian boatmen. They quarrel among themselves about anything or nothing, and scream in so diabolical a manner that a traveller who does not know them would believe they were at every moment cutting one another's throats. Their squabbles, however, are always bloodless, and it is very seldom that they lead even to a resort to the fists. Insolent to the traveller who allows himself to be bullied, they are the most docile fellows in the world when they see they have to deal with people who are not disposed to let them have their own way. When I saw that the quarrel which had delayed our departure from Melazzo was likely to be renewed on our passage to Faro, I gave them a piece of good advice, which was enforced by an intimation (uttered half in Italian, half in English) from the Irishman, that he would kill them if they did not proceed. This being supported by no less an argument than the production of a revolver, matters began to look serious. There were many exclamations of "Gesú Maria!" but at last the fellows pushed off, and away we went.

On approaching Faro Point—which we did after a few hours' rowing, without meeting any of the enchanting Sirens whom the Roman poets of old told us existed there—we saw the flotilla, consisting of hundreds of fishing boats, which had been collected by Garibaldi with a view to the passage of the liberating army across the channel into Calabria. The boats were either anchored on a sort of lake communicating by a small canal with the Straits once famous for the whirlpool of Scylla and Charybdis, or were moving about with stores and ammunition.

The scenery of the surrounding country increased the picturesqueness of the place.   Opposite to us was the mountainous Calabrian coast.   At the brink of the blue waters lay the villages of Gallico and Villa San Giovanni, with their hedges of cactus and their groves of orange and olive trees.   On the left, the fort of Scylla towered at the extreme point of the Straits on the summit of a mountain whose pointed rocks appear like so many pinnacles of a Gothic cathedral.   Further on, the eye follows the line of the coast, broken either by necks of land, or by deep ravines marking the course of the mountain torrents, which the people of that country call in their soft dialect *fiumare*.   On the right, almost facing Messina, the gay and pleasant town of Reggio is seen whitening on the declivity of a gentle slope, as if it were cradled in a garden of flowers and orange trees.   On the Faro side, the hills which bend gently towards Messina are marked by the square tower of the forts of Gonzaga and San Salvatore.   Opposite to the last-named town, the stern castle of Reggio frowns darkly, as if jealous of the surrounding loveliness.   A neck of land joins the citadel to the town of Messina; the boundaries of which isthmus were marked, at the time to which I am referring, by a double row of Neapolitan and Garibaldian sentries; for, according to the convention entered into by Clary and Medici, the ground was to be regarded as neutral.

Such was the magnificent scenery which we beheld from the lighthouse of Faro Point, where Garibaldi had by that time fixed his head-quarters.   It was there that he directed the movements of his fleet of

fishing-boats; it was there also that he organized that
singular army which was destined in a few days to rout
the well-appointed legions of Francis II., and to conquer
a kingdom by simply marching through the insurgent
provinces of Calabria and Basilicata. How strange a
spectacle did that army present! What a variety of
uniforms did it exhibit—flannel shirts of every colour,
white bournouses, and feathered Puritan hats! Here
comes by a well-known Countess in a half-hussar,
half-amazonian dress; there, the sharpshooters of
Colonel Peard are parading in their brown blouses.
Down below, several of Dunne's regiment are being
drilled by their English officers, the elegance of whose
red jackets contrasts with the rougher costume of their
comrades. On the left of a dirty osteria, towards the
beach, a hut has been constructed; and a large inscription tells the passer-by that the "Albion Club" has
been established there. British activity is never at
fault: where there are ten Englishmen there must be
a club. It is true that the "Albion Club" at Faro
was only a poor hut, the floor of which was covered
with a mat, while two rough wooden benches served
for divans. But there was always a glass of wine to
be had there, and a sausage and crust of bread were
never wanting. Towards noon, you had also a
chance of securing what at Faro in those days was
called a dinner; *i.e.*, an omelet, plenty of fried fish,
and excellent figs. A butler and a cook were attached to the club. The first was a half Maltese,
half Greek, who made a good profit from the sour wine
he sold; the second was a poor Neapolitan, who was
so afraid of the Royal cruisers steaming up and

down the Straits that he was continually over-frying the fish or burning the omelet, when the vessels approached too near the coast.

The suffocating heat of the intense Sicilian day at length abates, and the breath of evening begins to crisp the blue waters of that narrow sea. The fishermen of the neighbouring villages light their torches, and start on their night-fishing errand; and all becomes quiet at Faro. Nothing is to be heard, except the watch-cry of the sentinels, and from time to time the report of guns along the opposite coast. The "Albion Club" is then turned into a large bedroom, where the members lie down without distinction of rank or nationality. If the Neapolitan cruisers are not bent on mischief—if the guns on the forts of Pezzo and Alta Fiumara are silent—there is a chance of spending a quiet night. The bed is none of the softest; but weariness makes it comfortable enough for sound sleep. The sun rises early in August, and at sunrise the drums beat, the camp is busy again, and all around is life and movement.

The first to rouse the slumbers of the camp are the sword-fish fishermen; for they are numerous enough along the Straits. The look-out man has already climbed to the mast-head of his boat, whence he descries the much-desired fish, and calls out to the other fishermen in their boats, " To Scylla!" or, " To Reggio!" according to the course taken by the creature, in its ignorance of the danger which threatens it. The boats then proceed in the direction indicated, and a man, standing at the bow, with a harpoon in his hand, gives chase to the fish. When the exertions of the fishermen are successful, things proceed smoothly enough; but if the fish slips away—a case which is by no means rare—a squabble begins among the boatmen, which never fails to end in oaths and imprecations, and appeals to innocent saints and Madonnas.

From Faro Point to Messina is only a few miles. The road is dusty; but donkeys and *carrozzelle* are always in attendance, and with a few *carlini* the noisy driver is satisfied. Let us pass through the streets of Messina. The same liveliness is to be seen as at Faro. Everywhere, the state of things which prevailed under the sway of the Bourbons' has given place to the new *régime*. In the Piazza Ferdinando Secondo, the statue of that worthy Sovereign is no more visible, having been pulled down by the people. A large crowd is passing, shouting out, "Down with the tyrant! down with the tyrant!" A host of half-naked *facchini* are dragging along another image of his late Majesty. Mr. Gladstone was certainly right when he wrote to Lord Aberdeen that the King was anything but popular in his dominions. The Messinese, at any rate, have given unmistakeable proof of their dislike of the late monarch.

Political demonstrations are no doubt very interesting to those who have left the comforts of life to follow the great events of a revolution; but a man, whatever his curiosity, must look out for a lodging and a dinner. To secure the first, we naturally hastened to the hotel, or at least to a shabby house which was honoured by that name.

"We want four rooms," said Major Corte, the spokesman of our party, addressing a half-ragged waiter.

"Four rooms, Eccellenza! I have not a bed to spare in the whole house," replies the waiter, and immediately slips off like an eel, for he has been summoned by the oaths of a roaring French Colonel, who for many days has been the terror of the place.

What is to be done? We are ten in number : three Irishmen; an Oxford man, who answers to the name of Broffy; Lieutenant Colfield, saved from death in a wonderful manner during the Indian mutiny; two other more obscure Britons; Major Corte, his wife, and myself. We cannot sleep *sub Jove;* we must find a *gîte.* The Town Hall, which plays so great a part in political commotions and in warlike times, is near at hand; so we resolve on hunting up the Sindaco. To the Town Hall accordingly we go; but the stairs and rooms are thronged with applicants on the same errand. All have a right to a lodging—at least, they say so. The poor town-clerks are in a state of stupefaction, and can scarcely answer the questions put by scores of people at the same time. At last, the military rank of our spokesman, and his arm supported by a sling—for Major Corte was wounded at Melazzo— facilitate matters, and we are taken into the presence of the worthy Mayor of Messina. Sindaci are all alike in Italy; and if there were truth in their words, they would do anything to accommodate you, even to the extent of giving up their beds. The reception we met with on the occasion to which I am referring was very courteous. Many bows were exchanged, many exclamations uttered, when it was stated that the Major had been wounded at Melazzo; but neither the

Sindaco nor the Town Hall clerks ever came to the most important point of all.

Had I adopted the bar as my profession, I do not think I should have lost a cause for want of urgent pleading. My tongue is nimble enough, and I am seldom in need of arguments to support my views. I therefore began summing up our case, which the Sindaco had chosen to drop, either purposely, or in consequence of the propensity which characterizes southern natures to indulge in idle talk.

" Sir," said I, abruptly, " we have come here to ask you to billet us in some way or other."

" To be sure, my friends," replied the Sindaco. " We are all brothers, and it is but right that those who have shed their blood for us should be made as comfortable as possible. Here, Don Peppino!" continued the official, calling to some one in the crowd which thronged the hall; " make haste! Let us see where we can put the Major."

" That is all very well," said I, " but we are with him, and we also want a lodging."

Presently, Don Peppino came out from the crowd.

" Here I am, Eccellenza," he said, presenting to the Sindaco the list of the lodgings allotted to military men.

" Well, let us see where we can accommodate the Major," pursued the Sindaco, reading the paper.

" And his suite," exclaimed I.

" But who are you, gentlemen? You do not wear any uniform, and I suppose you do not belong to the army."

The Sindaco's observation was logical enough,

and it was difficult to answer him. Major Corte,
however, stood by our side, and we knew he would not
leave his friends in the lurch.   He therefore soon
conferred upon me the title of historiographer to the
expedition—a charge which I at once accepted with a
thankful smile.   As for our companions, it was difficult to persuade even a Sindaco that men who could
scarcely speak half-a-dozen words of "the sweet language of the *si*," as Dante calls it, had any official
capacity in the army of the Liberator.   The *canard*
was too big to be swallowed, and our English tourists,
to whom I had translated the observations of the civic
magistrate, were naturally enough alarmed; for to be
thrown on the streets of a strange city in a foreign
land does not present a pleasing prospect.   The
reader, however, will recollect that there were three
Irishmen amongst us, and where there are three
"Paddies" there is no difficulty which cannot be sur-
mounted. The sharpest of the lot spoke Italian decently
enough.   He therefore stepped forward, and said :—

"Sir Sindaco, your Excellency"— (Irishmen are
always quick enough to see when to apply the right
titles to the right men, or at least to employ them so
as to be of use)—"you must know that we are all
men of the highest rank, more or less charged with
diplomatic missions from our Government."

This was the flash of a genius.   The poor Sindaco
took it for granted that the Irishman was a cousin of
the great Agitator, and that the rest were sons,
nephews, or other connexions of the British Ministers.

This *coup de scène* produced its effect, and an hour
later we left the town, regularly billeted on a

Signor Domenico Rosso, or Russo, if I remember the name.

But, alas! our miseries were not yet at an end. Don Peppino accompanied us to the lodging we had had so much trouble in securing; but we found that the landlord had disappeared, taking with him mattresses, linen, plate—in a word, everything that was indispensable to our comfort. A sort of simpleton was the only person left in the house; and, had it not been for the kindness of Mr. Richards, the English vice-consul of the place, we should certainly have slept upon the laths of the bedstead, and dried our faces on our handkerchiefs.

Messina is not a town about which there is much to say. Except the interest which the warlike bustle and the preparations for crossing the Straits then offered, there was nothing striking in our mode of life. Day after day passed very much alike. A sermon in the open air, preached by Father Gavazzi or Father Pantaleo, and a great show of coloured lights and banners, formed the main features of Messinese life. The Garibaldian officers were to be found at the cafés or the *osterie*, or at a sort of club which had been opened by the Countess I have mentioned above. For myself, I had the good luck to make two valuable acquaintances, viz., Captain Stuart Forbes, who had chosen to follow Garibaldi's Staff as an amateur, and Captain Lambert of the *Scylla*, which was then in the roadstead of Messina. The hospitality of English naval officers is well known; and Captain Lambert exercised it with a kindness worthy of his nation.

In spite of the monotony of our life, night alarms,

G 2

and the excitement they brought with them, were not wanting. General Clary had been superseded by old General Fergola in the command of the citadel, and Fergola was a man who seemed disinclined to allow us to pass our nights in peace. Every now and then, we were suddenly roused by the report of the citadel guns, which, even without cause, sent shells and shot into the town. There was then a great running about, a general screaming of women and children, a rapid movement of Garibaldians, but seldom any killed or wounded. It was the old story of the mountain bringing forth a mouse — "much ado about nothing." In consequence of this, Captain Lambert frequently called on Fergola, and energetically protested against his proceedings as a violation of the convention. Fergola explained by saying that he had no control over his troops ; and thus the matter generally ended.

A ride or a walk to Faro was of daily occurrence, both for me and Captain Forbes, for we were almost considered as belonging to Garibaldi's Staff. With his invariable kindness, the General had furnished us with a pass which enabled us to go unmolested through the camp. When a carriage or a donkey could not be had, and when the dust of the road was too annoying, we tried to hire a boatman who would take us to Faro and back. This, however, was a very difficult affair to manage. The chance of getting a boat for love or money was not great, for the Messinese boatmen, as I have before stated, were such cowards that, at the first sight of a Neapolitan cruiser, or the first splashing of a cannon-ball in the water, they began to scream like children, and to pull the boat ashore as fast as they could. The practice was not very pleasant; yet one could scarcely help being amused at hearing the fellows address all sorts of prayers to the Madonna and the Saints as soon as they thought themselves in danger. In Sicily, as well as on the Neapolitan continent, the people are generally bigoted and ignorant. The Neapolitans boast of the liquefying blood of St. Januarius; and the Messinese enjoy the no less wonderful privilege of possessing an autograph letter of the Holy Virgin. What is still stranger, I have been told that the inhabitants of Teormina evince great devotion towards similar documents written, as they assure us, by the hand of San Diavolo. Where they have been able to find such a saint I cannot say; but, judging from what I heard from a priest at Messina, both letters are genuine, and their authenticity indisputable.

CHAPTER IV.

THE LANDING IN CALABRIA.

Communism at Bronte—Calabrese Deputations—Missori's Expedition—Failure in the Attempt to capture a Neapolitan Fort—
Anxieties and Hopes—Missori at Aspromonte—Night Alarms
—Narrow Escape of the Members of the Albion Club—Apprehensions of the Neapolitan Government—A Neapolitan Politician at Work—Garibaldi disappears—French Threats—Garibaldi's Army—His Generals—Return of the Liberator—The
Garibaldians Start for Reggio—Landing at Capo d'Armi—An
ill-fated Vessel—The Neapolitan Army in Calabria—Garibaldi's
March on Reggio—A useful Countryman—I leave Messina
on a dangerous Errand—Reggio—The Neapolitan General
Gallotti—Garibaldi's Attack on Reggio—Combat at Night in
the Town—General Briganti's threatening Movement—Capitulation of the Castle.

WHILST Garibaldi's mind was engrossed by the difficult task of organizing his army, and making the
necessary arrangements to cross the Straits, the population of the small town of Bronte, having a somewhat confused idea of liberty, thought proper to in-
augurate a communistical movement. Political assassinations began to stain the town, and such was the
exasperation of the Brontese against the *sorci*—as the
adherents of the Bourbons were called—that in less
than a week about fifty of them were slain in cold
blood. Nor was this all. Under the pretext of getting
rid of the supporters of the reactionary party, the

rabble of the town began to divide amongst themselves the property of their victims. Bourbon spies and Bourbon adherents only reaped what they had sown—hatred and bloody revenge : however, Garibaldi sent Bixio to put a stop to such atrocities. From the short sketch I have already given of the character of this intrepid companion and intimate friend of Garibaldi, the reader will infer that he accomplished his task with complete success. On arriving at Bronte, he had the ringleaders of the movement arrested, summarily tried by a court-martial, and despatched to the other world in less than an hour. At the time, a story was told at Messina, which, if "*non vera, era ben trovata,*" as the Italian proverb says, being very characteristic of General Bixio. It was stated that when the chief of the movement—a ruffian who had himself slaughtered ten *sorci*—was brought before the General, the latter was seized with such a fit of passion that, drawing his revolver, he shot the culprit at once. I do not vouch for the truth of this story : I only relate it as I heard it.

The *Jacquerie* of Bronte having been put down, Garibaldi's activity was wholly directed towards preparing for the safe landing of his army on the Calabrian coast. This was not an easy enterprise ; for the Straits were constantly guarded by the Neapolitan cruisers, and, on the other side of the channel, a powerful Neapolitan force was ready—or at least was supposed to be ready—to stand its ground. Calabrese patriots, however, were continually arriving either at Faro or at Messina, urging the Liberator to hasten his march, and free their country from the detested

soldiery.   One day, whilst we were taking our breakfast with the General at Faro, a deputation, composed
of twenty-six persons, the representatives of as many
towns in Calabria, came to lay the state of affairs
before the General, and arrange with him for future
action and reciprocal support.   Some of these deputies
were mere peasants, though very orderly, and exercising great influence in their mountain districts;
others were advocates, landowners, or Sindaci of
the towns.   Their dress was most picturesque.
Even the richest of the Calabrians are in revolutionary times proud of wearing the pointed hat trimmed
with velvet ribands, as a part of the national costume.
As for the peasants, they were clothed in their mountain garb from head to foot; velvet jacket and breeches,
coloured stockings, and goat-skin sandals.   The Calabrian deputation looked, therefore, more like a band
of actors, ready to appear in some operatic scene,
than political messengers coming on a grave and
important errand.   The news they brought to Garibaldi, however, was so promising, and the assurances
that Calabria would rise as one man, in spite of the
recent constitution granted by Francis II., were so
emphatic, that, on the night of the 8th of August,
Garibaldi made up his mind to send a column of *enfans
perdus* on the Calabrian coast, in the hope of sur-
prising the fort of Altafiumara just opposite to Faro
Point.

The officer selected for this dangerous enterprise
was Major Missori. A few days previously, he had gone
to reconnoitre the Calabrian coast, and had returned,
bringing information of the condition of Calabria and

the Calabrians which was perfectly in accordance with the statement made by the deputation.

Great was the excitement at Faro when we saw by the unusual movements of the boats that something was on the eve of occurring; still greater, when, about eight o'clock in the evening, the news spread that Missori, with two hundred men picked from the old Cacciatori, Guides, and Genoese Carbineers, was to cross over to the continent. At this announcement, all amateur soldiers and privileged correspondents hastened on board the vessels anchored at Faro, or took up a position on the shore, to witness the thrilling sight. By sunset, a south-west wind drove dense clouds towards the Calabrian coasts. A dark night was therefore pretty certain—a night favourable to the enterprise so long meditated by the General-in-Chief; and we were not deceived in our expectations. The rays of the rising moon were unable to pierce the heavy vapours of the atmosphere, and the whole tract of land which skirts the Sicilian coast was wrapped in a thick veil of mist. At nine o'clock, Garibaldi, who was on board the *Aberdeen* steamer, gave his last instructions to Major Missori and to Alberto Mario—two gallant fellows, each worthy of the other; and at a quarter past nine, all the men were on board the fishing-boats, ready to sail. But here a unanimous complaint was raised by the soldiers who were not of the envied number. They clasped the hand of Major Missori, and adjured Major Nullo not to leave them behind. One pleaded his having been wounded in the Lombard campaign of 1859; another urged, as a claim to being selected, the fact of his coming from the same part of Italy as Colonel Mussolino, or some other officer appointed to a share in that perilous undertaking. I well remember the face of a young Genoese carbineer whilst he was adjuring Major Nullo to allow him to follow the heroic band. It was, indeed, a moving sight to witness the grief of those who were to be left behind, and to hear their appealing supplications. Order, however, was soon restored, for the sentiment of duty was uppermost in the hearts of those noble fellows.

Half-past nine was pealing from the bell-tower of the Faro church, when the expedition started amidst the surrounding darkness of night. On sailed the little flotilla of twenty boats; but, at a certain point of the Straits, six of them, having lost the track, returned. The remaining fourteen kept well together, and made for the appointed spot; but, either from the darkness, or from the influence of that current which probably gave rise to the old story of the whirlpool of Charybdis, the boats were unable to approach the coast at the point designated, and so, landed the expedition a little to the left of the fort of Altafiumara. To reach its walls, Missori and his men had to make their way through the obscurity along the rocky paths of the coast. A signal had been agreed upon, to inform Garibaldi of the safe landing of Missori; and we all awaited with anxious expectation the appearance of the longed-for light—the signal of success. Minutes seemed hours; every sound which broke the stillness of the night a messenger of misfortune.

At last, the rattling of musketry, followed by the

roar of a gun, was heard, and it became painfully obvious that the brave fellows had failed in their enterprise. The expedition, having (as I have already stated) been thrown to the left of the fort, was marching in that direction when it was met by a patrol of Neapolitans, who at once opened fire, and put the troops in the fort on the alert. To surprise the garrison of Altafiumara was therefore out of the question; and Missori could do nothing but take his men across the mountain paths of Aspromonte, and get on to the high land of Calabria. Protected by the night, he pushed through the narrow ravines of the Fiumara, and passed unobserved the outposts of the enemy, who, believing that Garibaldi himself had landed with a considerable force, did not like to go forward at random towards the mountains. We, who were ignorant of the escape of the expedition, waited in an anguish of suspense to know the fate which had befallen our friends. The noise of firing had ceased, and the opposite coast was again buried in silence; yet no signal appeared. After a while, however, a faint light was perceived above the fort, slowly ascending in the direction of Aspromonte. It was believed to be the signal agreed upon between the General and Missori. The enterprise had failed, but the two hundred heroes—the flower of Italy—we had good reason to hope were safe.

When the wavering light first appeared, I was standing outside the Albion Club with some friends, already mourning the supposed fate of Missori and Nullo, whom we all liked exceedingly. Following the light with our eyes, as it appeared at intervals, we were discussing whether it was really the desired signal, or only a bonfire lighted by some shepherd, when an old man, who chanced to pass by, suddenly stopped, and, addressing me, said :——

"You have no reason to be alarmed; I am a Calabrian, and live in a village on the road to Aspromonte. I am well acquainted with the country, and can tell from here the very point where the light is moving. There is no doubt that it is the signal agreed upon; the expedition is now on its way to Sant' Angelo, where it will find the armed bands of my countrymen. Be tranquil. Major Missori, if he did not fall when we heard the musketry, is now safe."

As the old man was uttering these words, I recognised him. He was one of the Calabrian deputies whom I had met two days before at Garibaldi's headquarters. And he was right; for an hour afterwards the boatmen came back with the news that the two hundred patriots had reached, almost unhurt, the mountain paths of Aspromonte. This intelligence was confirmed next morning by a messenger sent from Sant' Angelo by Missori. The cry, "They are on Neapolitan soil, and safe!" was soon repeated by the crowd of soldiers, and we all lay down to rest with a hymn of thanksgiving in our hearts.

For myself, I could not sleep during the whole of that night. My mind could only dwell upon one thought : that, after eleven years of sorrow and despair, the national flag was again hoisted upon the misty tops of the Calabrian mountains.

Making their way through the defiles, the band of Missori stood their ground for many days, marching from village to village, everywhere spreading the revolution, and preparing the people for the triumphant progress of Garibaldi through Calabria. By the middle of August, the invading force was increased by 2000 Calabrians, and could therefore have defended itself had it been attacked by the Neapolitans. But the Garibaldians were in no way molested, General Briganti contenting himself with sending a column which never attacked Missori's band, and a despatch containing a haughty intimation to surrender: an intimation which was scornfully rejected by Missori, who wrote back that the soldiers of liberty were ready to receive the supporters of tyranny when they dared to come.

Until we crossed over to Reggio, it was our evening occupation to watch the large fires lighted up on the ridges above the forts of Scylla and Del Cavallo, and over the Villa San Giovanni and Gallico. These fires were signals made by Missori to intimate to Garibaldi that the revolution was spreading through the country he occupied. In this way the Neapolitans were kept continually on the alert, every now and then firing on our boats, or at the Faro batteries. Alarms, therefore, occurred almost every night, and they became still more frequent after the 10th of August, Garibaldi having permanently established his head-quarters at the Lighthouse of the Straits, from which the village of Faro derives its name. Endowed with restless activity, the General was everywhere, directing everything. He found time to occupy himself with politics, to superintend the organization of his army and navy, and to receive deputations; in a word, he was the very soul of that great movement.

At daybreak he left the *Aberdeen*, where he generally slept, and came on shore to resume the labours of the day; and from that time to nightfall his busy hand and brain were almost ceaselessly at work.

During those short nights, Neapolitan men-of-war were perpetually steaming up and down the Straits, exchanging signals, by means of coloured rockets, either with the forts on the coast, or with the citadel of Messina. On one occasion, whilst I was sleeping at the Albion Club, with Captain Forbes and some other Englishmen, a Neapolitan frigate thought proper to disturb our slumbers by sending some shells in the direction of the batteries close to the Lighthouse. The gunners, however, having pointed their mortars too far to the left, their shells, instead of falling into the batteries, exploded close to our hut. Such an unexpected accident naturally excited great confusion amongst the members of the club, whose committee the next day proposed that the institution should be dissolved, as it would be madness to risk ingloriously the lives of the sleepers. This resolution, however, met with great opposition. An American, who commanded a Garibaldian steamer, set forth that both the "Lion" and the "Stars and Stripes" would be "taken down a peg or two," were they to retreat. "What will the Garibaldians say?" pursued the Yankee; "they will say we have not only withdrawn before danger, but that we have even 'bolted' —'sloped'—'mizzled.'" This harangue of the transatlantic orator, strongly backed by the younger members of the association, carried the point. During the day, however, an order came from General Orsini to demolish the hut at once; and thus fell the Albion Club, never to rise again on the beach of Faro Point.

Missori's successful landing on the one hand, and the expected crossing of the Straits by the whole of Garibaldi's army on the other, naturally increased the apprehensions of Francis II. and his Ministers. To those alarming events were to be added the failure of the mission to Turin of Signor Manna (who had been sent to propose an alliance between the Neapolitan kingdom and Sardinia), and the respectful but firm refusal of Garibaldi to follow the advice of Victor Emmanuel contained in the letter which Count Litta Modignani had brought to Marsala. The revolution was also gaining ground in the continental provinces of the kingdom, and it was easy to foresee that, as soon as Garibaldi had set foot on Neapolitan soil, the three Calabrias and the Basilicata would at once rise. The Ministers of Francis II., and especially Prince Torella, De Martino, and General Pianelli, had no great faith in the army; for they knew by experience that the instruments of a base and ignorant despotism seldom prove good soldiers on the field of battle. Matters having come to such extremities, Commendatore De Martino (who, although a Liberal, felt that the duty of an honest man was not to desert his master in the hour of danger) consented to listen to a proposition made to him by an old conspirator who had long personally known Garibaldi. De Martino could not have believed that the plan proposed had any chance of success; but, to get rid of the man, as he had made himself troublesome, he consented to the proposal. A sum of money was paid to him (for without money such individuals do not put themselves out of their way), and he was sent to Calabria, charged to offer Garibaldi 50,000 troops and the use of the Neapolitan navy in the war for the liberation of Venice, if he would consent not to cross the Straits. The mission was of course a failure. But it was not the only means resorted to by the reactionary party of the Neapolitan court to get rid of Garibaldi. When I was at Messina, a rumour was current in the city that two men had been arrested, as being connected with a plot which, if successful, would have cost the General his life. I do not know what degree of credibility the story deserves; but it was generally believed at the time. At any rate, a Calabrian was arrested at Faro, who confessed that he had been sent by one of Francis II.'s uncles for the purpose of assassinating the General. The man said he had accepted the sum of 1000 piastres to this end; and that he had come to Faro, not to perpetrate the crime, but, on the contrary, to warn Garibaldi of the intention of the reactionary party, so that he might be on his guard for the future. But neither diplomatic expedients nor threats of assassination were likely to induce Garibaldi to desist from his patriotic enterprise.

Every day bringing new troops to Messina, to Faro, and to the minor towns or villages of the neighbourhood, it was to be anticipated that the crossing of the Straits would be effected at any moment. This, however, was delayed, owing to some unexpected news which came from Piedmont to Garibaldi at Faro. One morning, as I was standing with Major Caldesi and other Garibaldians at the door of the Lighthouse, discussing the probabilities of Missori's whereabouts, a Garibaldian steamer was seen to enter the Straits, and stop at the landing-place of Faro. The galley was lowered, and two persons came ashore. In a few minutes, the new-comers—who were no other than Dr. Bertani, the political agent of Garibaldi at Genoa, and the Marquis Trecchi, an orderly officer of Victor Emmanuel—made their appearance at head-quarters, and were ushered into Garibaldi's room.

" Big birds !" said Caldesi to me. " Those fellows must have some important mission to fulfil. I hope they are not come on the same errand as Count Litta."

Caldesi, however, had guessed rightly ; for, after the Doctor and Trecchi had been with Garibaldi a few minutes, General Sirtori was telegraphed to proceed without delay to Faro, Garibaldi being on the point of starting—though nobody but Sirtori knew for what place. And for a time the Liberator did really disappear from the island.

The cause of this sudden and mysterious departure from Sicily was simply as follows :—While Garibaldi was occupied with the organization of his army, Dr. Bertani had not been idle at Genoa. He had gathered together a division of 5000 men, which was apparently intended for Sicily, but which was really meant for the invasion of the Papal States. It was intended that this force should be commanded by the French revolutionary leader, Colonel Charras, then in exile in Switzerland, and that it should be sent to operate against the reactionary army under Lamoricière. Charras, however, either declined the offer, or was unable to accept it. The expedition therefore sailed from Genoa under the command of Colonel Pianciani ; but having arrived in the Gulf of Aranci, on the coast of the island of Sardinia, the Ministers of Victor Emmanuel, who had received reliable information as to its real course, sent orders to the Sardinian squadron to stop it, and to intimate to Colonel Pianciani that he would only be allowed to take his troops to Sicily. At the same time, the Marquis Trecchi was sent by the King to Garibaldi, to inform him that, in the case of Pianciani's force invading the Papal States, it would have to deal with the French, who had received orders to oppose any such attempts. On the receipt of this news, Garibaldi left the command of the army to General Sirtori, and hastened to the Gulf of Aranci, to settle the matter, and to come back in a few days, bringing the 5000 men with him. Before leaving Faro, he ordered Colonel Cosenz to do all that was possible to throw a force on the other side of the Straits, and thus afford help to Missori and his brave companions. Many of these attempts were made during the absence of Garibaldi ; and some companies even succeeded in getting to the Calabrian coast, though others failed.

Matters were now drawing near to a conclusion. The famous treaties of 1815 were threatened with another rent. "L'Armata Meridionale" had been greatly increased ; indeed, so much so that, aided by the insurrection, it could easily have matched the legions of Francis II. Its organization was of course somewhat irregular, as always is the case with armies which are hastily formed, and whose discipline has not been severe. In order to place his forces in accord with the army of Victor Emmanuel, Garibaldi gave to his four divisions the numbers which followed those of the Sardinian army, at that time consisting of fourteen divisions. The first brigade, under General Eber, a Hungarian of great literary and military merit, was about 2000 strong ; the second, commanded by Bixio, numbered 2500. These divisions had for their chief General Türr, the well-known Hungarian officer, so much liked by Garibaldi and by every one who comes in contact with him. Rather impetuous in his character, he is always to be found in the thickest of the fight ; amiable and generous, he was perhaps the most courteous officer of the Armata Meridionale. The second division was under Cosenz, a Neapolitan of distinction, and possessing great military knowledge. Count Milbitz, an old Polish officer, who had made himself famous at Warsaw in 1830, and at Rome in 1849 ; Sacchi, a Genoese exile, who had risen from the ranks to the post of Major in the Spanish army ; and Eberhart, a Prussian officer, were the three Brigadier-Generals of the sixteenth division, which was 8000 strong. Medici, a Lombard, rather heavy and rough, but undoubtedly the best General of the army, was in command of the seventeenth division. Its first brigade was under the orders of Simonetta, a countryman of Medici, a hard fighter, and a man endowed with all the qualities which make a good superior commander. The second brigade of this division had for its chief an old friend of Mazzini, Nicola Fabrizzi, a Modenese by birth, and a staunch patriot. This division numbered 4800 men. To

these three divisions was to be added that which
Colonel Pianciani intended to take into the Papal
States, but which joined the rest of the army in Sicily
at a later period.   Five hundred Hussars, under the
command of Carissimi ; 300 Guides, commanded by
Missori ; 450 Artillerymen, under Orsini and Scalia, and
160 Engineers,—completed this curious army, which
had been organized within a period of three months.

The navy was composed of the steam sloop *Veloce*,
and eleven steam transports.   The Marquis Anguissola,
the Neapolitan commander of the *Veloce*, had passed
over with his vessel to the National cause, and the
name *Veloce* was changed into that of *Tuckori*, from
the Hungarian officer who was killed at the taking of
Palermo.

With these forces, Garibaldi undertook and accomplished the annexation of a kingdom which might
have been defended by a well-organized army of at
least 80,000 men.   But the right cause was on his
side ; he had with him the majority of the Neapolitan
population ; and, above all, he was surrounded by that
prestige which is in itself an army.

On his arrival from the Gulf of Aranci at the
port of Teormina, on the 18th of August, Garibaldi found that the troops had almost completed
their embarkation on board the *Torino* and *Franklin*.
The force with which he was going to attempt the
first serious landing in Calabria was formed of Bixio's
brigade (2500 strong), 1000 volunteers of Colonel
Pianciani's division, and Eberhart's brigade, numbering 700 men.   At ten o'clock, the *Torino*, under the
command of Bixio, and the *Franklin*, on board of

which was Garibaldi himself, steamed off in the direction of Capo d'Armi. The two vessels were crowded in every part; bulwarks, paddle-boxes, and rigging, were all crammed with troops. To increase the difficulties of the voyage, the *Franklin* sprang a leak of a very serious character, the stoppage of which Garibaldi was obliged to superintend in person. Although the Neapolitan cruisers had given proofs that they were rather inclined to keep out of harm's way, the possibility of meeting some of them rendered the enterprise still more dangerous. To make them believe that it was from Messina and Faro that Garibaldi intended to start, troops were massed at those two points, and steamers were kept in apparent readiness to ship them. This device drew off the attention of the Neapolitans, and the expedition arrived unmolested on the Calabrian coast, at Capo d'Armi, a little before two on the following morning. Here the pilot of the *Torino*, in his anxiety to get the steamer near the shore, ran her on a sandbank, from which she could not be got off. But there was no great harm in this: the more important object had been attained, and the disembarkation of Garibaldi's troops was successfully accomplished two hours after the vessels touched the shore of the land they had come to liberate.

Before starting from Sicily, Garibaldi had sent orders to Missori to work down towards Capo d'Armi with the insurrectionary *squadre* he had collected in the districts of Aspromonte. Missori did all he could to arrive at that spot on the 19th of August; but the mountain tracks he had to follow were too arduous to permit of his succeeding.   The march of his force was besides delayed by the threatening movements of a flying column of Neapolitans, sent against the village of San Lorenzo, where he and his men had been entrenched for several days.   This intelligence was communicated to Garibaldi by a small detachment of Guides, despatched by Missori along the coast, to look out for the landing of the General.   Having sent back one of the Guides with an order to hasten Missori's march along the flank of Aspromonte, which overhangs Reggio, Garibaldi directed his men to lie down on the beach, and rest for a few hours.

There is an Italian proverb which seems to have been expressly invented to depict the course pursued by the Neapolitan navy during that wonderful campaign. When a man, whose duty it should be to run and help another, arrives too late, my countrymen say that he " carries the help of Pisa."   Such was the case with the Neapolitan Commodore on that occasion.   Scarcely had the Garibaldians lain down to rest when the ugly hulls of the *Fulminante*, and those of two other Neapolitan steamers, were seen coming up with all speed.   As at Marsala, the Neapolitan Commodore made signs to the ships to take up a position in .front of the beach, and a tremendous fire was opened on the Garibaldians.   Some confusion began to spread amongst the soldiers; but they were soon marched off towards the hills, and only two men were killed by the explosion of the shells.   The Neapolitan officer, who saw that his prey was certain to escape, then turned his wrath against the ill-fated *Torino*, which was lying on her stern, half-buried in the sand.

She was soon on fire, and the flames shed a ruddy tinge upon the glorious blue sky, and over the highest tops of the surrounding mountains. Old Etna saw the waves of the gulf in a blaze from the light of a burning furnace which was not its own. Night came on, and by that time Missori's *squadre* were working their way through the passes of Aspromonte in the direction of Reggio. From the lofty peaks of the mountains they could see the flames of the burning vessel, which, though far off, illuminated the paths they followed. The moon was just rising, and her soft rays spread a sort of airy veil over the whole of that wonderful picture—a picture which no artist's brush can paint, and no poet describe. Meanwhile, the merry songs of Garibaldi's troops, on their march towards Reggio, rose through the air, and contrasted with the booming of the distant guns of the batteries at Scylla and Faro.

It was somewhat late when Garibaldi's expedition, following the bridle-path of Aspromonte, arrived at a small hamlet above the Cape, at the foot of the classical cliff of Leucopetra. Here the General received a message from the insurrectional committee of Reggio, to the effect that 12,000 Neapolitans were echeloned along the coast from Bagnara to Reggio; while the 1800 which had been sent in pursuit of Missori had been recalled, and were expected to arrive at Villa San Giovanni next morning. These 12,000 troops were but the advanced guard of the 27,000 men who, under General Viale, formed the army of Calabria Ultra, the head-quarters of which were established at Monteleone. The town of Reggio was garrisoned by

1500 troops, partly holding the castle and the fort on the sea-shore, partly quartered in the city.   The messenger added, however, that, at the first tidings of the landing, Brigante had advanced from Bagnara to Villa San Giovanni, ready to support General Gallotti's force at Reggio, leaving, at the same time, Melendi's brigade to guard the coast behind from Scylla to Altafiumara.   This account of the enemy's numbers and plan of action had no influence on the mind of Garibaldi.   He gave orders that his troops should march next morning, and then went to bed, and slept as soundly as the Prince of Condé did the night before the battle of Rocroi.

On the evening of the 20th, Garibaldi arrived unmolested at a point about eight miles from Reggio, where he halted, and made preparations for attacking the enemy next morning, an hour before dawn.

Having been informed by one of Garibaldi's Staff-officers, who had been sent from Teormina to Faro on the 18th, that the expedition was to start that very evening, I made arrangements to cross the Straits, which I determined to do as soon as news reached Messina that the Garibaldians had succeeded in landing.   I had my English passport, which I then thought would protect me, even should I be caught by the Neapolitans; and besides, when a man has made up his mind to follow the operations of an army, he knows there is no interest without risk. Some Messinese tried to dissuade me from going to Reggio before it was known to be occupied by our friends; but prudence is not generally the counsellor an excited person is ready to listen to, and I persisted in my project. It was not, however, easy to find a boatman who would face the danger. Still, I knew that what the Americans call " the almighty dollar " had as great an influence with Sicilian sailors as with transatlantic traders. At Messina I had picked up a fellow Lombardian, who, although he pretended to belong to a certain battalion of Bersaglieri, was more fond of loitering about the town than of discharging his military duties. Francesco (for such was his name) was as sharp and active as our old acquaintance, my servant Antonio, who accompanied me through the campaign of 1859. He was not my servant, however, nor would I have allowed him to become so. He was merely a good-natured fellow, who would have done anything for me, simply because he knew my family, and had been brought up by an uncle who, in better times, was the manager of one of my grandfather's estates. Accordingly, Francesco spent a great part of the day at my lodgings; and he would not have disdained to drive me to Faro, or would even have spared me the annoyance of posting my letters during the scorching, sunny noons of Messina. On the 19th of August, I communicated to him my plan, not disguising, however, that I had experienced some difficulty in finding a boatman who would take me to Reggio on the following morning.

" Do not be alarmed at that," said Francesco, with a knowing smile. " If you are disposed to let your piastres flow from your purse, I can find a fellow who will undertake the job."

" Very well," answered I. " I give you *carte blanche;* do as best you can."

An hour afterwards, Francesco came back with the smile of a conqueror on his face, and informed me that the bargain had been concluded for six piastres, and that I was to have two rowers, who were from that moment at my disposal.

"Bravo!" exclaimed I. "I shall start as soon as we hear that Garibaldi has landed."

"Not alone, however," said Francesco; "for, if you have no objection, I will accompany you."

"But what will your Major say?"

"Oh, as for my Major, I think he has quite lost sight of me; and besides, I have heard that the battalion is not under orders to march, but will remain in Sicily. I don't like garrison life; so, when on the other side of the water, I will ask our fellow Mantuan, Major Boldrini, to accept me in *his* battalion."

There was nothing to answer to this patriotic resolve. Accordingly, I acceded to the request of Francesco, and asked him to sleep at my lodgings, in order to be ready to start at any moment.

On the evening of the 20th, news reached Messina that Garibaldi was already within a few miles of Reggio. I therefore decided to start next morning. The dawn of the 21st of August was not yet whitening the tops of the Calabrian mountains when we set out from the harbour of Messina. Nothing can exceed the beauty of the scenery which borders the Straits, and it is beheld to especial advantage on a fine summer morning, when the light of the rising sun begins to disperse the transparent mist of departing night. Innumerable hues creep over the mountains, and the orange and olive groves gradually become more distinct on the dark, wild background of the ravines. Streams of light pour forth from the gaps in the mountain sides, illuminating by degrees the villages and villas below. The lofty peaks of Aspromonte, which, breaking into numerous spurs, descend towards the sea, are either crowned by deep green woods, or rear their shapeless rocks to the sky. The ivy-clad walls of the gardens, and the cactus hedges which mark the roads or paths, slope down towards the sea in long zigzag lines; and, to increase the picturesqueness of the scenery, hundreds of boats spread their pointed lateen sails to the wind, like the wings of doves. Such is the panorama which the blue waters of the Straits reflect upwards, like a fantastic vision on the point of springing from the sea. There are days, though rare, when the scenery which I have attempted to sketch assumes a still more splendid beauty; days when the phenomenon of the mirage is beheld from either of those enchanting — I might almost write, those enchanted—coasts.

Francesco and I were contemplating that magnificent spectacle in silent rapture, when suddenly the roar of distant guns made us aware that Garibaldi had attacked Reggio. On hearing the boom of the artillery, the first movement of our boatmen was indicative of an intention to turn back. However, they were speedily compelled to relinquish any such design; for Francesco, seizing hold of his revolver, swore he would shoot them if they did not pursue their course. Between a distant danger and an imminent peril, the boatmen chose the first; so that by five o'clock we were drawing near the coast of Reggio without having

met with any accident whatever. But the fight was
not over, and there was no possibility of landing. We
accordingly kept rowing about for several hours, until
the tri-coloured flag, waving from the tower of the old
castle, told us that victory had once more smiled on
Garibaldi. The boatmen, being now reassured,
pulled towards the shore, and we made our entry into
Reggio.

The march of Garibaldi had been rapid. He had
started at midnight on the 20th, and long before
dawn his troops, divided into two columns, silently
made their appearance in the suburbs of the town.
On the previous day, he had sent orders to Cosenz,
who was left at Faro, to cross the Straits during the
night, and land his division between Altafiumara and
Scylla, so as to make a diversion, and facilitate the
main attack upon Reggio. This operation Cosenz
carried out before daybreak of the 20th.

Reggio is built almost opposite Messina, upon a
hill which slopes gently down towards the sea. Three
wide streets run parallel to the shore, one above another.
These three streets, or *corsi*, are intersected at intervals
by other streets, which run from the highest part of
the town in a precipitous descent towards the sea.
At the north-east end of the upper town, and commanding the whole city, stands a strongly-built castle
called the Fortezza Alta. It dominates the coast
below, and its guns can be equally well used to keep
down the population, and to prevent any stranger approaching from the Straits. To the left of the
castle is another and smaller fort, which, at the time
of its capture, was armed with four worthless

60-pounders. The country all about is one continuous chain of hills, formed by the last spur of Aspromonte; and these hills strike down in different irregular forms towards the Gulf. The consequence of this topographical conformation is that the two forts, which might prove efficient either against an assailing fleet or the town itself, can easily be attacked in the rear from the heights which overhang them.

Although the Neapolitan General Gallotti, the commander of Reggio, was fully aware of Garibaldi's landing near Mileto, he did not expect that he would attack him so soon. Moreover, the whole population of Reggio sided with the National army, and Gallotti could get no information concerning the movements of the invading troops since they had landed. I should also add that General Gallotti, not being a Wellington or a Jomini, had taken it into his head that Garibaldi would assault Reggio from the sea. He therefore retired to his lodgings in the town; so far was it from his thoughts that the National leader would be impertinent enough to attack him, without even a word of warning, in the rear.

General Gallotti had under his orders seven companies of the 14th regiment of the Line, a battery of seven field-pieces, and the castle, which was well armed with guns, besides being provided with ammunition and provisions for a month. How could he be blamed if he went to bed at his usual hour, to sleep off his anxiety? The poor old General was perhaps dreaming of his Marshal's baton when, at half-past two o'clock in the morning, the column under the command of Bixio reached the piazza without firing a musket, whilst the column led by Garibaldi himself entered the suburbs without being noticed by the enemy. The advanced guard of Bixio's column was formed of the battalion commanded by the son of Garibaldi, and two companies of Sacchi's brigade, under the orders of Major Chiassi. As soon as the Piazza was occupied, Garibaldi's son was sent to take up a position at the extremity of the wide street running parallel with the seashore, where he remained, ready to assail the Neapolitans whenever they should show themselves. At last, a patrol of the Royal troops, coming up from the Marina, or road by the shore, fell in with Chiassi's men, and the conflict began. It is impossible to describe the confusion which soon prevailed in the streets. The Neapolitans were flying towards the castle, and in other directions, calling upon all the saints of the calendar, and not listening to their officers. The moon had set, and the darkness which prevailed increased still further the confusion of the surprised troops. Major Boldrini had been by this time ordered by Garibaldi to skirt the farthest street of the town, try to get at the rear of the small fort on the seashore, and carry it if possible. This was soon done, for Boldrini's men rushed at its walls with such terrific cries of "Viva Garibaldi!" that the noise alone struck terror into the Neapolitans who ought to have defended it. Climbing up like cats, the Garibaldians jumped into the fort, leaving the Bourbonic heroes just time to lay down their arms and beg for mercy.

Garibaldi now turned his efforts towards the castle, where by this time Gallotti and his troops had sought shelter. A barricade had been erected at the entrance of the narrow lane leading to this stronghold; but grape-shot and shells were sweeping the streets, and bursting in every direction over the town. Bixio was wounded, and the struggle was becoming hot, when on a sudden the rattle of musketry was heard from the heights in the rear of the castle. It was the column of Missori, which, having just arrived, was engaged picking off the gunners from the ramparts of Gallotti's last vantage-ground. The first act of the drama was at an end.

Whilst all this was going on in the town, General Brigante, who was at Villa San Giovanni, having been informed by telegraph of the dangerous position of General Gallotti, hastened to his aid as fast as he could. He proceeded from the last-named village at five o'clock, and had passed the hamlet of Gallico (four miles from Reggio) when Garibaldi moved forward to meet him to the left of Santa Lucia. At the first news of the Dictator's movement, Brigante thought proper to fall back on Gallico, leaving his colleague at Reggio to extricate himself as best he could. Garibaldi thereupon returned into Reggio; and as soon as he arrived in the piazza (which was about the middle of the day), he saw that a decided attack against the castle would produce a good effect upon the frightened Neapolitans. He therefore sent orders to Lieutenant-Colonel Dezza, of Eberhart's brigade, to arrange a storming party, and try, in some way or other, to get within the castle. General Gallotti was anxious to escape from his dilemma as soon as possible; for, as he said afterwards, he was bound to consider his wife, to whom he had sworn to save his precious existence. A flag of truce was therefore hoisted, and the "gallant General" asked for a capitulation. This was soon granted, and it was agreed that the garrison of Reggio should retire to Naples by sea, with their arms.

As I have already stated, I arrived at Reggio a few minutes after the capitulation. Hastening to the piazza, I was fortunate enough to make the acquaintance of the defender of Reggio, who was then trying to prove to a crowd of Garibaldian officers that he had done his duty. "Che volete, Signorini," he was now and then repeating, "io sono un vecchio soldato, e perciò m'attendeva che Garibaldi m'attacchasse di fronte, ed invece m'è capitato alle spalle." This justification of the Neapolitan General—which was tantamount to saying that he expected Garibaldi would have attacked him in front, instead of in the rear —shows how great were the military attainments of the Bourbonic General. He was satisfied, however, with having kept the promise he had made to his wife, who was standing by his side, looking at him as if he were a second Achilles.

At sunset, the Neapolitan Commodore sent a French mercantile steamer to take the defenders of Reggio, as they called themselves, to their destination. When I remember the martial appearance of the men, I can even now scarcely believe that they could have capitulated to the dismal-looking soldiers of Garibaldi, who were hardly covered with serge, and were living upon a crust. But the love of liberty animated the breasts of the latter; they fought for a noble cause, and under the leadership of a man who knows how to make a hero even of a child.   This was the only secret of the wonderful victories which, since the landing at Marsala, had illustrated the modern epic of Garibaldi's campaign in South Italy.

CHAPTER V.

CALABRIA.

GARIBALDI was accustoming us to wonders. In three days he had started from Teormina with 4200 men, had landed on the Calabrian coast (running through his Sicilian Majesty's cruisers), and had captured Reggio. Were he as proud as he is simple, he would indeed have had a right to rank himself with the great Generals of former times. But with him the thought of glory always comes after that of duty; and he knew besides that he had yet the Neapolitan troops to vanquish, and the populous provinces of the mainland to free. There was accordingly no time to enjoy the illumination of Reggio and of the opposite Sicilian coast, which, from Messina to Faro, was one

uninterrupted line of coloured light. We were to be
ready to follow him at break of day next morning, for
the military movements of Garibaldi are extremely
rapid; he is always marching on the heels of the
enemy, to whom he allows no respite. At dawn on
the 22nd of August, therefore, after having bidden
adieu to Francesco (who had faithfully kept his word,
and enlisted in Boldrini's battalion), I joined the Staff
of the General, and off we drove towards the pretty
hamlet of Accerello.

If one were to make an exact calculation of the
quantity of oil and wax candles consumed for illuminating purposes during the revolution of Southern
Italy, I am sure it would reach a very large sum.
Although, when we arrived at Accerello, it was broad
day, yet the coloured lights of the preceding night
were still burning here and there, both along the
Sicilian coast opposite, and the Calabrese coast close
at hand. But let [us stop at Accerello, not only
because an excellent breakfast of ham (which is eaten
raw in Italy) and fresh figs is laid for us on the ground
floor of a cottage belonging to a jovial-hearted Calabrian miller, but because a Neapolitan *parlementaire*
has just arrived with a letter for Garibaldi.

"Good news," said Gusmaroli to me. "Brigante
has asked for an interview with the General. The
lesson we gave Gallotti at Reggio is bearing its fruits.
Brigante, I think, is anxious to capitulate."

The individual who had thus spoken, and whose
name I now mention for the first time, was a rather
interesting personage, owing to Garibaldi's great
liking for him.

Old Gusmaroli had formerly been the curate of a small hamlet in the neighbourhood of Mantua. In 1848 he was the chaplain of the Mantuan volunteers, organized by an uncle of mine—a fine battalion which distinguished itself in the war of independence of that year. Soon after the armistice of Milan, the Mantuan volunteers went to Rome, and became a part of that valiant army which, under the leadership of Garibaldi, kept in check the troops of General Oudinot, sent by the Republicans of France to put down the Republic which had been proclaimed in the Eternal City. Don Gusmaroli followed the battalion, and went through that short but glorious campaign, caring but little for the excommunication of the Pope. At the restoration of Pius IX., he returned to his parish, more for the sake of the scanty living attached to it, than from any earnest desire to perform the duties of his sacred ministry. Closely watched by the Austrian police, the poor curate spent, at intervals, several months in prison, charged either with having spread Mazzini's proclamations, or with having helped young peasants to pass the frontier in order to escape the Austrian conscription. At the breaking out of the war in 1859, Gusmaroli secretly formed a band of a hundred volunteers, and joined the Cacciatori, then being organized at Biella by Garibaldi. Our chaplain, having now changed the surplice of the priest for the tunic of the soldier, became a lieutenant; but, not being able to fulfil the duties of his rank, he was allowed to follow the Staff of Garibaldi, more in the quality of a useful man than in that of an officer. Though ignorant, Gusmaroli was sharp; and he knew so well how to obtain the sympathy of the General that in a few months he became one of his favourite attendants. He and an ex-Capuchin friar, named Froscianti, were the two janitors who night and day guarded the inner apartments of the General, anticipating all his desires, and providing for all his wants.

Gusmaroli was not wrong in anticipating the arrival of the Neapolitan General Brigante. We were in fact just finishing our ham and figs when a trumpeter of the Neapolitan Lancers made his appearance on the road, followed by two officers. One of them was Brigante. He was introduced into the small kitchen of the miller—the only decent room in the cottage—where Garibaldi was writing; and the two Generals remained in close colloquy for half an hour. The countenance of the Neapolitan General when he came out of the kitchen was such as to make it very evident that the conditions he had come to propose were rejected by Garibaldi. During the Southern Italian campaign, I scarcely met with a Neapolitan General whose appearance conveyed the idea of a soldier. The greater number were fat, heavy, embarrassed ; and looked more like priests or monks who had assumed the military uniform, than followers of the profession of arms. Arrogant and overbearing towards the feeble, they were humble as slaves when brought into contact with their superiors, or when they thought themselves in danger. To say the truth, Brigante possessed fewer of these qualities than his colleagues ; but, when he left Accerello, his face betrayed that he was far from being a hero.

The negotiations for the surrender of Brigante's column having failed, Garibaldi gave orders to advance; and on we went, ascending the hills which run beyond the ridge facing the Straits. Garibaldi at the same time sent Major Nullo with six Guides, to reconnoitre the road of Villa San Giovanni. Nullo, accompanied by Commander Forbes, pushed on without meeting the enemy; but, on reaching the first houses of the town, the reconnoitering party found itself in the presence of two squadrons of Neapolitan Lancers. The Guides of the "Armata Meridionale," and an officer like Nullo, were already accustomed to this sort of encounter, and knew that courage and audacity generally succeeded with the Neapolitan Generals. Acting on this principle, Nullo ordered his men to draw their revolvers, and, galloping towards the front of the Neapolitan cavalry, summoned the commanding officer to surrender. "Surrender to you!" disdainfully exclaimed the officer. "Where are your troops?"

"Garibaldi is at ten minutes' distance from here," replied Major Nullo, "and I advise you to spare useless bloodshed, which can neither benefit your Lancers nor the troops of your General, for they are already outflanked by General Cosenz." This bold narangue produced its effect. The Neapolitan officer wavered for a few seconds, and then said to Nullo that he had better go and speak to General Melendis, who was with a battalion of Cacciatori at the bridge which spans a deep water-course just at the extremity of Villa San Giovanni. The Garibaldian officer went to see General Melendis, and with his usual spirit asked him to have the Lancers marched back beyond the bridge, which would thus become the line of demarcation of the two armies. Audacity succeeded for the second time; the Lancers were ordered to retire, and it was agreed that messengers should be sent to Garibaldi to see whether there were not means of coming to some understanding, and avoiding a fight. Nullo with his Guides remained masters of the town, to the great astonishment of its population, who, relieved from the incubus of the Neapolitan soldiery, were enabled to show the National flag, and to shout out "Long live Garibaldi! Long live Italy!"

At dusk, Garibaldi's column, which we left marching from Accerello to the hills, took up a position on the heights of Mattiniti. We were there within gun-range of General Melendis' brigade, whose bivouac fires were to be seen along the ridge which slopes down towards the sea in the direction of Villa San Giovanni. The order to halt for rest was by no means unpleasant, for we were quite done up by the forced march we had made along the goat-tracks of the mountains, under the scorching sun of August. A distribution of cheese and biscuit was made. As for wine or rum, it was quite out of the question; for, in the hasty departure of the expedition, Colonel Acerbi, the able Commissary-General of the army, could not give the necessary orders for shipping provisions. Even water was not to be found in abundance, as the country all about was one continued undulation of dry hills, as far as the eye could reach, with only here and there tufts of Indian figs, and sunburnt patches of heath.

For my part, I was suffering so much from thirst that I went with some soldiers to explore the country, and see whether water could not be procured. The night was splendid, and we could easily see our way through the woods and wild ravines which run towards the coast. We had walked for about half an hour, hearing only the howling of the dogs in the distant farms, and the watch-word of the sentries of both camps, when the sweet breath of the night brought to our ears the murmur of running water. At that moment we felt what must have been the joy of the sons of Israel when the wand of Moses drew the refreshing spring from the mountain. Providence had led us to a hill through the wide crevices of which a clear, fresh, delicious spring was sparkling. Our miseries were at an end; we were enabled to drink, and did so with that avidity which can only be appreciated by those who have felt the torments of drought. Then, filling our flasks, we went back to camp, to tell our companions of the important discovery we had made, that they might profit in their turn.

Although the night, as I have said, was splendid, it was not only fresh, but decidedly cold; indeed, so cold, that, when we lay down to rest, dressed as we were in our thin summer suits, we found that there was no chance of sleeping. On those high lands the night breeze always blows keen and sharp, even in the summer season. It is a sort of compensation for the suffocating heat of the day; but the compensation was hardly welcome to us, who had no cloak to wrap ourselves in. A large fire was therefore lighted, and we passed the night chatting and smoking. Forbes, who, after the episode of Villa San Giovanni, had joined Garibaldi's Staff at Mattiniti, took a by-path in search of a cottage he had seen during the march. This nocturnal errand, I was told next morning, nearly cost him his life; for, having lost the right track, he not only got too near the Neapolitan outposts, but was subsequently arrested by a Garibaldian officer under suspicion of being a Neapolitan spy.

We had been seated round the fire not much more than an hour, when the repeated " Chi va là ?" of our sentries made us aware that somebody had passed through the line of our outposts. Two Garibaldian officers, who were as chilly as we had been an hour before, made their appearance; and welcome visitors they were, for they brought news of General Cosenz's expedition.

" Do you bring good news ?" asked Baron D'Ondes, addressing one of the two officers, a handsome young fellow belonging to a noble Milanese family.

" What a question !" exclaimed he. " Surely you must have learned by this time that the Garibaldian devils, as the Neapolitan soldiers call our red-shirts, always win."

" But had General Cosenz to sustain a fight ?" asked one of our companions.

" Of course," answered the officer. " Not a hard one ; but we came to blows, and worsted the enemy. We lost, however, some of our brave' fellows, and amongst them poor Colonel De Flotte."

" Sit down, sit down, and tell us the particulars of the fight. Light your pipe, and begin."

" You are no doubt aware," said the young fellow

thus addressed, " that, whilst you were engaged in the attack on Reggio, our expedition left Faro, caring but little for the Neapolitan cruisers which were in sight. Having safely landed our troops between Scylla and Altafiumara, we took the mountain tracks, and ascended the high lands according to the orders received from Garibaldi. Our march was not much interfered with by the enemy; for the small body of Neapolitan troops we met now and then do not deserve to be noticed, inasmuch as they fled as fast as they could whenever they saw us. The advanced guard of our column, however, was getting near the village of Solino, when it was met by some Calabrian volunteers, who told Colonel De Flotte, under whose orders the guard was placed, that the village was then occupied by the 5th battalion of the Neapolitan Cacciatori. De Flotte was not the officer to wait for reinforcements, and he knew, besides, that the two small companies of Frenchmen and Englishmen he had with him were quite strong enough to meet and rout a battalion of Francis II. On entering the village, they were attacked by the enemy, whom they repulsed after a short combat. The positions had just been carried at the point of the bayonet, when poor Colonel De Flotte, anxious to make prisoners of a few Neapolitans, ran towards a lane of the village, sword in hand, summoning them to surrender; but at the corner of the lane one of the Neapolitan Cacciatori, who was concealed in a house, shot him dead on the spot. You may take my word for it that the French fully revenged the death of their brave commander. As soon as Solino was occupied by our troops (who, after De Flotte's death, were led by Captain Goodall, a dashing young Englishman, whom you must have noticed at Faro), the Neapolitan sharpshooter fell into their hands, and was shot on the ground, without the benefit of a court-martial."

"Well done!" we all exclaimed in chorus.

" But what has become of the main body of General Cosenz?" asked Gusmaroli.

"We were allowed to follow our march without being further molested, and I have been sent with my comrade to inform Garibaldi that we are occupying a position above Villa San Giovanni, whose church you can distinguish amidst the grove of orange trees below."

"And what have you done with the body of poor De Flotte?" asked I.

" We buried it in the churchyard of the village, and a subscription has been opened amongst the officers of our brigade to erect a monument worthy of him. Garibaldi, too, told me just an hour ago that he will pay a tribute to his memory in to-morrow's order of the day."

By this time the bivouac fire had died out, and dawn was fast appearing. Garibaldi had already made his appearance amongst the moving groups of the camp, and the order to march was given. We went down a steep declivity of the mountain towards the Neapolitans, who were posted in the plain opposite to us. To reach one of the *fiumare*, or beds of the torrents which rush through those mountains, we had to pass within gun-range of the Neapolitan brigade under the command of General Melendis, which was well provided with artillery. At the time we left our camp, this brigade was massed before the village of Piale, and seemed disposed to contest our march, and to prevent our turning the road of Fort Pezzo be-low. Such was indeed the case; for the moment our advanced guard made its appearance on the spur of the mountain, the Neapolitan skirmishers opened fire upon us, their artillery shelling our little army to some purpose. The enemy's cannon-balls killed half-a-dozen of our men, and their rifle-bullets wounded as many as double that number, without, however, interrupting our steady advance. In less than two hours, Melendis' brigade was entirely outflanked, and we were in a position to threaten the main road leading from Villa San Giovanni to the forts of Pezzo, Altafiumara, Torre di Cavallo, and Scylla. Nor was this the only result obtained by the bold and well-combined movement of Garibaldi; for General Brigante, whose troops were occupying the coast be-low, had his communication cut off from the main body of Melendis' brigade.

Garibaldi, having accomplished his object, and se-cured the result of his strategical manœuvre, sent to General Melendis two officers, summoning him to sur-render. The agents chosen for this purpose were the Marquis Trecchi and Major Vecchi—the latter an inti-mate friend of Garibaldi, and the owner of the villa at Genoa where, as the reader will remember, the expedi-tion of the first thousand had been decided upon and organized.

A flag of truce was hoisted, and the two officers proceeded to the enemy's camp. As we were halting to wait the result of Trecchi and Vecchi's mission, Captain Forbes came up to tell us his misfortunes of the preceding night—misfortunes, however, which ended in a satisfactory manner. Forbes, as I said before, had been arrested by a Garibaldian officer under suspicion of being a disguised Neapolitan; but, fortunately for him, Captain Granchi, a common friend of ours, chanced to pass, and liberated him, though not without some difficulty.

When Trecchi and Vecchi reached Melendis' camp, they found it in a state of total demoralization. Some of the Neapolitans were shouting out " Long live Garibaldi! Long live Italy!" The countenances of others showed that they were not very well disposed to fight. This state of things having been pointed out by the two Garibaldian officers, Melendis denied at first that he was in a bad condition, and said that he could not give an answer to the demand made on him before he had referred to General Viale, the Military Commander of Calabria Ultra. Four hours' delay was therefore asked for by him, and granted without difficulty. It had been arranged, however, that the chief of Melendis' Staff, accompanied by two officers, should proceed to Garibaldi's camp, and discuss with the General the conditions of the capitulation. Marquis Trecchi and Major Vecchi therefore took the three officers to the head-quarters of the Liberator, and the negotiations were at once entered into.

On a sudden, one of the negotiators thought proper to ask Garibaldi whether he would raise them a grade if they consented to join him. With words of reproof which can be imagined by the reader, he dismissed the

Neapolitan officers without coming to any conclusion,
but not without telling them to remind their General
that, at the expiration of four hours, he would begin
the attack, if the conditions of the capitulation he had
proposed were not accepted.

We had therefore four hours to wait, which was not
very pleasant, seeing that our appetites were keen :
however, it was not long before a host of girls and
women, laden with baskets full of bread and figs, came
into camp.   Such occurrences were not rare during
our march through Calabria.   It was the season of
fruit ; and fruit is plentiful in that country.   To relieve the monotony of our momentary inactivity, a
Neapolitan frigate and a war-steamer thought proper
to entertain us with the spectacle of a brisk fight
with our batteries at Faro Point.   The scene was really
magnificent.   From the place where we were encamped, the whole line of the Straits spread in all
its beauty before our eyes.   The fantastic pinnacles
of the rock upon which Fort Scylla is built rose on
our right, dominating the coast line, which follows the
various levels of the projecting masses of cliff, sometimes descending to the sea-shore, sometimes rising
many hundred feet above it.   Here and there, the
empty beds of the torrents, winding down like deep,
wide ditches towards the sea, crossed the main road
beneath the red-brick bridges which span them.   The
small straggling villages of Porticello and Cantinello
showed their white walls amongst the terraces of
vineyards, olives, and orange trees.   Right and left
were the high ranges of mountains on whose shelving
slopes the luxuriant cultivation appeared like enormous

baskets of flowers studding the rocky frame of the mountains.

More beautiful than any other village, Villa San Giovanni stood at our feet on the extreme edge of the coast, seeming as if it were actually rising from the waters, owing to the ground on which it is built being concealed by the ascending houses. Further on, the eye could catch the opposite line of coast, from the distant town of Melazzo to a point beyond Messina, the sand-bank of the ancient Pelorus marking the spot at which the open sea ceases, and the Straits begin.

Such was the scene we witnessed from our camp on the slope of the mountains, many hundred feet above Villa San Giovanni, while the contest between our batteries at Faro and the two Neapolitan men-of-war was going on. It was a sharp fight, lasting long enough for some to be killed and wounded on both sides. At length, the Neapolitan vessels succeeded in passing the Straits by hugging the Calabrian coast, not, however, without receiving some cannon-balls in their hulls.

The four hours asked for by Melendis having expired, Garibaldi ordered a soldier to go up to the roof of a neighbouring farm, and for the second time to hoist the flag of truce. This was quickly done; but the poor soldier had no sooner got on the roof than he was struck through the head by a Neapolitan sharp-shooter. So great was the indignation of our men at hearing of this cowardly act that they were on the point of rushing off, and attacking the Neapolitans at once. Two new messengers from Melendis were in the meanwhile announced, and to these gentlemen Gari-

baldi read such a lecture as made them turn pale
more than once—I do not know whether from fear or
shame.   He told them that they were in command of
a set of brigands ; that to shoot the bearer of a flag of
truce was one of the most infamous actions a soldier
could do.   To these words, which would have fallen
upon any honourable officer like melted lead poured
upon a wound, the two Neapolitans had nothing to
answer but that the man who committed the act was
" some wag of a sentry who had let off his musket in
a freak."   After this incident, Garibaldi ordered the
two messengers to return to their General, and tell
him that if by three o'clock he had not surrendered,
he would attack him, and drive the whole of his brigade
into the sea.   The consequence of this peremptory
summons was that Melendis was obliged to accept the
conditions imposed upon him—an act which was the
signal for the total breaking-up of his brigade. The Neapolitans, when made aware of the capitulation, threw
away their arms, and came up to our lines to fraternize
with the soldiers of liberty.   Fear, more than bro-
therly feeling, was the great mover of this enthusiasm ;
but, when a favourable result has been obtained, it is
useless to look too closely into the causes which have
determined it.   Thus it was with us.   We were glad
that 2500 men had been forced to lay down their
arms before a corps of so-called filibusters.   Kissing,
screeching, and hugging then began, with the usual
obligato of " Eccellenza," and " Signorino," till I
almost repented that I had followed Garibaldi.   After
witnessing this disgraceful scene, I could understand how, with soldiers who had not the slightest

notion of the dignity of men, it was impossible to maintain a position against the impetuous onslaughts of Garibaldi.   Not only did the soldiers try to kiss our hands, but even some of the officers did so too; there was, in truth, no humiliation they would not have undergone.   Had "our Excellencies," as they called us, desired to have our shoes kissed, they would have satisfied such a wish without much difficulty.

No doubt these servile habits will disappear with the progress of education and the influence of liberal institutions; but it will take years before the lower classes of the Neapolitan provinces will be brought up to the level of their more manly brethren of the North.   Dignity and self-respect are rather the results of example and education than gifts of nature.   In Southern Italy, the children generally receive at a very early age the impression of numberless superstitious stories, which fill them with a sort of mysterious fear.   They contract the habit of trembling at the least manifestation of authority, till pusillanimity and fear become a fixed condition of their minds.

An important result of General Melendis' surrender was that his colleague Brigante was also obliged to capitulate before night.   When I descended with Garibaldi's Staff into Villa San Giovanni, the embarkation of the Neapolitan troops had begun, and there was such enthusiasm amongst the townspeople, such shouting and clamour, that I might have fancied myself at the entrance of hell, as described by Dante.   Night had not yet set in when news arrived that the garrison stationed at the fort of Pezzo had

capitulated in its turn ; and this announcement caused
the joy to redouble.

Fatigue is always felt in proportion to the excitement we have gone through. It is not to be wondered at, therefore, if when night came I was quite
exhausted. I searched far and wide for a lodging,
but in vain ; and was at length obliged in despair to
stretch myself under a sort of lobby attached to the
cathedral. While I was lying there, the rector of the
parish came by, and, catching sight of me, asked if
I were ill. On being informed of the true state of the
case, the kind-hearted priest promised that, if I would
follow him to his uncle's house, I should have at least
a sofa to lie down on. He then conducted me
through a labyrinth of lanes, rugged with sharp-
pointed stones, to the dwelling of which he had
spoken ; but, on arriving there, we found every part so
full that my newly-kindled hopes died within me. In
one room on the ground-floor, Cavaliere Gallenga was
busy writing his letters for the London newspaper to
which he is accredited ; in a second, Colonel Vecchi
was enjoying his supper ; and all the other apartments were in possession of officers and soldiers.
While the rector and his uncle were debating how
matters could be arranged, the wife of the latter came
into the room, and, observing my really exhausted
condition, kindly bid me go with her, and she would
find me a mattress. And she was as good as her word.
The kind old lady gave up her bed, and I was allowed
to sleep through the night as comfortably as if I had
been a king.

At five o'clock next morning, after having sipped

a cup of coffee, and bidden adieu to my host, I
hastened to head-quarters, well knowing that Garibaldi is a bird who takes wing with the rising sun.
In fact, I had scarcely reached the house where he had
passed the night, before I saw him riding towards
Altafiumara at the head of two battalions of General Cosenz's brigade. Gallenga had succeeded in
buying a horse, and so had the officers of the Staff;
but as for me, Forbes, and a few others, we were still
pedestrians, and had to take our chance of finding
some donkey or *carrozzella* which might give us a lift.
Both these, however, we were unable to procure at
Villa San Giovanni; for, at the first shot fired at
Reggio, the peasants had taken all their donkeys and
horses to the mountains, being aware that, in case
of the Neapolitans retreating, they would have
seized them without paying a *carlino*.   Forbes and I
therefore made up our minds to follow Garibaldi
on our own legs; but at that moment old Gusmaroli,
who had also been left behind, came up, and told us
that the *corriere* for Naples had just arrived, and that
we could go together by that conveyance. The heavy
carriage was at once taken by storm, to the great astonishment of the conductor, who was frightened to
death, knowing that he had to make his journey
through Calabria amidst the half-disbanded Royal
troops and the insurrectionary *squadre*.

The *corriere* had only taken us a distance of about
three miles when, at a turn of the road, we saw Garibaldi, who had halted with his Staff at a bridge
near the fort of Altafiumara.   On leaving the carriage, we strongly recommended the conductor, should

he arrive in Naples, not to forget to announce our appearance there on an early day of the next month.
My friends of the Staff told me that the General
had sent Colonel Baggi to summon the garrison of
the fort to surrender, General Cosenz having at the
same time occupied the heights hanging over the
road.   Medici's and Türr's divisions had by that
time also started, either from Messina or from Faro,
and had landed on the Calabrian coasts.   Our army,
therefore, was reinforced, and the experience of the
previous days had taught us that summonses to
surrender were mere matters of form.   Accordingly,
we were not at all surprised when, after an hour,
Colonel Baggi came back, accompanied by a young
Neapolitan officer, with news that the garrison of
Altafiumara had capitulated.   Orders were then given
to push on towards Scylla.

I was at last enabled to follow the Staff of the
General, owing to the kindness of Captain Mario, who
had lent me a horse.   The young Neapolitan officer
rode with me; and he seemed so enthusiastic about
the National cause and Garibaldi that I could not help
asking him how it happened that he was on the
wrong side.

" Your question is just enough," answered he ; " but
you will not be surprised when I tell you that I am
the only son of a General who was an intimate friend
of Ferdinand II.   Brought up at the military school
of the Annunziatella, I was compelled by my father
to follow the career of a soldier.   Having joined my
regiment, it was not long before I discovered that
many of my brother officers were secret agents of the

King's police, continually bent on eliciting the liberal feelings of their comrades, in order to denounce them. I was so disgusted at finding that the military uniform covered such degraded beings, that I wrote to my father to say I was determined to resign my commission. At this intimation he fell into a violent passion, and wrote back that, if I dared to do such a thing, he would not only, as they say in England, cut me off with a shilling, but have me imprisoned at once. So I was compelled to remain, and to go through many hard trials; for, my liberal opinions having been detected, I was looked upon as one of the black sheep of the flock. Although I am grieved to see an army disband in this shameful manner, yet I assure you that this is the happiest day of my life."

The officer was indeed, as he said, a true patriot; for on that very evening he enlisted as a private in one of our regiments, and a month afterwards he was killed under the walls of Capua.

We had by this time ascended the steep coast road which leads up to the town of Scylla. Bad examples are always contagious; and so it was with the castle which at that point frowns over the town at its foot. At ten o'clock, Scylla was in our power; a part of its garrison went to their homes, and the rest embarked for Naples. Even this formidable stronghold—a diminutive Gibraltar in its way—was given up without firing a shot. The wonders Garibaldi had achieved in so short a time had excited such dread amongst the mercenary and demoralized instruments of Francis II., that Generals and soldiers completely forgot all military rules except those which are laid down in the treatises on Capitulation.

Now that Scylla was ours, we hastened through the zigzag streets of the town in search of the osteria; for the northern breeze which generally sets in during summer had made our stomachs keenly sensible of the want of breakfast. An establishment which shows the sign of the "Aquila Nera" was soon found out, and was fortunately discovered to be tolerably clean. The breakfast, too, was excellent, consisting of the frightful-looking but delicious sword-fish, figs, almonds, and water-melons—all in perfection, and the wine cooled by the snow of Aspromonte. To make our repast still more enjoyable, groups of beautiful girls were standing at the fountain opposite, singing hymns of liberty, or shouting out their " Vivas ! " with unrivalled enthusiasm. The girls of Scylla, however, seemed not very fond of some of the red-shirted heroes. The Irishman, who (I do not know why) had adopted the Garibaldian costume without belonging to the army, went to the fountain with the apparent intention of courting the damsels; but he was received with such a shower of imprecations that he was obliged to decamp. When he came back, and told us the reception he had met with, I observed to the two girls who were waiting at our table that their countrywomen had perhaps shown their displeasure because they were grieving for the departed Neapolitans. Such, however, was not the case; for, shortly after I had ventured on the remark, the handsomer of the two cried out, with all sorts of gesticulations :—" No, Signorino, no ! If we are angry with you, it is because you have allowed the wretches who have tormented us so long to go away in peace."

"But what could we have done?" asked I.

"You ought to have killed them all," replied the girl, her eyes flashing with anger.

"Don't show yourself so cruel," said one of my companions. "We are all brothers; and, besides, military honour cannot be set aside by the soldiers of liberty."

"Why do you talk of brothers and honour? Did not the *Borbonici* show that they had forgotten both? 'Garibardo' is too good; he ought to have killed them all."

The girl was evidently so determined in her opinion that we left her to her own way, and, having paid our bill, went to stroll about the town.

Scylla has not only a claim to be remembered on account of the famous verse of the Latin poet—

Incidit in Scyllam qui vult vitare Charybdim;

but is equally famous for the awful catastrophe with which it was visited in 1783. The shock of earthquake experienced by all that portion of the Calabrian coast, on the morning of the 5th February in that year, partly destroyed the upper range of the town, and greatly injured its castle, then the residence of the feudal lord of that country. Indifferent to the fate which seemed to threaten his life, the old Prince of Scylla was calmly awaiting death before the altar of his chapel, when his attendants persuaded him to leave the castle, and go to his safer residence of La Melia.

The catastrophe, however, had been so sudden that almost all the horses had perished under the ruins of the fallen walls. It was therefore decided that the Prince and his suite should start the next day, when horses could be got from La Melia. These arrangements having been made, the Prince of Scylla retired to his bark, which was anchored in the largest of the two creeks forming the harbour of the town. Some 4000 people were gathered on the beach, terror-stricken, and invoking the mercy of God upon their condition. These were the whole of the surviving inhabitants of the place. At sunset, the chaplain said the Ave Maria, and invoked the blessing of God upon Prince and people, whom a common misfortune had united on that shore. Grief, terror, and fatigue soon plunged these unfortunate creatures into a state of bodily and mental languor. But, alas! sleep had no sooner descended on their eyes than a damp southerly wind began to blow from the sea, heavy, and impregnated with offensive effluvia: it was the sirocco, which is almost always the herald of earthquake in those regions. An hour later, a distant but loud crash roused the sleepers to a sense of new misfortunes. The shock had severed a large portion of Mount Baci, and dashed its shivered mass into the sea. The water, impelled by the pressure of the fallen mass, rushed with immense force over to the opposite side of the Straits, inundating the Faro, and then retreating upon the Calabrian coast. It swept along the shore of Scylla like an immense hurricane, carrying with it the whole population which had gathered there. Only a few were thrown back unhurt upon the scene of the calamity; but the Prince disappeared into the whirlpool of the gulf with the others.

The details of this catastrophe are preserved by tradition amongst the population of Scylla, and are mixed with many fantastic episodes which add a mysterious horror to the story. The vivid imagination and superstition of some go so far as to assert that every year, during the night of the 5th of February, voices are still heard coming from the bosom of the waters; and it is further averred that a bluish flame is seen on that evening, wandering about the rock where the chapel of the castle stood—a flame which the women of the town seem inclined to believe is the soul of the old Prince, coming from the other world to visit the ruins of the castle in which he was born.

For a pedestrian, as I was, to follow Garibaldi's Staff would have been a matter of total impossibility. The tactics of the General chiefly rest on rapidity, and no man's legs could stand such harassing marches. Acting, therefore, on the advice of a friend, who assured me that the innkeeper of Messina had a horse to sell, I left Scylla for that town, hoping to rejoin my friends next morning at Bagnara. Fate, however, had decided otherwise. On my arriving at Messina, I found that the innkeeper had no horse to sell, for the simple reason that he had already sold it to an officer of General Türr's Staff. My disappointment was great; but Captain Forbes, who had also returned to bid adieu to Captain Lambert, of the *Scylla*, consoled me with the assurance that I should pick up one on the road at the first encounter we might have with the Neapolitans. It was therefore arranged that at daybreak next morning we should return to Villa San Giovanni, and thence push on till we reached the General.

As we found the café of Messina deserted (for, with the exception of Colonel Dunne's regiment, the Garibaldians had left the town), we went to pay a last visit to our friend Lambert, who on that very morning had had an angry discussion with General Fergola, on account of the annoying fire which his men had kept up during the previous night, indiscriminately discharging their rifles on to the decks of the British ship and of a French war-steamer anchored by her side.

Like all English naval officers, Captain Lambert was a great admirer of Garibaldi. He bade us adieu very cordially, hoping that we should enter Naples before the month of September was over. Shaking hands with me and Forbes, he left us, saying :— "Look sharp, lest you should fall into the hands of the Neapolitans." Who would have imagined then that, thirty-five days afterwards, I should have an opportunity of remembering the kind warning of Captain Lambert in his Sicilian Majesty's dungeons of Gaeta?

CHAPTER VI.

GARIBALDI'S MARCH THROUGH CALABRIA AND BASILICATA.

To Messina and Back—Shooting at Fish—Bagnara—The Women of Bagnara—Palmi—A Grocer's Shop—Melito—The Bishop's Palace—Murder of General Brigante—The Convent of Monteleone — Recollections of Murat — Maida — Another Capitulation — Rogliano—Cosenza — Albanian Colonies — Colonel Pace—Albanian Funeral—A Night March—Basilicata—The last Capitulation—Val di Diano—Sala—The Two Committees.

SAILING from Messina at four o'clock in the morning of the 24th, Forbes and I reached Villa San Giovanni again in about two hours. The voyage was pleasant, the morning bright and fresh, the boatmen less quarrelsome than usual, and my enthusiasm for the beauties of the Straits the same as ever. I say "*my* enthusiasm," for my companion was more occupied in watching the course of the boat than in contemplating the panorama which rose to the right and left. On our arrival, we found Villa San Giovanni less busy and crowded than when we had left it on the preceding day. A few Garibaldians, however, and some of Missori's Guides, forming the extreme rear of the army, were still strolling about

the town.   Major Missori himself had not as yet left
the place, but was taking a few hours' rest in the
house of Mr. Hallam, an English gentleman whose
kind hospitality had been offered to us.

The voyage to Messina and back having consumed
some precious time, we were naturally anxious to
move forward as speedily as possible, and to reach
Garibaldi either that evening, or, at latest, next
morning.   The difficulty, however, was to find boatmen who would take us to Bagnara, which the two
we had hired at Messina had promised to do, though
now, either from fear of falling in with the Neapolitan
cruisers, or for some other reason, they declined to
perform their contract.   Mr. Hallam, however, was
too kind to leave us in a dilemma.   Forbes also had
grown savage with impatience, and seemed to have
made up his mind to undertake the journey at any
rate, following the main road of the coast, *pedibus
calcantibus;* an exploit which my legs, disabled with
fatigue, must have declined.   Mr. Hallam, however,
removed all difficulties, and tranquillized the agitated
spirits of the naval officer by placing his galley at our
disposal.   At three o'clock in the afternoon, we were
enabled once more to plough the waves, and gently to
coast along the Calabrian shore in the direction of
Bagnara.   The voyage was as pleasant as that of the
morning, though it was not without danger.   It is
true that the Neapolitan cruisers were out of sight,
and that we had very little contention with the
currents whirling round between Scylla and the spot
where the river Crataci falls into the sea.   But a
veritable amount of peril arose from the freaks of some

Garibaldian stragglers who were marching on the road our boat was coasting. To remove the monotony of their march, these red-shirted fellows amused themselves by discharging their muskets at the huge fish which occasionally came to the surface, and plunged again immediately afterwards into the water. The shots, though little likely to have effect on the fish, might at any moment have proved fatal to some of us, as the bullets passed close to our boats. Night came on, however, and the game was put an end to; for even the rays of a splendid moon were not sufficient to enable the obnoxious sportsmen to aim at the leaping dolphins. We were therefore permitted to enjoy in peace the exquisite scenery we were passing. I will not attempt to describe it in all its details, but will only beg the reader to imagine a coast walled by stupendous rocks, sloping down in shelving promontories, or retiring in irregular creeks. Let him call to mind that the vegetation which grows at the feet of those mountains is of tropical luxuriance and splendour, whilst the tops of the cliffs are crowned with the timber trees of northern climates. Below, palm and olive groves alternate with aloes and Indian figs; above, chestnuts and oaks spread their shade in almost pathless forests. Amidst these varying aspects of nature our boat sailed on, passing now through broad zones of moonlight, now through the deep shadows of the rocks. We kept steadily on our way, and at length came near a massive cliff, on turning which we beheld the town of Bagnara in a blaze of light, rising like an enchanted amphitheatre above the strand of classic Portus Balarus.

Although Garibaldi had already gone to Palmi, the lively population of Bagnara were still *en fête*. I therefore proposed to Forbes to proceed at once into the town ; but my friend was for an early start, and for sleeping on the sand, which, in his opinion, would offer a capital bed.   As I did not agree with him on this last point, we separated, and I subsequently obtained a lodging for the night, together with some members of "the English colony," at the house of a gentleman of the place.   Our host was apparently accustomed to, and much pleased at receiving, visitors.   His house, furnished with luxury, had a suite of rooms specially set apart for the reception of friends and strangers.   Inns which can offer a decent resting-place to the traveller are seldom met with in Calabria ; and it is almost a necessity that hospitality should be exercised in a generous manner by its inhabitants. It is therefore customary in Calabria for any one who brings a letter of introduction to be considered at once as the guest of the house.   When he leaves, the host gives him another letter addressed to some friend in the town or village where he will stop the following night ; and by these means he can travel through these provinces, certain of finding a bed to lie upon, and good food to eat.

Although the sun had risen above the horizon when we awoke next morning, we did not start at once for Palmi, owing to our desire to see something of the renowned women of Bagnara.   There is a proverb which thus points out the three rarities of Southern Italy :—" Sicilian wines, saffron of Cosenza, and women of Bagnara."   For the two first we did not care much ; but we were anxious to judge whether the proverb was true as far as the third was concerned. It was Sunday, and our host, hearing of our wish, said :—

" You will not object to go to church, when I tell you that you will there have an opportunity of seeing the greater number of our women."

Although my companions were all Protestants, they did not belong to any of the Exeter Hall sects ; so they made no objection to hear mass, especially as it was the best means of satisfying so natural a curiosity. Mass being over, we remained in the churchyard, that we might see pass before us the gentle rarities of Bagnara as they returned to their homes. The women walked one after another, in groups or alone, with a majesty in their movements I had rarely seen before. They fully justified the words of the proverb, being tall and erect, with noble, dignified features. In their countenances there was a curious mixture of sadness and gaiety, of severity and grace. Their soft, dark blue eyes glowed beneath black eyebrows, and their smooth, low foreheads, of the Greek classical type, were shaded by a profusion of undulating brown hair. Even the old women retained a matron-like comeliness. As for the young ones, whose charms I have attempted to describe, they really looked, as Maxime Du Camp observes, as if they were daughters of the Egyptian Sphinx and of the Minerva of Athens. It was a half-sweet, half-savage beauty ; a strange mixture of the Saracenic race with the purer blood of the Hellenes.

Time is pressing, however, and we must push on,

for General Orsini, whom we have just met in the
piazza, tells us that Garibaldi will leave Palmi before
noon.   A *carrozzella* is hired with great difficulty.
The nag is half starved; but we must do as best we
can.   The road ascends the rocky flanks of the mountain, now turning abruptly in an elbow-like form, now
winding up again, to descend anew in zigzag lines
towards the sea-shore.   We have already left Bagnara
a long way behind : for more than an hour our horse
has been trotting up and down, and we are lamenting
that we shall not have an opportunity of seeing the
town again.   But on a sudden the road opens, and
the flat-roofed houses are seen at our feet, as in the
hollow of a gulf.   We have turned and turned round
the rock, and have only just reached its top.   Farewell, enchanting city ! farewell, old Portus Balarus ! farewell, beautiful women !   The loveliness of
Calabria, however, is inexhaustible.   Here are again
coming in sight olive groves, cultivated gardens,
Indian fig hedges, and palm trees.

A pyramidal cliff rears its grey peaks through the
chestnut woods, and our driver tells us that we are
getting near Palmi.   Here is the Tenuta di Pietro
Faliscarpi; there, the more elegant Casino di Giovanni Sanpolito.   We rattle on amidst olive trees,
which cannot be said to form groves, but wide forests.
They are no longer the graceful, gentle plants we have
admired in Sicily, or along the coast as far as Bagnara ; but noble and majestic trees, whose luxuriant
branches rival those of the Lebanon cedar.   We
have now arrived at a spot near Palmi, where the
rocks prolong themselves in the shape of a promon-

tory. The Lipari Islands are seen in front. Turning
to the right, the eye ranges over the whole Gulf
of Gioia, as far as Capo Vaticano; to the left, the
line of the cliff extends from the entrance of the
Faro down to Punta del Pezzo. The Sicilian shores
are visible from Melazzo Point to Messina; and old
Etna, towering majestically in the distance, sends up
its thin pinnacle of smoke towards the cloudless
sky.

But here comes a merry band of girls and young
peasants, clad in festive attire—a pretty blending
of the Greek and Calabrian costumes. They are
coming from church, but are singing the song of
the Garibaldians, which they have already learnt by
heart. The verses are not altogether correct, nor is
the pronunciation strictly Italian; for the words
" Italia " and " Garibaldi " have been transformed
into " Talia " and " Garibardo." But, after all, it
does not much matter, for the utterance comes from
the heart. " *Viva la Talia! Viva Garibardo!*" we
answer, therefore, to the pretty girls of Palmi.
For at Palmi we have arrived; glorious Palmi
in its outskirts, but dirty, exceedingly dirty, Palmi
within. Morning service is over, and all the folks of
the town are cramming the piazza and the streets,
pell-mell with the soldiers of Türr and Medici. The
priests are also in great force, for Palmi is a town
of seminaries and convents. As we proceed, asking
for the osteria, the people gaze at us with curious
eyes, as if they knew intuitively that we are followers of the great General who has just left their
city. At length we reach the osteria; but there is

no hope of getting in, the house being crowded in every part. What are we to do? where can we look for a dinner?

"Here, Eccellenza!" cries our coach-driver, "here is a *pizzicagnolo*; I am certain you will find an excellent *pizza*."

Pizza, if the reader is not already familiar with the name, is a sort of dry cake, made of flour, garlic, and oil—a horrid composition, of which, nevertheless, the Italians of the South are particularly fond. The stomach which can tolerate such stuff may defy indigestion for ever. Without any intention of regaling ourselves on this fare, we enter the shop, whose board informs the passer-by that "*Antonio Scarinelli vende olio, salami, e vino Greco.*" I knew that the grocers of those towns have always something to sell besides what the board sets forth; so I asked without hesitation if Signor Antonio could undertake to satisfy our hunger with anything better than a *pizza*.

"Certainly, Eccellenza," he replied. "Go into the kitchen, and speak to my brother; he will give you all you want."

Glancing round the place, I soon discovered that I was not mistaken. The shop of Antonio Scarinelli was, in fact, a receptacle for all kinds of things. Cheese, bread, sausages, fruit, and lard were piled up on the same shelves with tallow candles, lump sugar, bottles of *rosolio*, and many more or less tempting articles. As we entered the kitchen, we could not at first discover the individual to whom the *pizzicagnolo* had referred; for the only person in the place was a man in his shirt-sleeves, and we soon inferred from his black breeches and buckled shoes that he be-longed to the community of the clergy. However, he was not occupied in any of the offices of his sacred calling, for he was at that moment stirring with a spoon something which was boiling in a pan.

" May I ask you, reverend sir, where the brother of Signor Antonio is to be found?" said I to the greasy *sacerdote*.

" Here I am, signorino," answered he. " What can I do for you? Command me! We are all brethren."

There was no mistaking the truth; the priest was to act as our cook. And a good cook he was, too. In less than an hour, the pan which he was stirring when we entered produced some excellent stewed beef, with enough *sughillo* to dress a large dish of maccaroni. Sweet Greco wine and fruit were also set before us, and we sat down to do the honours of the table with all the earnestness of people who have their teeth still in their heads, good fare, and excellent appetites. There was plenty, not only for us, but for Major Guadagni, of Sirtori's Staff, and for Mr. Vizitelly, the able correspondent of the *Illustrated London News*, who, having dropped in by chance, had an oppor-tunity of appreciating the culinary talent of our cook, who by this time, however, had modestly retired, the vesper-hour having been chimed by the church bells.

Having finished our dinner and paid our bill, we began to think once more of the *carrozzelle*. We were all completely done up, and not at all disposed to walk. Our negotiations to secure donkeys or carriages,

however, failed.   Signor Antonio came back with the
sad news that the *Garibardini* had taken them all. What
was to be done?   We were informed that the General
had gone ahead, and would pass the night at Nicotera.
A portion of Medici's division was already steaming up
towards that town, and the troops of Cosenz were on
their march towards Rosarno, where they would halt
for only a few hours, and then push on to Monteleone
—a distance of forty Neapolitan miles, equal to at
least forty-seven English.   Signor Antonio evinced
his despair by calling on all the saints of the calendar;
but we had more occasion to be desperate than he, for
it was our legs that were in question.   I felt like the
English Richard III. in Shakspeare's play, when he
offers his kingdom for a horse.   I had no kingdom to
dispose of; but I would have given almost anything
I possessed, and so would my companions, for some
means of conveyance.

Ultimately, Vizitelly and I decided to trust to our
legs, and started at once, taking the flat, dusty road
leading to Rosarno.   To reach this place, however,
was by no means an easy task.   On we walked, nevertheless, leaving behind us the old forests which crown
the heights forming the northern boundary of the
valley of Gioia.   We halted for a few hours' sleep at
Rosarno, in spite of its heavy air, impregnated with
malaria; and, on the next day, having crossed the
Messima—probably the ancient Medama, mentioned
by Pliny and Strabo—reached (God knows in what
state) the insulated hill on which stands the town of
Melito.

Though a miserable and dirty place, this city may

lay claim to some renown, not only because it was founded by Roger, Count of Sicily, but because Greek colonies still inhabit the numerous villages in its neighbourhood. These people have preserved their ancestral language, and, to a certain extent, their costume. The name of Melito also calls to mind one of the most terrible episodes of the earthquake of 1783, with which the story of the unfortunate Prince of Scylla, related in the preceding chapter, is connected. Completely destroyed, but built again upon the old site, Melito possesses the advantage of having a wealthy Bishop, who, on the first tidings of Garibaldi's arrival, had fled, lest his eyes should be horrified by seeing the excommunicated of the Vatican. The reverend Monsignore had left behind his Vicar-General and his agent, to look after his palace, from which he had taken with the greatest care everything of value, such as linen and plate. Garibaldi and his Staff were therefore obliged to put up with the bare mattresses of Monsignore's beds.

On our arrival at Melito, we found Forbes quartered in the first floor of the café commanding the wide piazza of the town. The view from the window of this room was anything but pleasant, for the eye looked straight down on a half-dried pool of blood, mixed with the cinders of a fire which had been lighted there only two days before. On that spot, General Brigante had been murdered by his soldiers, and half burned, together with his horse. After the capitulation of Villa San Giovanni, Brigante took with him to Melito the disbanded soldiers whom he had picked up on the road. The word *tradimento*, however, had never ceased to be uttered by the soldiers; and the cry grew so threatening after his arrival in that town that he thought it prudent to disguise himself, and start for Naples. He had a son amongst the officers of that band of rascals; and before leaving Melito he wanted to give him some instructions. Trusting in his disguise, he rode towards the piazza; but he was there recognised. The words, " Here is the traitor !" were uttered again and again, and in a few minutes the infuriated soldiery had despatched the General, and thrown his corpse and his unoffending horse upon a funeral pyre.

Leaving Melito about noon, we, the non-combatants, made our solemn entry into Monteleone at three o'clock in the afternoon of the 28th of August. I say " our solemn entry," for at Melito we had been able to procure donkeys. On our arrival at Monteleone, we found that the Neapolitan corps under General Ghio (which, according to a rumour we had heard at a shop in Palmi, intended to stand its ground) had decamped the evening before.

Monteleone is full of classical recollections, and is allowed by most antiquarians to stand on the spot where rose the magnificent Hipponium of the Greeks —a name subsequently changed by the Romans into Vibo Valentia, or Vibona. During his banishment from Rome, Cicero passed many months at the villa of his friend Sicca, the walls of whose gardens are yet to be seen, bordering the shore of the gulf at the foot of the smiling hill where the present town stands. A ruined castle, built by Frederic II., still rises at the top of the promontory, together with a convent of

Augustinians, which seems to have been once a part of the castle. On this convent, our party had been billeted by the Sindaco of the town, and the reader may guess the amazement of those tranquil monks when we made our appearance at its gates. The reception we met with, however, was very cordial; cells were soon allotted to us, and a good supper was offered and accepted. Excepting the monks of Monte Cassino, of La Cava, and of two or three other orders, monastic communities in Southern Italy do not shine with respect to learning; and the Augustinians of Monteleone were in the last category. Father Guardiano was an old man, who had already touched that degree of decrepitude which seems like a second childhood at the threshold of the tomb. The other monks appeared to care but little for the books of the convent library, but were fond of their pipes, and of the good meals the brother cook prepared for them. As to their politics, they had turned to the wind which was then blowing, and had become liberal to the backbone. Their patriotism even went so far after our arrival, as to induce Father Provveditore to concoct an address to Garibaldi, which was presented to the General by a deputation of monks. Father Provveditore was a man of gigantic frame, and so strong that, having once struck a donkey with his fist, he killed it on the spot; for which feat we were tempted to give him the name of Cain. Nature had not developed his brains in the like proportion; and the address he undertook to write turned out such a failure that he was obliged to ask the assistance of one of our party, whose style, his brethren thought, would answer better

for the exceptional occasion.   Though Father Provveditore was not a learned man, he was an excellent
fellow, who doubly endeared himself to me by finding
a good horse, which I hastened to buy.

Mounted at last, and free to follow more closely the
Staff of the General, I rode next day to Pizzo, where
I was desirous of visiting the church in which the
remains of the unfortunate Murat were buried in the
autumn of 1815, after he had been shot in the castle
of that town, where he had landed with a few followers.
In the preceding winter, during my short stay at
Ravenna, I had had the honour of becoming acquainted
with his daughter, the Marchioness Rasponi, in whose
house are religiously preserved many things which
belonged to this gallant General of Napoleon I.
Great was my pleasure when, after having visited the
platform of the castle where he received the fire of the
soldiers, for which he himself gave the order, I heard
that a Signor Rossi had sent to Garibaldi, for presen-
tation to the Marchioness, the banner which Murat
carried when he appeared in 1815 in the public square
of Pizzo, the star which he wore on his uniform, and
two balls which Signor Rossi had picked up on the
spot where the hero fell.

Türr had by this time arrived at Pizzo, and he told
me that I ought to hasten my progress if I wished to
join Garibaldi, who was to sleep at Curinga, and early
next morning to push on towards Maida.

Galloping along the winding road from Pizzo to the
river Angitola, I passed through vineyards, gardens,
and olive-groves, overtaking on my way several Garibaldians marching in the same direction, or encamped

in the roadside fields. The sun was fast setting, and, from the natural platform I was riding on, the whole Gulf of St. Eufemia was visible, and my ear could distinctly detect the Ave Maria, chimed by the bells of the numerous villages scattered on the mountains which form its northern boundary.

The hour of midnight had struck when I began to mount the detached wooded hill on which stands the little town of Maida, facing Nicastro on the southern extremity of the valley; but I was so tired that I at once joined the bivouac of Medici's column, and spent the night there. With the morning light I was again in my saddle, passing through the field on which was fought the battle between the English, under Sir John Stuart, and the French, under General Regnier, in 1806—a battle which ended in the total defeat of the latter.

General Türr was right in what he had told me; for, when I entered the miserable city, I found that Garibaldi, who had exchanged his wide-awake for the Calabrian sugar-loaf hat, was on the point of leaving Maida with Baron Stocco. The Neapolitan *squadre* of Calabria, organized by Baron Stocco, had been bivouacking in the outskirts of Maida since the day before, according to an order given to the Baron by Garibaldi himself, with a view to allowing Ghio's column to retreat in peace, and thus avoid bloodshed among brethren. Had the volunteers of Stocco been left in that tract of country between the rivers Angitola and Lamato, where they were encamped on our arrival at Monteleone, there can be no doubt that Ghio's troops would have been completely destroyed. I mention this inci-

dent because it shows how glad Garibaldi was whenever he could carry out his plans without useless loss
of life.

At nine o'clock, Garibaldi, Stocco, and Captain
Forbes started in a post-carriage in the direction of
Tiriolo, a small town in the Apennines, between
Nicastro and Catanzaro, from which a view of the
Tyrrhenian and Ionian seas may be obtained.   The
Staff and army were to follow, and proceed as fast as
they could, for Ghio was only a few miles off, and
Garibaldi had decided that he would make him capitulate as his colleagues, Brigante, Gallotti, and Melendis, had done.   Passing through the picturesque
Calabrian villages, here and there peopled by Greek
colonies, our modesty had to go through a great many
trials, for the women and girls wished to kiss the
liberators of their country, as they called us.   Some
of my companions did not decline the offer; and in
this they showed their good taste, for many of the
girls were exceedingly pretty, still preserving the
beautiful features of the classic race from which they
are descended.

On arriving at Tiriolo, we were greeted by the enthusiastic cries of the National Guards, and of other
Calabrian volunteers, who informed us that Ghio was
at a distance of only seven miles, and that Garibaldi had
hastened towards San Pietro with a few National
Guards in pursuit of him.   The first columns of our
army had not yet appeared, and I was far from tranquil
on hearing that the General had ventured on so
dangerous an errand.   We hurried forward, however,
according to instructions, and on entering the village

learnt that Garibaldi had arrived there at nine o'clock, whilst the rear-guard of the Neapolitans was leaving it.   Had Ghio been a man of the smallest courage, he could have taken Garibaldi and all of us prisoners; for the few National Guards placed in the outskirts of San Pietro could not have resisted a squadron of well-organized cavalry.   All went smoothly enough, nevertheless ; our sleep was only interrupted by a slight shock of earthquake, and at daybreak next morning the Calabrese scouts brought intelligence that Ghio had stopped with his column at Savoria Manelli, a town of Neapolitan notoriety, being the birthplace of the famous brigand Caliguri.   The town is situated near the village of Passaggio, and commands the high-road from Catanzaro to Naples.   By this time, news had also reached us that Türr was advancing with part of his men.   Sending to him an aide-de-camp with orders to hasten his march towards Savoria, Garibaldi took the mountain tracks, throwing out as skirmishers the Calabrese volunteers, whom the priest Don Ferdinando Bianchi had organized.   By ten o'clock we arrived at a little farm half a mile from Savoria.   As soon as the Calabrese, emerging from the mountains, got sight of Ghio's troops, who were huddled together in the town like sheep in a fold, they opened fire.   No videttes having been placed by the Neapolitan General to guard his camp, the consequence was that the sudden attack spread terror amongst his troops. Such was their dread, that Colonel Peard, having boldly advanced with a few Calabrese into the town, instead of being made prisoner, was begged by some Neapolitan officers to go to Ghio, and persuade him to

capitulate.   Ghio did not require much pressure on
the matter, for Peard had scarcely addressed him on
the subject when he consented at once to send the Chief
of his Staff to Garibaldi.   At noon the capitulation
was signed, and we were enabled to enter Savoria.   To
describe the scenes of confusion which we witnessed
that day would be impossible.   What we had beheld
at Reggio, Villa San Giovanni, and Scylla was bad
enough ; but this was even worse.   The town contained
7000 infantry, cavalry, and artillery, who were screaming, shouting, and cursing.   Loose horses wandered
about, kicking furiously right and left, whilst the Garibaldians were trying to catch them.   Ghio and his
officers were spectators of that miserable scene, and
they seemed as unconcerned as if it had been a Chinese
army which was breaking up.   To add shame to shame,
General Ghio and the Chief of his Staff begged
Garibaldi to order that a few hundred piastres, due to
them as arrears of pay, should be handed over to them,
as well as the expenses of their journey to Naples. Such
were the Generals of Francis II.! What wonder, then,
if the army they commanded dwindled down to
nothing in a few days, and the whole of Calabria
was lost ?

Starting from Savoria on the last day of August, we
followed the main road, passing through picturesque
glens, bordered by lofty rocks, and in the afternoon
arrived at Rogliano.   Here we halted at the house of
Avvocato Morelli, a wealthy gentleman who, like
Baron Stocco, had been prominent in bringing about
the insurrection of Calabria.   From Rogliano, General Türr was ordered to go to Paola, and take the

command of the body of 4000 men forming Pianciani's expedition, which, owing to the exertions of
Colonel Frappolli, had by this time landed there.

After being entirely destroyed in the earthquake of
1638, Rogliano was rebuilt, and now presents a
much greater appearance of neatness than Calabrese
towns generally do. Avvocato Morelli gave us a
princely reception; such a reception as we could
hardly have ventured to expect in those Apennine
countries.

Leaving the towns of Amantea, Foscaldo, Bel-
monte, and Maratea, on the northern side, and following the main road, either bordered by mulberry
trees or running between well-cultivated fields, we
arrived at nightfall at Cosenza. This town, the
capital of Calabria Citra, is seated in a hollow at the
confluence of the rivers Crati and Busento. The
olive-trees, which since we left Palmi had almost
ceased to adorn the landscape, here again made their
appearance, giving once more to the country the charm
of eastern vegetation. The effects of the last earthquake, which partly destroyed Cosenza and the
neighbouring villages, were still to be traced here and
there as we made our way down the gradual descent
which leads to it. I will not tire the reader with a
description of the illuminations and feasts which
marked the short stay of the Dictator at Cosenza.
They were like all the others : a great deal of shouting, a heartfelt enthusiasm, and no economy of flags
or of lamp-oil. Baron Gozzolini volunteered to be
the host of the amateur followers of the war, and desired to detain us for a few days ; but Garibaldi was not

the man to allow even a day's respite.   Our march,
moreover, was accelerated by the news which Father
Pantaleo brought from Naples.   The break-up of
Francis II.'s government was imminent—so imminent that, according to information supplied by
Alexandre Dumas, Don Liborio Romano, then the
Home Secretary of his Sicilian Majesty, had repeatedly
expressed a desire for the Liberator to arrive in the
capital as speedily as possible.

At daybreak on the 1st September, Garibaldi started
in a post-chaise, with Cosenz, Sirtori, Trecchi, Nullo,
Missori, Stagnetti, Gusmaroli, and Basso, leaving
orders for his Staff to follow him.   Since the capitulation of Ghio at Savoria, we had not met with any
Neapolitan troops; for there was in Calabria only the
column of General Calandrelli, which, having capitulated to the Provisional Government of Cosenza,
and promised to retire from the province, was then
on its way to Lagonegro, trying to get to Naples as
fast as it could.   It was important that Calandrelli
should be prevented pursuing his retrograde march.
Garibaldi therefore sent orders to Türr (who, the
reader will recollect, was at Paola with the men
belonging to Pianciani's division), to take his troops
to Sapri by sea, land there, and march on Lagonegro,
thus placing his division between Calandrelli's column
and Naples.

A few hours after the departure of Garibaldi's
Staff, I was riding along the road to Spezzano Albanese, hoping to overtake the General, either at that
village, or farther on at Castrovilleri.   I had started
from Cosenza with one of our English companions;

but before reaching Tarsia I met Prince Nisceme, Baron Cuzzo, and other Staff officers of General Cosenz, with whom I traversed that wearisome road, so often the theatre of the bloody deeds of brigands, and in the ravines bordering on which many travellers have found their graves. On arriving at Tarsia—a village which enjoyed the reputation of being still attached to the Bourbons—my companions were obliged to quarrel with the Sindaco, on account of his having refused to provide for the wants of a few Garibaldian stragglers. Leaving Tarsia, we fell in with Pace's column of Calabrese volunteers, and followed it to Spezzano Albanese. We were now approaching the centre of those singular Albanian colonies which in the fifteenth century settled in the villages then under the sway of the Prince of Bisignano, who had married the daughter of the Albanian *condottiere* Scanderbeg, the latter having come to Calabria to assist Ferdinand I. at the siege of Otranto. It is a curious fact that, though four centuries have now passed away, these colonies still retain the Greek religious rites, together with their original tongue, though the Roman Catholic Bishops have done their utmost to convert them to the orthodox faith. The Albanians (for such they may be called) have even got a college in one of their villages, in which the sons of the landed gentry are brought up under the control of their learned and liberal priests. In consequence of this education, the young men of those villages have always turned out bitter enemies of the Bourbon despotism. The influence exercised by the gentry over the peasantry of the country is very great; and whenever a revolutionary attempt has taken place in Calabria, the Albanians have been prominently connected with it.   Being a fine people, who still maintain the warlike habits of their ancestors, they know how to use their muskets against any oppressor of their country.   Now that they have got rid of the government they detested, they have been organized in five bodies of National Guards, to whom may be chiefly ascribed the merit of having put down the brigandage spread by the agents of Francis II., in that branch of the Apennines which overhangs the valley of the Crati.

The chief of the Albanian volunteers we overtook on leaving Tarsia.   Giuseppe Pace was a native of Castrovilleri, and suffered imprisonment for many years at Procida.   I had known him in London, to which he came in 1859, with Poerio and the other Neapolitan exiles ; and he now kindly invited me to his house, which we were to pass on our road to Lagonegro. Having spent a few hours at Spezzano Albanese, we started on the same evening for Castrovilleri.   As we were leaving the town, a funeral was coming up the road which descends into the valley.   The corpse of a young woman was lying on the open bier, and was being carried to the grave attired in a red silk dress, with a wreath of flowers round the head.   The hair was hanging loose, and in the hands, which were clasped together as if she had been praying, was a bunch of flowers.   A group of weeping women followed in silence, whilst a train of bearded priests chanted the Miserere.   Now and then, the mournful procession stopped, and the bier was lowered to the ground before the house of some friend or relation of the deceased. It was an Albanian funeral, conducted according to the rites of the Greek religion. These rites assume a still more curious character in the case of the funeral of a married man ; for then the widow follows as chief mourner, plucking at regular intervals two or three hairs from her dishevelled tresses.

The night was splendid, and the moonlight so brilliant that the valley where ancient Sybaris stood was clearly descernible on our right. We could even see the remains of those Roman structures which perhaps mark the place where the town of Copia (so called from the fertility of its territory) was built on the ruins of Sybaris. The lower slopes of the mountains (which, to the right and left, are richly cultivated and wooded) are enlivened with villages and churches. Lucanian Muranum was on our right, half concealed by umbrageous trees at the extremity of the valley that lies beneath the western flank of Pollino. The rivers Esora and Cocitello were winding their lucid waters southward through the valley, hastening to unite and form the Cocile, the Sybaris of the ancients. Our road lay amongst woods of olives and ancient elm trees. Behind the fertile fields, lofty and cultivated hills emerged in the far distance ; whilst the marching columns of Calabrian volunteers, dressed in their national costumes, heightened the beauty of the scene, and brought vividly to one's recollection the pictures of Salvator Rosa.

At a place called the Rivolta we halted. It was indeed a heavenly spot. Large groves of ancient

oaks, ornamented with festoons of vines, spread their
shade on all sides ; fields of corn appeared in the distance ; country houses showed their white walls here
and there in the meadows ; and a large stream of
fresh, clear water flowed through the landscape.   The
bivouac fires had been lighted by those unhappy
Neapolitan soldiers who were disbanded after the different capitulations.   Forsaken by their chiefs, and left
in a state of total destitution, the poor fellows would
have starved on their way home, had it not been for
the charitable feeling of the Calabrian population.
As soon as our column arrived, the volunteers scattered themselves about the fields, gathering round the
several bivouac fires, and sharing their scanty piece of
bread with the wretched Bourbon soldiers.

In the uncertain light of morning, we entered the
town of Castrovilleri.   We hoped to find Garibaldi ;
but he had started for Lagonegro, so earnest was he to
overtake Calandrelli's column, which was already intercepted by Türr's corps, now appearing on its rear.
Although to follow Garibaldi's movements was not an
easy task, yet, after having spent a few hours at Pace's
house, I left Castrovilleri with two of my friends—the
only ones who, besides Cavaliere Gallenga and Captain
Forbes, were spirited enough to endure that harassing march.   My poor horse, which was completely
done up, having scarcely had twenty-four hours' rest
since I quitted Monteleone, was left at Spezzano
Albanese.   Major Lucci had been, however, kind
enough to lend me one of his—an excellent nag which
had carried my weary bones to Castrovilleri, and was
to take me to Rotonda on that very evening.   As for

my two English companions, they followed in a post-carriage.

We had now entered the province of Basilicata, the ancient Lucania; for, at the summit of the Apennines, which we had reached by ascending the long and steep defiles of Maranno, we bade farewell to Calabria. An early ride took me on the same day to Lagonegro, where I heard that, in spite of a boastful order of the day, in which Calandrelli announced to his troops that the Austrians were arriving, the gallant General had capitulated. But the tax-collector, in whose house I put up, added, as a sort of corrective, that Francis II. had decided to make a regular stand at Salerno, where he had massed the remainder of the army, about 30,000 strong. This news increased my desire to push on as fast as I could; and, having procured a fresh mount, in less than three hours I descended the last spur of the Apennines, which brought me to the entrance of the lovely Val di Diano, celebrated for its fertility. I was now riding down hills, or galloping across meadows, as fast as I could; for I was anxious to get to Sala before dusk.

As I was approaching the suburbs of that town, I met Baron Cuzzo and another of General Cosenz's Staff officers, who told me that there was excellent news from Naples, and that in all probability we should enter the capital in two or three days.

He also stated that Garibaldi had just received a Neapolitan deputation, sent by the so-called *Comitato dell' Ordine.* In saying this, the officer laughed.

" What are you laughing at, Cuzzo?" said I, " and what do you mean by this *Comitato dell' Ordine?*"

" Well, you must know," replied my friend, " that Cavour has taken it into his head to have a Sardinian Provincial Government proclaimed before we enter Naples. The committee have sent Dr. Tommasi and two or three others to announce the news to the General."

" And what was Garibaldi's answer ?" asked I.

" You may easily imagine. The General told them that he had landed at Marsala and crossed the Straits to free the Neapolitan kingdom from the Bourbonic tyranny, and that he would not hear of annexation till Venice and Rome had been conquered for Italy. The gentlemen of the *Comitato dell' Ordine* pro- mised Cavour to get up a revolution, in order to secure the success of his plan, and boasted that they would shed the last drop of their blood in the prose- cution of that design ; but *altro è parlar di morte, altro il morire.*"

To understand the words of the last speaker, the reader must know that some of the Neapolitan exiles, who, after the amnesty granted by Francis II., re- turned to Naples, established the *Comitato dell' Ordine,* the object of which was to make the people of Naples rise, hasten the departure of the King, and then establish a Provisional Government, with a view to proclaiming at once the annexation of Southern Italy to Sardinia. Possibly owing to the want of organization of the Neapolitans, Dr. Tommasi and his friends were unable to keep their promise. To check the influence of this political party, another committee was established by Garibaldi's friends, called the *Comitato d'Azione,* whose members, having more energy than those presided over by Tommasi, out-stripped them by securing the ascendancy of Gari-baldi's name throughout the whole of the Neapolitan kingdom. Dr. Bertani was the very soul of this second committee, which proved far more successful than the first.

Such was the state of things which preceded the arrival of the Liberator in the Neapolitan capital.

CHAPTER VII.

THE LAST HALT IN GARIBALDI'S MARCH.

Ride to Auletta—News from Salerno—A Telegraphic Trick—
Ignorance of the Priests at Basilicata—Political Condition of
the Neapolitan Kingdom in 1860—Inexperience of Francis II.
—A Constitution granted—Spinelli's Ministry—Diplomatic
Failures—Alexandre Dumas—The Neapolitan Minister of the
Interior becomes a Conspirator—The Crisis—The Terrace of
the Royal Palace—The Young Queen of Naples—Proclama-
tion of Francis II.—A *Coup d'État* meditated—The Nea-
politan Deputation starts for Salerno—An accommodating
Sub-Prefect—Garibaldi's Officers at the Railway Station of
Salerno—We start for Naples.

THE early light was just appearing above the mountains of Sala, when, on the 6th of September, I regained
the high road which was to take me to Eboli. At
La Petrosa (where the river Negro, breaking in different cataracts, passes under the rocky promontory on
which the town of Auletta stands), I fell in with one
of our brigades bivouacking by the road-side in a most
romantic glen, surpassing by far the natural beauties
I admired the previous day in riding through Val
di Diano. I was told that Garibaldi had been seen
just a few minutes before, driving in the direction of
Eboli, but that General Türr and his Staff were at

Auletta. I therefore ascended the steep mountain road leading to that town, thinking it better to get some information about the further movements of our army before venturing on the road to Eboli.

Although the people of Basilicata are not a fighting race, like their brethren of Calabria, yet the insurrection was here also in full swing. Colonel Boldone, formerly in the service of the Neapolitan Government, and a country gentleman named Mignona, were in command of the insurrectionary bands of Basilicata, which numbered about 8000 men. These, added to the Calabrians and the 25,000 troops forming the regular army of the Revolution, enabled Garibaldi to bring into the field a respectable force, one-third of which, at least, would have matched an equal number of any European army. In the general and well-developed insurrectionary element lay the true secret of those bold movements of the Dictator which ended in so signal a triumph. Garibaldi, with only a few of his followers, was always thirty or forty miles in advance of the leading column of his army. Had it not been for the insurrection, and the dread which his name inspired in the Neapolitan soldiers, he might have been made prisoner a hundred times, without his army knowing it till days after.

On my arrival at Auletta, I found the place occupied by a few companies of our men, and heard that Garibaldi had been summoned to Salerno by the unexpected tidings that the Neapolitans had abandoned that town, and had fallen back on Capua, by way of Nocera. No doubt, the bold march of the Dictator, and the well-combined movements of his regular

troops and of the insurrectionary bands, had had great
weight in bringing about the sudden disappearance of
the 12,000 Neapolitans and the thirty guns which
General Afant de Rivera had under his command.
But this astounding and happy result—for the *corps
d'armée*, with the aid of its powerful cavalry, could have
arrested the advance of the Garibaldians on the plain
it occupied—was also partly attributable to a successful trick which some of Garibaldi's followers
played on his Sicilian Majesty's Ministers on the 4th
September. On that evening, Colonel Peard, Gallenga,
and Forbes unexpectedly arrived in the town of Eboli,
where they met with a warm reception, the townspeople being under an impression that Colonel Peard
was Garibaldi himself. Forbes employed all sorts of
arguments to persuade at least the Sindaco and other
officials of the delusion under which they laboured; but
all was of no use. Peard and Gallenga, thinking that
they might turn their reconnoitering excursion to the
benefit of the National cause, went at once to the telegraph office. In 1859, Gallenga followed the march
of the Tuscan army (then commanded by Ulloa), and
was therefore on the best terms with that General,
who, according to the last news received from Naples,
was supposed to have succeeded General Pianelli as
Francis II.'s Minister of War. On entering the
office, Gallenga, having exchanged a few words in
English with Colonel Peard, thus telegraphed to
General Ulloa :—

"Eboli, 11.30 P.M.—Garibaldi has arrived with
5000 men, and 5000 Calabrese are momentarily expected. Disembarkations are anticipated in the Bay

of Naples and the Gulf of Salerno to-night. I strongly advise you to withdraw the garrison from the latter place without delay, or they will be cut off; and let me beg of you, as a personal friend, but a political enemy, to abandon a sinking cause, which must be your ruin."

This telegraph had only just been transmitted along the wires when a Minister of Francis II. telegraphed to Eboli, "Any news of the division of Calandrelli?" To this, Peard and Gallenga answered, "General Calandrelli and his division passed yesterday under the orders of Garibaldi at Lagonegro, and now form a portion of the National Army." This trick, together with other telegrams sent by these two gentlemen to the Sindaco of Salerno, ordering him to prepare an imposing number of rations for the next day, determined—as I was myself afterwards told by the Minister of Francis II., Commendatore De Martino— the backward movement of General Afant de Rivera's *corps d'armée.*

It was no wonder that, on hearing such exciting news, I was anxious to leave Auletta, and get on the track of Garibaldi as soon as possible. My horse, however, was tired, and a few hours' rest was necessary. I had found all I wanted at the house of a priest, a good-hearted man in his way, but the very incarnation of ignorance. The circumstance, however, did not surprise me, for when at Lagonegro I was enabled to judge the intellectual condition of the clergy of Basilicata—a condition which may be further illustrated by the following story.

On my way to Lagonegro, I met with two priests of

Castelluccio, of whom I inquired what cause had prevented the wealthy people of their province from joining Victor Emmanuel's army in 1859, whilst all the rest of the Peninsula had sent volunteers to the Sardinian camp. As the two priests seemed not to understand me, I asked them whether they were well informed of the battles fought the year before in Lombardy. The answer I obtained was such that I felt convinced they knew very little about the matter, and seemed still to be ignorant that one of the richest and most flourishing provinces possessed by Austria had been lost by her. To say the truth, I thought at first they were making a fool of me; but, after a quarter of an hour's conversation, I came to the conclusion that they were really no better informed of those events than a Chinaman might have been. The ignorance of my host of Auletta was fully equal to this; for he had not even an exact knowledge of the great achievements of Garibaldi in his own country. To such of my readers as have never travelled in the mountainous districts of Southern Italy, this statement may perhaps seem incredible; but I am certain I may venture to say that not one of those three priests could have written a letter in correct Italian, or have read any other book than the breviary. Such being the ignorance which prevails amongst the clergy of the Neapolitan provinces, the reader may easily infer the moral and intellectual condition of the peasantry. I shudder when I reflect how long and difficult will be the work of regeneration in a community which for centuries has been kept in so disgraceful a condition. When travelling among those wild mountains, where all

intercommunication is a matter of the utmost difficulty, the stranger may be excused if he should think
himself in one of the remotest parts of the known
world.

Starting from Auletta at five o'clock in the
evening, I arrived at Salerno at ten A.M., on the
7th of September, just half an hour after Garibaldi had left for Naples, accompanied by thirteen
officers of his Staff, some English amateurs, and the
Neapolitan deputation, who had reached Salerno on
the preceding night, shortly after the arrival of the
Dictator at the same town, where he was received
with all that display of popular enthusiasm which had
marked his *promenade militaire* through Calabria and
Basilicata. When I entered the city, traces of the
phrensied joy of its people were still to be seen,
and they surpassed all the manifestations I had
witnessed in Lombardy and Central Italy during the
preceding year. It was a sort of madness, such as
only southern races ever fall into. The demonstrations were those of a people who had abruptly
passed from a state of utter slavery to freedom, from
inaction to action, from death to life. The moral
resurrection of a country long crushed under the vilest
of despotisms was visible in those ebullitions of delight
and gratitude.

On his accession to the throne of his father, Francis
II. found the kingdom he had inherited in a state of
complete moral dissolution, chiefly brought about by
the ferocious system of government which had sig-
nalized the reign of Ferdinand II. Corruption on
a large scale had been carried on by every class of

functionaries, from the highest to the lowest. There were few magistrates, Generals, or Government officers who could not have been bought; the only question was as to the best way of offering the required price. The Administration was consequently thrown into a state of utter confusion, and the army reduced to a body of prætorians, who only cared for their private interests, honour and courage having deserted their banners. Favours were bought, impunity secured, political and private revenge countenanced—nay, encouraged—by the Government. Thousands of good citizens were driven from their native country, carrying with them into foreign lands, or into the free State of Piedmont, a lively picture of the sufferings of their fellow-countrymen, and of their own miseries. The all-powerful, cruel, and corrupt police were aided in their tyranny by the influence of Austria and Rome; and all this while, the northern part of the Peninsula was prospering under the rule of a constitutional King, and progressing towards the unification of the country through the valour of the army and the wisdom of the people. The difference between the two systems was the more striking, because the standard of comparison was to be found within the common country. Happiness and gradual amelioration had become the lot of Piedmont; misery, moral degradation, and constant threats of revolution continued to be the fate of Naples. Such was the state of the Two Sicilies when Francis II. was called to rule the patrimony of his ancestors.

The new King, young, without experience, ill educated, and badly trained by a step-mother who had inherited from her Austrian parents all the hatred which the Princes of the House of Hapsburg have invariably shown to Italy and to liberal institutions, came to the throne only to follow the fatal path which his father had trod with apparent success, owing to that iron will with which he had been endowed by nature. But this power was wanting in his son. Brought up by Jesuits, heir to a kingdom which he believed he had derived from God, and totally unacquainted with the wants of our epoch, he was led to believe by his ignorant courtiers that he could successfully carry out a system which was in itself an absurdity. England, Sardinia, and France did not fail to warn him of the perilous road on which he had entered. But their counsels fell heedless on his ears; and the advice of his anti-national Ministers, the intrigues of a mischievous priesthood, and the support of the Austrian Camarilla were preferred to the suggestions of wiser and more liberal teachers.

For Francis II. and his minions, England and Sardinia were only the upholders of revolutionary principles; while France was ruled by a *parvenu*, the nephew of a pretender whom his grandfather had condemned to be shot in the castle of Pizzo. It was therefore natural enough that Francis II. should only have had ears for the advice which came from St. Petersburg, from Rome, and above all from Vienna.

The hour, however, had struck in which the supremacy of Austria was held at bay. The guns of Magenta and Solferino had set at nought her overwhelming power in Italy. No sooner was Francis Joseph humiliated than the petty sovereigns of Central Italy were swept away, and the position of Francis II. became more perilous every hour. The rising of the Sicilian patriots, though quenched in blood for a time, was renewed with greater force on the appearance of Garibaldi in the island. After having failed to satisfy the popular demands by charging General Filangieri with the formation of a hybrid Liberal Government, the young King saw the necessity of evoking from the tomb the Constitution of 1848, which his father had stifled after the 15th of May of the same year. But, unfortunately for him, though fortunately for Italy, the day had passed for any such compromise.

The men called by the King to work out the problem of constitutional rule, were all, with one exception, honest and respected citizens ; some of whom had been openly persecuted by the Government of Ferdinand II., some watched by his police, others employed in the army or as diplomatists in foreign countries, on account of the suspicion in which they were held for entertaining liberal opinions. Prince Torella belonged to the first of these categories; the Marquis La Greca, Count Spinelli, and the famous Don Liborio Romano, to the second ; Commendatore De Martino and General Pianelli to the third. To save a rotten monarchy, already tumbling into pieces, was the task which these men courageously undertook ; a task almost as difficult to carry out with success as, according to first appearances, was that of Garibaldi. Nevertheless, most of them set to work with the earnestness of honest men who were determined to fulfil their duty to the last. Prince Torella and Commendatore De Martino were foremost

among the new Ministers. The first was imprisoned by the police of the young King only a few
days after his accession to the throne; while his
brother, the Marquis Bella, had been in exile since
1848. De Martino, formerly Neapolitan Ambassador
at Rome, was a man who, though serving faithfully his master, had never shrunk from pointing out
to him the dangers he would incur if he persevered
in a system so scornfully denounced by the whole of
liberal Europe.

The first step taken by the new Ministers of Francis
II. was to send Signor Manna to Turin, charged
to negotiate an offensive and defensive alliance between the two kingdoms — an alliance which had
been contemptuously rejected by the Neapolitan court
when proposed by Sardinia only six months before.
In the mind of the constitutional advisers of the
young King, this would have resulted in dividing Italy
into two powerful States, and hastening its total
liberation from the yoke of Austria. But it was too
late. Garibaldi had already entered Palermo, and the
cry " Down with the Bourbons !" was re-echoing
through the land. Though a good patriot, an excellent administrator, and an able diplomatist, Manna
failed in his mission at Turin, and the same fate
awaited De Martino at Paris, and the Marquis La
Greca at London. Ministers and diplomatists knocked
at every door, but no door was opened. At Turin,
Cavour told Manna that negotiations were now useless; Lord John Russell washed his hands of the
whole business ; and as for the Emperor Napoleon, he
answered as the oracles of old. These, moreover, were

not the only dangers of the situation.   Amongst the
new Ministers there was one (Don Liborio Romano)
who, since the landing of Garibaldi at Reggio, was
secretly conspiring against his inexperienced master.

Two days after the victory of Melazzo, Alexandre
Dumas volunteered to go to Naples on board his
yacht *Emma*, in order to watch the course of events,
and try to hasten the revolution.   On his arrival at
Naples, the famous romance-writer began to carry out
his revolutionary projects, and turned the deck of his
yacht into a perfect tailor's shop, where red shirts
were openly manufactured under the windows of the
King.   With all the activity of his nature, Dumas
enlisted new conspirators, secretly spread Garibaldi's
manifestoes, distributed arms and ammunition, and, in
short, became the most active agent of the National
propaganda.   So far, indeed, did he go, so openly did
he act, that the French Admiral and the French
Ambassador intimated to him that, if the Neapolitan
Government should order his arrest, they would not
protect either his yacht or himself.   Dumas, however,
is not easily frightened; so he pursued his work all
the same.

In the meanwhile, Garibaldi had crossed the Straits,
had captured Reggio, and had begun his progress
towards Naples.   Don Liborio Romano, seeing that
the first throw had been gained by the Dictator,
thought it expedient to lay down the conditions on
which, if Francis II. should lose the others, he would
step in, and serve the new master.   Knowing that
Dumas had been sent to Naples by Garibaldi, Don
Liborio went to see him, declared himself a warm

Garibaldian, and offered his co-operation. This, of course, he professed to do for the good of his country; for there is no man, however cynical he may be, who does not try to justify a reprehensible action by alleging the uprightness of his intentions. The practice is said to be held in great favour by the Jesuits; and Don Liborio seems to have studied in that school with great effect. All the arrangements for the conspiracy were therefore discussed by the Minister and the French author. They were to communicate through Signor Cozzolongo, Don Liborio's private secretary, and, in case the plot should be discovered, a safe refuge for the Minister was negotiated by Dumas with the commander of a foreign man-of-war, who was told that Don Liborio might find himself under the necessity of applying for his protection.

The conspiracy, though carried out with the greatest secrecy, was, however, detected by the secret police of the Court. A few days before the flight of the King, Francis II. called his Home Secretary into his cabinet, and abruptly said to him:—"Don Liborio, I know that you are keeping up secret relations with Alexandre Dumas, and that you are treating with Garibaldi."

"Yes, sire," answered Don Liborio; "it is my duty to watch the intrigues of your enemies, and, in order to follow them the more closely, I have resorted to the artifice of assuming the character of a conspirator."

Count Pallhen gave a similar answer to Paul I. the day before the Emperor was strangled.

Whilst Francis II. was at once abandoned by his

army (which, as the reader knows, did not even try to
oppose the march of the revolutionists through Calabria), and deceived by one of his Ministers—whilst
he was losing power every day through the influence
of the two rival, yet equally anti-Bourbonic, committees, named respectively "*Azione*" and "*Ordine*"—
the telegrams sent by Gallenga and Peard from Eboli
came to precipitate the crisis.

The clock of the Arsenal had just struck the first
hour of the 5th of September, when two ladies were
walking up and down the terrace of the Royal Palace
which faces the Gulf.   It was a glorious night : the
waters of the Tyrrhene sea were calm and silvery ;
and old Vesuvius, with its eternal spire of smoke,
towered over the splendid bay.   The youngest of the
two ladies was distinguished by a sad and stately
beauty.   Her eyes and hair were dark ; while her
figure, tall, erect, and queenly, showed that she could
unite vivacity with dignity, force with grace.   The
eldest, in appearance more matronly, had the stamp of
a noble simplicity upon her kind and gentle countenance.   Both were silent, as if absorbed in the beauty
of the scenery.   But they were not looking at the
swift sails of the *speronare*, coming from Capri or
Amalfi, nor at the falling stars which now and again
darted their sudden brilliance along the heavens, and
vanished into the bosom of the sea.   They were not
listening to the harmony of the fishermen's song, nor
to those strange, soft sounds which give so melancholy yet so sweet a charm to the Neapolitan nights.
The thoughts of the two ladies were not so bright ;
for they knew that perhaps this was the last time

they would walk through the alleys which border the sweet flower-beds of the terrace.

Presently, a short, grey-haired man made his appearance, and advanced towards the ladies.

"What news do you bring, Commendatore?" asked the younger of the two, with a sad smile. "Is the council of the Ministers over?"

"Yes, your Majesty," answered Commendatore De Martino; "the council is over, and the fate of the monarchy—at least for the present—is decided. The King will leave Naples to-morrow for Gaeta."

"So, then, Garibaldi is advancing on Naples?" said the Queen.

"Yes, your Majesty; we have received intelligence that he will arrive at Salerno to-morrow, and an order has been already sent to General Afant de Rivera to retire with his Majesty's troops on the Volturno."

"Sad news!" exclaimed the Queen, turning to her lady-in-waiting, the Duchess St. Cesario; "but we must bend with resignation and dignity to the will of God. Let us retire; the King must be in need of consolation."

In this way did the unfortunate companion of Francis II. receive the news that she had lost a crown, together with the country of her adoption and her affections. The details of that mournful scene were the frequent theme of conversation when we arrived at Naples. Most truly may it be said that the Royal lady was worthy of a better fate; for devotion and unbounded goodness are not wanting to her brave heart. In looking back on the glorious drama of the

N 2

Italian revival, the imposing figure of this noble woman erects itself bright and serene amidst the darkness of the last days of the Neapolitan Bourbons.

At the Council of Ministers of which De Martino had spoken to the Queen, Don Liborio Romano was charged to write the Royal Proclamation announcing the departure to Gaeta, which I shall perhaps be excused for inserting in this place :—

"ROYAL PROCLAMATION.

"Among the duties prescribed to Kings, those of the days of misfortune are the grandest and the most solemn, and I intend to fulfil them with resignation, free from weakness, and with a serene and confident heart, as befits the descendant of so many monarchs.

"For such a purpose, I once more address my voice to the people of this metropolis, from whom I am now to depart with bitter grief.

"An unjust war, carried on in contravention of the law of nations, has invaded my States, notwithstanding the fact that I was at peace with all the European Powers.

"The changed order of government, and my adhesion to the great principles of Italian nationality, were not sufficient to ward off the war ; and, moreover, the necessity of defending the integrity of the State entailed upon me the obligations of events which I have always deplored : therefore, I solemnly protest against this indescribable hostility, concerning which the present and the future will pronounce their solemn verdict.

" The diplomatic corps residing at my court has known since the commencement of this unexpected invasion with what sentiments my heart has been filled for all my people, as well as for this illustrious city, with a view to securing her from ruin and war, to saving her inhabitants and all their property, her sacred churches, her monuments, her public buildings, her collections of art—all which forms the patrimony of her civilization and of her greatness, and which, being an inheritance of future generations, is superior to the passions of a day.

" The time has now come to fulfil these professions of mine. The war is approaching the walls of the city, and, with unutterable grief, I have to depart with a portion of my army, to betake myself whither the defence of my rights calls me. The remainder of my army remains in company with the honourable National Guard, in order to protect the inviolability and safety of the capital, which I recommend as a sacred treasure to the zeal of the Ministry; and I call upon the honour and the civic feeling of the Mayor of Naples and of the Commandant of the said National Guard, to spare this most beloved country of mine the horrors of internal discord and the disasters of civil war; for which purpose, I concede to the above-named the widest powers that they may require.

" As the descendant of a dynasty which has reigned over this continent for one hundred and twenty-six years, after having preserved it from the horrors of a long Viceroyalty, the affections of my heart are here. I am a Neapolitan, and could not without bitter grief address words of farewell to my most dearly beloved people, to my fellow-citizens.   Whatever may be my destiny, be it prosperous or adverse, I shall always preserve for them a passionate and affectionate remembrance.   I recommend to them concord, peace, and strict observance of their civic duties.   Let not an excessive zeal for my dynasty be made a pretext for disturbance.

"Whether from the fortunes of the present war I return shortly amongst you, or whatever be the time at which it may please the justice of God to restore me to the throne of my ancestors—a throne made all the more splendid by the free institutions with which I have irrevocably surrounded it—all that I pray from this time forth is to behold again my people united, strong, and happy.

"FRANCIS II."

This was a dignified document, such as one can hardly believe could have been written by the same man who, the very next day, three hours before the departure of his Royal master, telegraphed to Garibaldi these words:—"All' Invittisimo Dittatore delle Due Sicilie.—Napoli vi attende con ansia per affidarvi i suoi futuri destini.—Tutt' a voi, LIBORIO ROMANO." I have given this famous despatch in the original Italian, lest my translation should be doubted; but it may be put in English thus:—"To the Invincible Dictator of the Two Sicilies.—Naples expects you with anxiety, to confide to you her future destinies.—Entirely yours, LIBORIO ROMANO."

Talleyrand said that there were certain statesmen who could be judged at once by reading any two lines they had penned.   The reader has the opportunity of judging Don Liborio by comparing the documents I have just quoted.

At six o'clock on the evening of the 7th of September, Francis II. and his Queen, accompanied by the gentlemen of the Royal household, and the Ambassadors of Spain, Austria, Prussia, and Bavaria, went on board a Spanish man-of-war, and steamed along the bay towards Gaeta. The only tears which accompanied the son of Ferdinand II. in his flight were shed by a few fisherwomen of Santa Lucia, whose curate had told them that the miraculous Madonna of the neighbouring church was bitterly weeping for the cause of the fugitive King. But not a man of the populous city was seen to mourn; not one bade a last farewell to the departing vessel. Except the Ministers and the courtiers, there was no one beneath the deserted porticoes of the Royal Palace, to pay the last tribute of compassion to an unfortunate Prince. In the apartments above, however, a touching episode had occurred. Among the Ministers assembled in the hall was Prince Torella, who, as I have before mentioned, had been persecuted, and even arrested, by the cut-throats of Francis II.'s police. When the King and Queen made their appearance on the landing of the stairs which lead to the harbour, they noticed the tears which Prince Torella could not conceal. Stepping forward, the Sovereign offered his hand to his faithful subject, and, with deep emotion, said to his wife :—

" You see, Maria, who are our true friends in misfortune; they are those who would have a right to remember that in other times they have been wronged by my government. Thanks, Prince," added the King; "I shall never forget the kindness you have shown to me on this trying day."

But Prince Torella was perhaps the only one amongst that large community who had paid the noblest of tributes to misfortune by forgetting the unjust persecutions of an earlier day. Almost all had deserted the young monarch; even those whose duty it was to be his companions in exile. God forbid that I should needlessly disturb the ashes of a man who is now lying in the Campo Santo of Pisa; but even the Count of Syracuse was not there to soothe the agony of the fallen monarch. He had quitted Naples a few days before, after exhibiting, under circumstances which I will proceed to relate, an almost incredible heartlessness.

A fortnight before the events I have just recorded, the King, repeating the old trick of his father, had listened to the suggestions of his half-brothers, the Count of Trani and the Count of Caserta, who had decided upon a *coup d'état*. General Cotrufiano, one of the most active agents of the Camarilla, was appointed military governor of Naples, and Prince Ischitella, a friend of the Queen Dowager, was made commander of the National Guard. An anti-constitutional proclamation was seized on a French priest named Souchèrs, who had been arrested. It seems that this reactionary manifesto was dictated by the brothers of the King themselves, at the instigation of of the Queen-mother, who was then at Rome, and of whom the French priest was a secret agent. The *coup d'état* was almost brought to bear, and the King was to drive in the evening through the Toledo and the Chiaia, to judge the effect it had produced on his people.   On that day, Dumas was on board his yacht, when a man, who had assumed the name of the Marquis Presti, made his appearance, and told the novelist that he and a friend were prepared to throw an incendiary bomb into the Royal carriage that very evening.   Dumas thereupon sent one of his friends, Signor Muratori, to the Count of Syracuse, to warn him of the danger which threatened his nephew. The Count of Syracuse, on receiving the message, answered that, after the appointment of Cotrufiano and Ischitella, it was evident that the King was meditating a *coup d'état*, and that he no longer considered him his nephew, nor cared what might or might not happen to him.   The Duke of Laurito was then sent for, and through him Francis II. was made aware of the intention of the assassins.   I need not dwell more on this subject ; the story which I have related speaks for itself.   The other uncles of Francis II. were no better.   Except the Count of Trapani (the youngest of them), not one of these princes shared the hardships of the siege of Gaeta.   The Count of Aquila was in Paris ; and the Prince of Capua was at some German bath.   As for the Queen-mother, she had been sent out of the country when the constitution was granted, lest she should die of grief at seeing the National flag wave on the top of the Royal Palace of Naples.

When the Spanish man-of-war, which carried the last Bourbon Sovereign of Naples to Gaeta, was leaving the harbour, the Neapolitan frigate *Guiscardo* was lying hard by.   Francis II. asked the Spanish commander to stop, and put the galley to sea, as he desired to go on board the latter vessel, with a view to persuading the commanding officer to follow him with his ship to Gaeta.   In a few moments, the King was on the deck of the *Guiscardo*, but only to experience another disappointment.   He harangued the crew, he adjured the officers ; but the crew were silent, and the officers answered that they could not recognise the Royal authority.   Great exertions, and even threats, were employed by the gentlemen of the King's suite to induce the seamen to return to their duty ; but all was in vain.   The commander of the *Guiscardo* was not to be moved, and Francis II. left the deck in despair, muttering now and then the words—" I have been betrayed, I have been betrayed !"   It was the story of James II. of England over again.

In the meanwhile, fearing that the interval between the breaking up of the Royal Government and the entry into Naples of the Dictator might be seized upon as a favourable opportunity for popular disturbances, the Prefect of the city issued the following address to the Neapolitans :—

" Citizens !—The King is leaving.   In the presence of a great misfortune, and of another principle which triumphs, your conduct cannot be doubtful.   The former imposes on you reserve in the presence of fallen majesty ; the other demands of you self-denial, prudence, and civil courage.   No one of you will disturb the development of the heroic destinies of Italy ; no one will think of lacerating the country with flagitious or vindictive hands.   Rather you will calmly await the memorable day which will open a path to our country, by which it may escape from dangers and difficulties without new convulsions, or the shedding of the blood of our brothers.   That day is near, but meantime let the city remain tranquil ; let commerce pursue its course with confidence ; let every one continue the ordinary occupations of life ; let all opinions unite in a sublime agreement to save the country. For your protection, the police is in permanence ; the National Guard watches under arms.   Thus acting, citizens, you will not render useless the magnanimous sacrifices of those who, whilst confronting the cruel uncertainties of the position, have sacrificed themselves for the public good, and who, whilst evading the dangers which threatened your liberties and the independence of the nation, were at the same time its watchful and persevering guardians.   They will continue that sublime mission, and I am persuaded that your agreement, your orderly conduct, will help them to overcome such difficulties as remain.   I am persuaded that they will not be compelled to invoke the severity of the law against the senseless agitation of extreme parties.   In this manner our fortunes will be completed, and, if history recounts the patriotism of our rulers, it will also be the generous dispenser of glory to the wisdom of this truly Italian people."

This address having been published, the Ministers whom the King had left behind to provide for the public tranquillity, assembled at the house of the President of the expiring Cabinet, Count Spinelli. At that meeting it was decided that Prince d'Alessandria, then Sindaco of Naples, should go at once to Salerno with General Sazepano, in order to see

Garibaldi, and make the necessary arrangements for his entry into the capital. As I have already stated, a deputation of the National Guard, headed by General Desoget, its commander, joined the chief of the Municipal Administration, and all arrived at Salerno during the night of the 6th of September.

Some attempts had in the meanwhile been made by the leading members of the *Ordine* Committee to urge the expiring Ministry and Municipal Council to organize a sort of Provisional Government, and at once proclaim the annexation of Naples to Piedmont in the name of Victor Emmanuel; but the attempt had no better success than the mission of Dr. Tommasi at Sala. The Marquis Villamarina (the Minister of Piedmont at the Neapolitan court) had never left his post, but, keeping apart from the political events of the last few days, had retired to his house at Capo di Monte, lest he should be charged with having hastened the downfall of Francis II., as his colleague Buoncompagni had been accused of accelerating that of the Grand Duke of Tuscany. His position was extremely delicate; but he succeeded in combining the interests of his sovereign with the respect due to the King to whose Government he was accredited.

Having thus summarily reviewed the events which prepared—nay, hastened—the entry of Garibaldi into Naples, I must turn to the Palazzo of the Prefect of Salerno, where I had now arrived. This official was absent; but his *alter ego* had just returned from the railway station, where he had accompanied Garibaldi and his suite. How anxious I was to reach Naples the reader will understand. The only ques-

tion was how to get a train, for the next did not
leave Salerno before noon. To pay my court to the
sub-prefect was the only chance left to me. In those
days, the ascendancy of Garibaldi's followers, whether
fighting men or not, was so great that even the humblest of our soldiers could have dared with success the
most absurd impositions. Without entering into long
explanations as to who I was, I set to work to impress upon the official mind that I was in a great
hurry to get to Naples as quickly as possible, hinting
that I was one of the General's Staff followers. The
sub-prefect therefore volunteered at once to provide
me with a carriage, saying that my horse could follow
next day. But a drive was the very thing which did
not answer my purpose; so I begged the worthy man
—I am almost ashamed to confess it—to send me on
by rail. He accordingly drove with me to the station, which was crammed with Garibaldian officers of
every rank, all wanting conveyance to Naples, all in-
sisting on immediate departure. It was no use for
the railway official to repeat that without the authorisation of his superiors he could not start a special
train. The Garibaldians had only one answer :—
" We must go to Naples at once." The appearance
of the sub-prefect cut short the discussion, and it was
agreed that they would telegraph to Naples to obtain
the required authorisation. But the answer we got
after forty minutes was that the director was not to
be found. At this announcement, a general outcry
burst forth, and matters began to look rather
threatening.

An officer of the National Guard of Salerno—appa-

rently a man of great influence—entered the room
at that moment, and observed that the railway official was perhaps grieving for the departure "del Borbone," and therefore could not understand that it
was his duty to accede to the demands of the Garibaldians. The sarcasm fell upon the poor railway inspector like a spark of fire on a heap of powder. He
jumped up with sudden energy, and exclaimed that he
was the greatest of patriots, and would prove it by
having a train ready at once. In less than twenty
minutes it was at our service, and, after a general em-
bracing of the sub-prefect, inspector, railway-guards,
and other more or less important bystanders, we
departed. The train was soon in motion, passing
through villages and towns inhabited by hot-headed
and quarrelsome fellows, who, owing to the vol-
canic soil on which they dwell, and the heady and
heating wine they drink, are the most noisy in the
world. From Torre del Annunziata to Naples, we
saw nothing but a succession of triumphal arches,
festoons of flowers, hangings, and flags. At Torre
del Greco, the same spectacle was repeated; for the
idol of the people had just passed through that
town. Then came picturesque Resina, built on the
lava which buried ancient Herculaneum under its
torrent of fire. Next to that, Portici made its appearance, with its splendid palaces, the autumnal residences
of the Neapolitan nobility. An interminable scene of
movement and gaiety was everywhere visible along
the line; a continual shouting of "Viva Garibardo!"
"Viva l'Italia!" filled the air. How the lungs of the
people could endure so much, I cannot tell; for

assuredly, by the time we reached Naples, we had almost lost the sense of hearing. But the long, sharp whistle of the engine made us aware of our arrival. In front, behind, everywhere, arose the same deafening cry—one constantly repeated shout, uttered in such discordant tones that the howling of a pack of hungry wolves could not have been worse. The noise, however, came with still greater intensity from Porta Capuana, under whose arch Garibaldi was then driving towards the Toledo.

CHAPTER VIII.

NAPLES UNDER GARIBALDI.

Entry of the Dictator into Naples—The Foresteria—Formation of the New Government—Palazzo D' Angri—Aspect of Naples on the Night of the 7th September, 1860—The Café dell' Europa—Pie di Grotta—The " Carrozzelle " Drivers—Efforts to check their Cruelty—Neapolitan Lazzaroni—Mr. Elliot and Garibaldi on board the *Hannibal*—Difficulties of the Political Situation—Mazzini at Naples—Conflicting Parties —Cavour's Policy—English Tourists—Mr. Edwin James's " Diplomatic Mission"—Lord Llanover and the Hon. Evelyn Ashley—Visit to the Neapolitan State Prisons—Prisons of the Prefettura—The "Stone Box" of Santa Maria Apparente— Subterranean Gaols—Prison System under Ferdinand II.

THE triumphant progress of Garibaldi was destined to receive no check. Led by victory — urged onwards by the applause of Italians, nay, of all liberal Europe—the warrior of Freedom made his entry into Naples, accompanied by only a few followers. What had he to fear as he drove through the populous city, or passed under the guns of Castelnuovo and Sant' Elmo, still garrisoned by the troops of the departed King? He is aware of his moral force; he knows that the people of Naples are thronging the streets and piazzas only to see and cheer him, and that not one of those soldiers would dare to fire a gun or a musket at the man of fate, the assertor of the people's rights.

His carriage makes its way through the dense masses of applauding spectators. He has just reached the Church of the Carmine, in front of which once rolled the severed head of the Suabian Corradino, and in whose holy precincts flowed the blood of the young revolutionary fisherman, Masaniello. The crowd grows thicker and thicker; the wide roads of the Mandracchio, of the Largo di Castello, and of the street of San Carlo, are so choked with people that it is almost impossible for the carriage to break through. Missori, Statella, and Nullo are the heralds who precede the modest *cortége*, and succeed in opening a path. They pass the corner of the Toledo, and at last reach the Palace of the Foresteria. Garibaldi alights from the carriage, and is received by the National Guard and the *Eletti*, or municipal councillors. Don Liborio Romano had already joined him at the station. But an immense multitude, almost wild with joy, are assembled in the vast piazza. They call upon the Dictator to show himself, and Garibaldi appears on the large balcony of the palace. Addressing the people, he tells them that they must prove to Italy that they are the worthy descendants of Masaniello. He then retires, for he has more important work to do.

The kingdom was at that time literally without any government whatever; and the difficult task of forming one devolved upon Cosenz, who, being a Neapolitan, was acquainted with the men who could best be called upon to act. In the meanwhile, the Marquis Villamarina, accompanied by the Sardinian Admiral Persano, had arrived at the Foresteria, to confer with the Dictator, and to explain to him the political situation of the country.

Shortly after the arrival of Garibaldi, I went to the Palace, in whose apartments I found a crowd of people ready to kneel before the rising sun of power. There were persons of every class, from nobles down to lazzaroni. All had petitions to present; all wanted to see the great man. There is perhaps no country in Europe where the habit of asking favours is more prevalent than in Naples. The beggar sues for a *grano*, the gentleman for employment, the nobleman for honours. The only difference between the petitioners is in the thing asked for; the form is almost always the same. " Eccellenza, I want this,"—" Invittissimo Dittatore, I have a right to that "—such were the expressions I heard constantly repeated amongst the crowd besieging the halls of the Palace. To judge by their words, all had suffered martyrdom for the cause of liberty: all had been victims of the " Borbone." It was indeed sad to see human nature thus fallen to the lowest standard of humiliating forms. Immediately after his arrival at the Foresteria, Garibaldi was moved to great rage because half-a-dozen priests—a deputation from I do not remember what religious community—wanted to kiss his hand, with that servility to which they had been accustomed from their youth. Dismissed from the Dictator's presence with words of reproach, the poor ecclesiastics were still in the hall, bewildered, when one of Garibaldi's officers told me the cause of their astonishment. I approached them, and asked why they wanted to kiss Garibaldi's hand; upon which, each producing a petition, they proffered the same demonstration to me.

"Do you not understand," asked I, "that a man who respects himself cannot permit in his fellow creatures such humiliating manners?"

"Eccellenza, we only wanted to show our respect for the Invitto Dittatore, and to ask him to redress the wrongs we have .sustained from the Bourbonic Government."

"Kiss *my* hand if you like," said one of our English companions, laughing. "I am a Protestant, and you will prove in doing so that you are tolerant and Christian men."

At these words, the priests, pocketing their petitions, walked away as if they had seen the devil. For them, our English friend was a rank heretic, and superstition was even more powerful than the desire to obtain what they had come to ask.

Whilst Cosenz was occupied in forming the Administration, Garibaldi was writing his proclamation to the citizens of Naples. Although his secretary, Signor Basso, enjoyed his unlimited confidence, Garibaldi always himself wrote these documents, which reflected the originality and force of his character. He now issued the following address, recommending harmony and union, and at the same time reassuring the clergy of the capital :—

"To the beloved Population of Naples, offspring of the People !—It is with true respect and love that I present myself to this noble and imposing centre of the Italian population, which many centuries of despotism have not been able to humiliate, nor induced to bow the knee at the sight of tyranny. The first necessity of Italy was harmony, in order to unite the great Italian family; to-day, Providence has created that harmony through the sublime unanimity of all our provinces for the reconstitution of the nation; and, for unity, the same Providence has given to our country Victor Emmanuel, whom we from this moment may call the true father of our Italian land. Victor Emmanuel, the model of all sovereigns, will impress upon his descendants the duty that they owe to the prosperity of a people which has elected him for their chief with enthusiastic devotion. The Italian priests who are conscious of their true mission have, as a guarantee of the respect with which they will be treated, the ardour, the patriotism, and the truly Christian conduct of their numerous fellow ecclesiastics, who, from the highly praiseworthy monks of Lagrancia to the noble-hearted priests of the Neapolitan continent, one and all, in the sight and at the head of our soldiers, defied the gravest dangers of battle. I repeat it, concord is the first want of Italy; so we will welcome as brothers those who once disagreed with us, but who now sincerely wish to bring their stone to raise up the monument of our country. Finally, respecting other people's houses, we are resolved to be masters in our own house, whether the powerful of the earth like it or not.

"GIUSEPPE GARIBALDI."

At Naples there is no lack of men who are disposed to accept office. General Cosenz was therefore only embarrassed as to the choice. Liborio Romano of course retained his post of Minister of the Interior; the honest man was so desirous to serve his country. Cosenz became Minister of War, Pisanelli was charged with the portfolio of Justice, and the Marquis D'Aflitto accepted that of Public Works. The formation of the new Ministry was a second check to the *Comitato dell' Ordine*, which had once more tried to seize power for itself.

One of Garibaldi's first and most important acts was to decree that the Neapolitan Navy should from that day form part of the Sardinian Squadron, under the orders of Admiral Persano. These matters having been settled, the Dictator asked his Ministers where he should fix his residence.

" Here, in the Palace of the Foresteria," answered one of them.

" No," rejoined Garibaldi ; " I have not come to Naples to dwell in Royal residences. Is there any house in the city belonging to a Genoese family?"

" Yes, there is the d'Angri d'Oria Palace, which is just empty, the Prince having gone to Paris with his family," answered one of the bystanders.

" Very well," said the Dictator, " we will proceed to the Palazzo d'Angri, after we have shown the Neapolitans that we are Christians. Let us first go to the cathedral, to hear the *Te Deum*."

In those days, so full of great events, time did not creep as usual—it flew. Night, therefore, soon came, and with night the illuminations. The people of the nearest villages had flocked into the city, and some of the Garibaldian troops had also come up from Salerno. The population of Naples was consequently increased by several thousands. From the Palazzo Reale to the top of the Toledo was one compact mass of men, women, and carriages, walking and driving in all directions amidst the most frantic shouts. Although the sun had set for some hours, the ragged lazzaroni were not asleep as usual in doorways or under the porticoes, but were mingling in the crowd of gaily dressed gentry, monks, priests, and soldiers. Here, a Garibaldian was carried in triumph upon the shoulders of two of the National Guard; there, Father Pantaleo was borne from one place to another by the eager crowd, who wanted to kiss him. A grey-haired man was making himself understood by pantomimic gesticulations, conveying perfectly the meaning of the words which his hoarse voice had no power to utter. Neapolitans do everything by means of pantomime : they express joy, grief, despair, or indifference, merely by lifting up the shoulders, turning the head with a peculiar movement, or making signs with the hands. The tongue seems almost a useless member to them ; and yet they are terrifically noisy. When, however, they were no longer able to shout out " Viva Italia una !" they held up the fore-finger of their right hand, and thus expressed their meaning. Women, men, beardless boys, old men with bowed figures and trembling steps, were there, shouting and gesticulating. Here comes the carriage of the Duchess Bovino : it stops, and a travel-worn, dust-covered Garibaldian is invited to take his seat near the lady. Other Garibaldians are rolling along in the elegant carriages of the aristocracy ; others, again, in the humble *carrozzella,* or in the *corricolo* of Portici and Resina. Nobody would have thought that so many vehicles could be found in Naples.

The crowd streams slowly through the Toledo, on its way to the Palazzo d'Angri. Garibaldi has been obliged to appear on the balcony, and address the people, more than once. It is getting late, however, and the General has retired to rest. But how is it possible to sleep amidst the cries which rend the air? What is to be done? The officers of the Staff hold a consultation, and it is decided that the Neapolitans shall be implored to be less noisy. Gusmaroli is charged with the negotiation. He appears on the balcony, and makes a sign that he wants to speak. The clamour suddenly ceases; the carriages stop. "The Dictator is gone to bed," says Gusmaroli; "please do not disturb him."

From that moment, as if the whole multitude had been struck dumb, the people become silent; not a cry is heard through the Toledo. The crowd bend their heads on the palm of the right hand, thus expressing that the dweller in the Palazzo d'Angri is reposing. The sign makes its way from one end of the Toledo to the other, like an electric spark, and no one again ventures to break the silence.

Down at Chiaia, however, the crowd may be as noisy as they like, for their screamings are out of the reach of Garibaldi's ears. At the Café dell' Europa, at the balcony of the Casino, at every window of the six-storied houses, there are incessant cries, and a unanimous waving of flags and garlands. Bengal lights are thrown up, casting their tricoloured radiance on the opposite buildings, and on the stream of human heads below. The Royal Palace, and the theatre of San Carlo, are also glowing with hundreds of torches, and, from the terrace on which the Queen was walking only

forty hours before, variegated balloons are sent into
the air.   The vessels in the harbour below are in a
blaze of light, which is reflected in the sea, together
with the stream of lava pouring from the side of
Vesuvius ; and forty thousand coloured lamps, hanging in festoons from the trees, have converted the
gardens of Villa Reale into fairy land.   But let us for
a moment enter the Café dell' Europa, which seems to
have been turned into a sort of Bedlam, so terrific is
the noise of the assembly.

" Here, waiter !" exclaims one, " bring an ice to all
the Garibaldians who are present."

" Don't let them pay," ejaculates another ; " put the
ices down to my account."

" Let me embrace our liberators !" shouts out a
third, jumping on to the neck of Missori, who has
just entered the café.

Carriages are sent for to take the volunteers to
their lodgings ; but it is of no use to ask the driver
what is the fare.   He lifts up his head, gives a hori-
zontal cut in the air with the back of his hand, and
says " Tutto pagato, Eccellenza !" and off he goes.

On the day of my arrival I met Mr. Percy French,
the attaché of the British legation, who kindly offered
me a room in his house.   A few hours afterwards, on
entering the Café dell' Europa, I was assailed by
half-a-dozen Neapolitans, who all wanted me to
accept apartments in their own homes.   I of course
declined, adding that a similar offer had been made by
an English friend whom I had met in Naples.

" No, no," they said, " it cannot be.   It would be
a disgrace to us were you to put up at the house of a

foreigner. It is true that Mr. French is a good friend of Italy; but he must renounce his claim to you."

Then they began to pull me about in all directions, each wanting to have the preference. Fortunately, they soon got to quarrelling amongst themselves—a circumstance which enabled me to make my escape from the café. On the next day, as I was entering the Palazzo d'Angri, I met one of them, who, getting hold of my arm, stopped me, exclaiming, with marked gesticulations, "Gesù! why did you leave the café so suddenly last evening? Why did you reject the offer of your brethren for that of a foreigner?" He appeared so angry that I really thought we should have come to blows. However, I got out of the difficulty by telling him that, to avoid displeasing any one, I had put up at the Hotel di Roma with my friends Forbes and Caldesi. This tranquillized him, and I was allowed to go upstairs, where I found Garibaldi and his Staff ready to start for Piè di Grotta.

The 8th of September is a great day at Naples. It is the day on which is held the religious festival of the Nativity of the Virgin, which is celebrated in the church near the entrance to the Grotto of Posilippo. Tradition relates that one night the daughter of a poor fisherman, being asleep in the grotto, saw the Madonna appear to her, wrapped in a white dress, with an aureole of glittering stars round her head. The Virgin told her that a painting of her would be found close by, and then disappeared. The fishermen of Posilippo carefully cleaned the wall above the place indicated, found the picture, and built there a modest chapel. So many won-drous tales were told about the miraculous power of this painting, that in the fourteenth century the chapel was greatly enlarged, and became a beau-tiful church. Judging by the votive offerings which adorn the altar of the Madonna of Piè di Grotta, the number of miracles wrought by her must really have been great. There are trinkets of every shape and metal; silver arms and hearts, *agnus deis*, gilt palms, painted wax-candles, and an endless gallery of bad pictures, representing, or pretending to repre-sent, the supposed miracles. I would not undertake to say that the shrine of the Madonna of Piè di Grotta is as popular as that of San Januarius; but at any rate it comes next after the saint so famous for the liquefaction of his blood. Many women of the Piè di Grotta quarter, however, when San Januarius is not quick enough in effecting his miracle, do not hesitate to throw upon him a certain amount of disrepute, boasting that their Madonna is more powerful than the *gialluto* saint, whose relic is preserved in the shrine of the Cappella del Tesoro. I will not, however, enter into any discussion on the subject, lest I should wrong either the one or the other.

But, putting aside all controversies, what is certain is that the Neapolitans evince great faith in this supernatural picture of the Piè di Grotta. Not a sovereign, from the bigoted Bourbons to the Vol-tairian Murat, has failed to pay homage to both these sacred pets of the Neapolitans. It would therefore have been unwise had Garibaldi shown any disrespect to the Madonna by refusing to witness the grand ceremony of the 8th. He consequently went to the church of Piè di Grotta, as others had done before him. As we drove along the Riviera di Chiaia, bands of lazzaroni and fishermen were drawn up, with flags and music, to welcome the hero of the day, who, judging by their repeated shouts, seemed to have entirely dethroned San Januarius. Along a great part of the way leading to the grotto, lofty green, white, and red poles were fixed in a double row in the ground, with flags waving from their summits. Hundreds and hundreds of *carrozzelle*, gaily dressed with hangings and banners, and crowded with more people than the half-starved horses could well pull along, followed our carriages. As the day was splendid, the women of Margellina and Posilippo inferred that the Madonna was by no means against the Dictator, which they would certainly have supposed had it rained. This inference they expressed by their gesticulations, and by running after the General, and screaming out, "*O Beata Vergine, sta con voi, Eccellenza!*" Thus we proceeded along that magnificent road; but, having arrived at the church, we found it no easy matter to get to the altar. The crowd pressed so close upon us that we were in some danger of being suffocated. However, we reached it at length; but, when the ceremony was over, an equally difficult task presented itself, for the General and his suite had to get back to the Palace. Such was the rush of people when we left the sacred edifice that some of Garibaldi's officers and I could not get to our carriage. We therefore hired a *carrozzella*, which took us by the back streets into the Toledo. To

those who have not been at Naples, it is difficult to
form a correct idea of this sort of Neapolitan conveyance, or of the drivers.   The first is a light, four-
wheeled, hooded carriage, painted in showy colours ;
the second, a sort of brute, who seems to have been
created for the torment of the poor animal over which
he is placed.   The barbarity to which animals are
daily and hourly subjected in the city of Naples surpasses all imagination. . In other countries, no doubt,
much cruelty exists ; but generally speaking it is the
exception—in Naples it is the rule.   When a car-
penter drives a nail into a block of wood, he strikes at
it no harder than suffices to send it home ; but a Neapolitan, having knocked the life out of an animal, will continue to beat it after it is dead, from a feeling of anger
and revenge at losing his victim.

" Why do you use your horse in that way ?" asked I
of the driver of the *carrozzella*, on seeing him striking
with the butt-end of his whip on the sore the poor
beast had on its right shoulder.

" I do it, Eccellenza, to make him run faster," answered he, still persisting in his cruel treatment.

" Villain !" exclaimed my Garibaldian companion,
" if you do it again, I will teach you how to leave off."
And he accompanied these words by a well-applied
blow on the man's neck, the only means of bringing
a Neapolitan driver to reason.

" Gesù, Eccellenza !" exclaimed the man, " I do it
to drive you the quicker, for horses are made to be
beaten as long as they can bear the blows."

The brutality of the cab-drivers of Naples had already, in those early Garibaldian days, attracted the

attention of an agent of the society which exists in London for the protection of animals. This was Mr. Adam William Smith, who, soon after the entry of Garibaldi into Naples, went there, and took up the question with an energy which, whilst it gratified all sensible and humane people, roused against him the utmost animosity of the drivers of the city. He called the attention of Garibaldi and of Prince Carignan to the subject; but Rome was not built in a day, nor will a people, whose callousness is the inheritance of ages, become considerate all at once.

Another great evil which existed at the time of Garibaldi's arrival was the almost incredible number of impudent beggars who thronged the principal thoroughfares of the city. The bad government which so long weighed upon that unfortunate country purposely forbore to check a habit which was calculated to keep the mass of the population in ignorance, and therefore to serve the selfish interests of their rulers. The governing classes knew well enough that a man with an empty stomach and worn-out limbs cares but little for his political or civil rights; and they acted accordingly. As experience has proved since the National Government has set to work, the evil is too deeply rooted to be removed at once; it is only by the beneficent action of education that anything can be done in the matter. Laws and regulations can effect but little for a society which is completely demoralized. Besides, where is there to be found a Neapolitan lazzarone who will obey the law? The well-known phrase, *Non te n'incaricare*, which is always on Neapolitan lips, expresses in brief the very essence of their nature. The

words duty, obligation, laws, have no meaning among
the lowest classes of the Neapolitan community; all is
Non te n'incaricare—that is to say, "Never mind! we do
not care about it." If the police are coming up, one
lazzaro will say to another, "*Non te n'incaricare.*" If
you tell a lazy boy, who is amusing himself by da-
maging some fine monument in a street, or throwing
dirt on the façade of a newly-built house, that he must
not do it, the answer is sure to be, "*Non ve n'incari-
cate.*" The very galley-slave working in the public
streets has stamped upon his face those cynical
words; for he shows that the shame of dishonour
is not felt by him. Here is a poor man who wants
a letter written to some of his relations or friends.
He walks to the little desk of the public *scrivano*, under
the portico of San Carlo, and dictates the letter in the
ear of the writer. When the epistle is penned, the
scrivano reads it aloud; but the poor man not unfrequently discovers that the scribe has written down
quite the reverse of what he wanted to say. "*Non
te n'incaricare!*" is the answer he gets; "your relation, or your friend, will understand all the same!"

These incidents of Neapolitan life, however, have
led me from the main subject of my narrative, to which
I must now return.

The troops we had left behind began to arrive,
and were marched off to the banks of the Volturno, to watch the Royal army which was encamped under the walls of Capua. At Naples, the
Bourbonic garrisons of the Castles Sant' Elmo, dell'
Ovo, and Nuovo, as well as several minor forts, had
given up those strongholds in spite of the orders

secretly issued by Francis II., before his departure from the capital, to hold them to the last. Political intrigues were in the meanwhile at work in every quarter. Part of the diplomatic body, as I have already said, followed the King to Gaeta ; but the French Ambassador and the Papal Legate remained at Naples, and their presence was felt in the mysterious influence they exercised on the Bourbonic party of the capital. The latter of these diplomatists at first openly conspired ; but the attitude of the Dictator's Government was such as to induce him to join the King at Gaeta. Baron Brennier did not conspire ; but he took no pains to disguise his dislike of the new rulers. The Russian Government was represented by Count Poggenpolt, who remained at Naples, but who neither directly nor indirectly interfered with the new order of things. Mr. Elliot, the English Minister, took up his quarters at Castellamare, watching events without any undue bias, either towards one side or the other.

Chance, however, brought him in contact with the Dictator. Since the capitulation of Palermo, Admiral Mundy and Garibaldi had shown great sympathy and respect for one another, and had become fast friends. It was therefore natural that the English Admiral should call upon the Dictator, as a mark of personal respect ; and he did so three days after the entry of the General into Naples. On the following day, Garibaldi, accompanied by Dr. Bertani, Major Missori, Lieutenant-Colonel Baggi, Captain Canzio, and myself, went on board the *Hannibal*, to return the visit. When we appeared on deck, Mr. Elliot had just arrived from Castellamare, where he gene-

rally stayed during the hottest days of the summer.
On seeing Garibaldi, the English Minister walked
astern, screening himself behind the row of soldiers
who were paying military honours to the Dictator.
But Garibaldi had scarcely entered the Admiral's
cabin when the English commander came out, calling
for Mr. Elliot.   The diplomatist seemed much embarrassed, and at first declined to enter the cabin.   At
last he yielded, and the three remained together for
about half-an-hour—a circumstance which is said to
have made the French colleague of Mr. Elliot very
angry.

At a quarter to twelve we left the *Hannibal*, and
went on board the Sardinian Admiral's screw-frigate
Maria Adelaide, to pay a visit to Admiral Persano.
On reaching the ladder of the frigate, Garibaldi was
saluted by the Sardinian vessels in port, as the custom
is when a general officer goes on board.   It was the
gallant Admiral of the future King of Italy who
thus paid due honour to the Dictator of the Two
Sicilies.   This mark of respect to a revolutionary
chieftain, as Garibaldi was sometimes called, still further increased the displeasure of the French Admiral
and Minister—a displeasure which was changed into
positive anger when it became known that the Dictator had begged Admiral Persano to land the battalion of Sardinian Bersaglieri and the two companies
of gunners he had on board.   Diplomatic intrigues
and French anger were not, however, feared by a man
like Garibaldi.   His programme was too settled for
him to alter it, and, with God's help, he boldly proceeded towards his object.

A real cause of annoyance to Garibaldi was the discontent of those who wished to hasten the annexation to Piedmont—a feeling which manifested itself more and more every day, hampering the regular march of public affairs, and opposing the organization and stability of the Dictatorial Government. The party which caused these embarrassments—a party composed of those patriots who emigrated to Piedmont in 1848, or who had been condemned by the tribunals of Ferdinand II., and which was called by the more advanced supporters of Garibaldi " the Piedmontese party "— was not disheartened by the defeat it had already sustained. Its members, though no doubt honourable men, wanted to get into power, and did not possess sufficient philosophy to stand on one side, and await the solution of the political question. Whether rightly or wrongly, they were accused of desiring to demolish the influence of the Dictator, and to insure the supremacy of their own. To judge from facts, it would appear that the action of this party was carried so far that Garibaldi thought it necessary to send out of the country Silvio Spaventa, who was believed to be the most intelligent and active leader of the Piedmontese propaganda. There is no doubt that the annexation of the Two Sicilies to Sardinia was in itself a high political necessity; but it ought to have been brought about with the consent of the man who had conquered the country, and not in the way adopted by his adversaries—a way which to a certain extent, justified Garibaldi in having it postponed. On the other hand, the Dictator was surrounded by

patriots, whose Republican opinions were no secret to
any one.   Dr. Bertani had been appointed Secretary-
General—an office which made him in fact the arbiter
of the Government, as far as politics and administration were concerned.   Carlo Cattaneo, another distinguished Republican, had also come to Naples, and
his advice was thought to be all-powerful with
Garibaldi.   In Sicily, the Pro-Dictator Depretis—a
sort of moderator between the two contending influences—had quarrelled with Crispi, and the dis-
agreement led to the resignation of the former, and to
the appointment of Mordini, another Republican,
highly respected in private life, but much disliked on
account of the extreme opinions he was thought to
entertain.   To increase these difficulties, Mazzini
made his appearance at Naples.   Garibaldi, of course,
could not banish from the country the man who
had been the first and most constant upholder of the
unity of Italy, then already half realized.   His
presence, however, produced such an effect, and the
influence he was said to exercise upon the Dictator
was so great, that, according to his opponents, Italy
was lost by the mere fact of his having set foot on
Neapolitan soil.

The admirers and the opponents of this Republican
leader may both point to certain facts which to some
extent justify their respective opinions.   On the one
hand, it may be urged that the conception of Italian
Unity, as we now understand it, is a modern one,
and that to Mazzini is due the merit of unceasingly
developing it.   Before him, Italy, as a single political

body, with a common feeling of nationality, never existed, even in idea; or at least no such idea was openly promulgated. In antiquity there was the Roman Empire; in the Middle Ages, the Italy of the Popes and of the Municipalities; but the union of the Italian family was utterly unknown to both, and the force of cohesion which could alone effect such a result was as yet to be discovered. Cæsar Borgia and Machiavelli may have thought it possible; Gabrielle Montrone at Naples, and Lahoz at Ancona, may have cherished the same idea; it may have flashed before the mind of the unfortunate Ciro Menotti; but it is nevertheless an undeniable fact that the thought and the desire of a united Italy only began to grow in the minds of the Italians after the publication of the Mazzinian paper, *La Giovine Italia.* On the other hand, it is impossible for any man of moderate views to sympathize with many of the opinions and acts of Mazzini. The impracticable character of his political ideas—the virulence of his opposition to Cavour and to Piedmont generally—the recklessness of the various insurrections he has organized, and the violence of some of his followers—have naturally associated with his name an amount of unpopularity which the services of his earlier life are not sufficient to counteract.

The fear lest the ex-Triumvir should use his influence to drag Garibaldi on to the perilous path of the Republic arose naturally enough in the mind of Cavour, seeing that the Dictator was surrounded by several of Mazzini's adherents, who had nevertheless accepted Garibaldi's programme of the Unity of Italy under

Victor Emmanuel.   During Bertani's Administration,
which was considered to be but a disguised nursery of
Mazzinians, many things occurred which all moderate
men must blame; but Garibaldi, as soon as he was
convinced that the Government of Bertani had lost the
confidence of the Neapolitans, and had given rise to a
justifiable opposition, begged him to resign, and named
the Marquis Giorgio Pallavicini as Pro-Dictator of
the country.   Bertani left office without being much
regretted; for, though he had rendered great services
to the National cause in organizing Garibaldi's expedition, he had allowed himself to be surrounded by
men whose personal interests were often preferred to
those of the nation.

In politics, the question of the "outs" and the
"ins" will always exist, and be at times a source
of embarrassment.   It was therefore natural enough
that the new opportunities suddenly opened to the
intelligence of the Neapolitans should arouse an eager-
ness for power among those who, saturated with
pride and vanity, think themselves wronged because
they are set aside by their political adversaries.   Many
of the opponents of Garibaldi and of his Government
were doubtless honest men; but the long years they
had passed in exile had left them ignorant of the real
wants of their country.   Most of them were, besides,
far from popular.   Openly hostile to the Dictator, they
encouraged an agitation which might have proved
fatal to Southern Italy, had not the popularity of
Garibaldi kept it in check, at the same time that he
made a sort of compromise by sacrificing Bertani (the

pretext for, if not the real cause of, that opposition), and allowing the Pro-Dictator, Pallavicini, to write to Mazzini, requesting him to leave the country. . Palla-vicini's letter I here append, together with the answer of Mazzini :—

"To the Illustrious Giuseppe Mazzini.

"Self-denial has always been the virtue of the generous.   I believe that *you* are generous, and I now offer you an opportunity of showing yourself so to your fellow-citizens.   Representative of the Republi-can principle, and indefatigable defender of that prin-ciple, you arouse, by remaining among us, the mistrust of the King and of his Ministers.   This is why your presence in this country creates embarrassment to the Government and danger to the nation, by compromis-ing that concord which is indispensable to the advance and triumph of the Italian cause.

"Even without intending it, you divide us.   Per-form, then, an act of patriotism by leaving these pro-vinces.   Add to former sacrifices a new one which the country demands from you, and the country will be grateful.

"I repeat it : even without so intending, you divide us, and it is necessary that all the national forces should be united in one bond.   I know that your words preach concord, and I doubt not your acts respond to your words.   But all do not believe you, and there are many who misuse your name with the parricidal intention of hoisting another banner in Italy.   Honour commands you to put an end to the

suspicions of some, and to the machinations of others.
Show yourself great by leaving Naples, and you will
take with you the praises of all honest men.

" I subscribe myself your devoted

" GIORGIO PALLAVICINI.

"Naples, Oct. 3, 1860."

Mazzini's answer ran. thus :——

" TO THE PRO-DICTATOR GIORGIO PALLAVICINI.

" I think I possess a generous mind, and it is for
that reason that I reply by a refusal to your letter of the
3rd, which I only read to-day in the *Opinione Nazionale*.
If I merely yielded to my first impulse and to fatigue
of mind, I should leave a land which I encumber, and
withdraw to one where liberty of opinion is left to
every one, where good faith is not doubted, and where
he who has laboured and suffered for the country does
not think it his duty to say to the brother who has done
the same, 'Begone!' You give no reason for your
request, unless it be the affirmation that, without
wishing it, I cause division. I will give you the reason
of my refusal.

" I refuse because I do not feel myself guilty, cause
danger to the country, or conceive projects which
may be disastrous to it, and I should appear to avow
such to be the case by yielding ; because, as an Italian
in an Italian land which has recovered liberty, I think
I ought to represent and support in my person the
right of every Italian to live in his own country when
he does not attack its laws, and the duty of not yielding to an unmerited ostracism ; because, after having
contributed to teach, as much as was in my power, the

people of Italy to make great sacrifices, it appears to me that it is time to raise them to a consciousness of human dignity too often violated, and to the maxim forgotten by those who style themselves preachers of concord and moderation; because no one founds his own liberty without respecting that of others; because it would appear to me that, by voluntarily exiling myself, I should be guilty of insult to my country, which cannot, without dishonouring itself in the eyes of Europe, render itself guilty of tyranny—to the King, who cannot fear an individual without admitting himself to be weak, and not secure of the affection of his subjects—and to the men of your party, who cannot be excited at the presence of a man declared by them to be alone and abandoned, without contradicting themselves; because the desire comes, not, as you think, from the country, which labours and combats under the flag of Garibaldi, but from the Turin Ministry, towards whom I have no debt, and whom I think fatal to the unity of the country: it comes from intriguers without conscience, without honour, and without national morality—without creed except for the existing power, whatever it may be, and whom I consequently despise; it comes from the vulgar mass of credulous men, who swear without examination by the word of the Almighty, and whom I consequently pity. Lastly, because on arriving I received a declaration from the Dictator of this country that I was free, in the land of the free. The greatest sacrifice I ever made was when, interrupting the apostolate of my faith for the sake of unity and concord, I declared that I accepted monarchy, not out of respect for ministers or monarchs, but for the satisfaction of a blinded majority of the Italian people; that I was ready to co-operate with the monarchy, provided it founded the unity of the nation, and that, if I ever were to take up my old flag again, I would honestly avow it, and publicly too, to my old friends and enemies. I therefore cannot spontaneously make another sacrifice. If honest men, as you say, believe in my word, it is their duty to convince my adversaries that the path of intolerance which they pursue is the only existing fomenter of anarchy. If they do not believe a man who has been struggling for the liberty of the nation for these thirty years, who has taught his accusers to stammer out the name of unity, and who never told a falsehood to any living being, let it be so. The ingratitude of men is not a reason why I should voluntarily bow before their injustice, and sanction it.

"GIUSEPPE MAZZINI.

"Naples, Oct. 6."

Cavour could not but be alarmed at the turn things were taking in Southern Italy even before the date of these letters; and he saw that the best means of thwarting the danger was by striking a blow which, whilst it would prove fatal to the temporal power of the Pope in Umbria, would re-establish on a firmer basis the *prestige* of the Constitutional Monarchy throughout the Peninsula, and hasten the annexation of the Neapolitan provinces to Sardinia. The mercenary legions which, under the command of Lamoricière, were gathered in the Roman States, and the dissatisfaction of Pio Nono's subjects, were enough to justify the course which the Cabinet of Turin had

adopted. An assurance that France would not effectually oppose the crossing of the Papal frontier had
been obtained from Louis Napoleon at Chambéry,
when it was urged by Farini that, if Sardinia were
not allowed to enter the States of the Church,
Garibaldi would undertake the task in the name of
the Revolution. The campaign in Umbria having
been decided upon, Sardinia again took the lead of
the Italian movement, substituting her influence for
that of the party of action, rightly or wrongly
charged with subversive tendencies. On the night
of the 10th of September, Cialdini crossed the Papal
frontier at Saludeccio whilst Fanti marched from
Arezzo on Foligno. Military operations against the
so-called army of Lamoricière had therefore begun,
and they were to be carried out with vigour until
Victor Emmanuel should be enabled to effect his
junction with Garibaldi on the Volturno. Having
thus explained the political situation of the Southern
provinces after the arrival of Garibaldi at Naples, I
may resume my personal narrative.

Wherever there is anything worth being seen,
there is an absolute certainty of meeting English
tourists. The victories of our gallant volunteers in
Sicily had caused a perfect inroad of brave Britons,
always ready to fight; and the entry of Garibaldi into
Naples brought a still further host, somewhat less
warlike, but equally friendly to our cause, and equally
enthusiastic in their admiration of the great Italian
Chief.

One day, as I was writing at the Hotel di Roma,
the waiter ushered into my room an English gentle-

man of corpulent proportions, who, handing to me a
letter of a friend, said he was no less a personage
than the *then* honourable member for Marylebone.
I had more than once seen Mr. Edwin James
at a celebrated trial at the Old Bailey; but I now
scarcely recognised him.   Although not altogether
dressed in a Garibaldian costume, the pistols which
were visible at his belt gave him something of a
redoubtable appearance, which did not help to bring
back to my remembrance the Q.C. whom I had
only seen before in his professional gown.   The
learned gentleman had already paid a visit to Garibaldi, and—as he said—had given him some salutary
advice, together with Lord Palmerston's opinion
on the state of affairs in Italy; an opinion which
the noble Viscount had expressed to him before his
departure from England.   Mr. James, however,
had not come to give *me* any advice, but to see
whether I would accompany him to the front of our
lines, and obtain for him and Lord Llanover the
necessary order to see the much-talked-of political
prisons of Naples.   To this I could only answer in
one way; so I told him that I would myself call
upon Lord Llanover, and have the order ready for
the next morning.   At the dinner-hour, I went to the
Palazzo d'Angri, where I requested the desired per-
mission.   On hearing for whom I was applying, one
of the Staff officers said to me, in a rather mysterious
manner :—

"Oh, you have seen Mr. Edwin James?   You
know therefore that he has brought excellent news
from England?"

"Well," answered I, "he told me what I knew already from the papers—that the people of England sympathize with our cause; which I have never doubted."

"It is not only that," rejoined my friend. "Mr. Edwin James has been sent here by Lord Palmerston on a very important mission, and I am informed that he has told the General that we may reckon upon the support of the British Government."

"This may or may not be true," observed I.

"There you are with your habitual incredulity," said my friend, with a gesture of impatience.

"I am no more incredulous upon this matter than any man who has lived long in England would be," answered I. "If Lord Palmerston had anything to communicate to the General, he knows that he has an excellent Minister here, and he would beg his noble colleague, the Secretary for Foreign Affairs, to write to Mr. Elliot about it, instead of sending Mr. James. That is the way in which diplomatic matters are transacted in England."

"I have certainly never been in England myself," answered my friend; "but what I know is, that the nephew of Lord Palmerston has accompanied his diplomatic agent in the quality of secretary, to give more importance to the transaction."

I was of course as far as ever from being convinced; but to bring the discussion to a close, I recommended my friend, whenever he saw a lawyer connected with a case, to follow the Lombard proverb, which says, "Believe the half of the half of what an advocate tells you." That this advice was not altogether wrong,

I had no great trouble in ascertaining when I met Lord Llanover and the Hon. Evelyn Ashley (the so-called nephew of Lord Palmerston) that same evening. Both heartily laughed at the credulity of my friend; but the latter seemed a little annoyed that his name should have been mixed up with that of the learned gentleman.

The story of Mr James's "mission" is well-known, and I shall not dwell upon it at any length. The report was got up only for the sake of satisfying his vanity, and after all there was no great harm in it beyond its untruthfulness. The only person who was put to inconvenience on that occasion was the commander of a Sardinian steamer, which Count Cavour, who seemed to have been as completely taken in as my friend, had put at the disposal of the pretended diplomatist. For myself, I should say that Mr. James only acted upon the well-known principle of De Maistre :—" L'ex-agération est le mensonge des honnêtes gens "—a proverb which could not now be strictly applied in his case.

The necessary order to inspect the prisons having been obtained, I went with my friend Mr. Percy French on the 14th of September to the Hotel Victoria, where Lord Llanover, the Hon. Evelyn Ashley, Captain Forbes, Mr. Edwin James, and Mr. Adam Smith—the friend of the poor Neapolitan animals—were waiting for me. Our steps were first directed to the Prefettura, a sort of transition place where political prisoners not yet judged were shut up with the worst class of criminals under the paternal *régime* of his Sicilian Majesty. Having arrived

at this building, we were taken to a low archway,
where an open door admitted us into a dark room,
about twelve feet square. Although the room had
been cleaned some time before, the smell was bad
enough to make us feel uncomfortable. This, however, was but the ante-room of a more horrible den
of the same dimensions, into which no light or air
could enter. At a few feet from the door, the roof
sloped downwards until it touched the pavement; and,
as the highest elevation of the vault was no more
than nine feet, it may be imagined how dreadfully the
inmates of that horrible "lock-up" passed the long
days of their imprisonment, and their sleepless nights.
It is indeed a matter of wonder how the victims of
Ferdinand II., who were shut up in that prison
during the hottest days of summer, could have lived
to tell the tale.

The worst, however, had yet to come. We crossed
the yard of the Prefettura; another door was opened,
and we entered a chamber, or, more correctly speaking,
a tomb, without any light or air, and from which came
out so horrible a stench that not one of us could
stand his ground for more than a minute. As Lord
Llanover was visiting those dwellings of sorrow, not
out of mere curiosity, but to ascertain whether the
statements published by the English papers were ex-
aggerated, he was very close in his observations, and
very minute in the questions he put to the officer who
accompanied us. Mr. James, who did not speak
Italian, as his Lordship did, requested me to ask the
gaoler whether human beings had really been shut up
in that hole. To this question the man answered

with a cynical smile:—"Oh, Eccellenza, many and many; but not for a long time, seeing that, at the expiration of eight or ten days, they were removed to other prisons, lest they should be gnawn by rats."

Knowing well that the Neapolitans of the lower classes are inclined to tell lies, or at least to exaggerate, I said to the gaoler:—"Now, speak the truth, for these gentlemen do not like falsehoods."

"I assure you, Eccellenza," replied the official, "that during the political trials of 1849, I saw more than one prisoner come out from this place partly devoured by the rats and vermin with which it swarmed."

The gaoler had really told the truth; for I afterwards ascertained from a Calabrese officer that one of the pretended members of the secret society of the Pugnalatori had been removed from that place covered with rat bites, which had put his life in actual peril, the want of air and proper food having nearly caused his sores to mortify. It appears that the sect of the Pugnalatori was organized in 1852 with the object of assassinating the famous Minister of Ferdinand II., Peccheneda. What is more curious is, that General Viale, one of the most influential friends of the King, seemed to have encouraged its formation, or at any rate to have protected one of its most active members, named Fortunato. This, it is believed, the General did in order to get rid of the Minister, of whose authority he was jealous.

But our sad journey is not at an end: we have only visited the first circle of this infamous *Inferno;* let us proceed to the other.

Santa Maria Apparente was in former times one of

the numberless convents of Naples. It stands on a height above the principal part of the town, and commands the beautiful panorama of the bay. Cape Misenum lies to the right; the Island of Capri rises in front; and the whole coast, from Vesuvius to Sorrento, spreads to the left. Having entered the great gate of the building, we ascended the steps of the large staircase, which are about a hundred in number. The inner door was opened by a dirty fellow, who, although he had no inmates to guard (for Santa Maria Apparente was then undergoing repairs), still retained his unenviable office of a gaoler. A long gallery, used formerly by the monks, runs in a southerly direction through the buildings, opening into the cells previously occupied by the brotherhood, and since 1848 by the victims of tyranny. Let us enter No. 1; it is the cell which was occupied by Poerio during his trial. It is about fourteen feet long by twelve wide, and would have been airy enough had not the window from which the monks enjoyed the view been denied to the prisoner. Heavy shutters were placed against the glass, and these shutters were locked night and day, the room being scarcely lighted by the four round holes pierced at the top. Boards were fixed in the wall at the side of the cell, on which a filthy mattress, about six feet long and two feet wide, was placed. Though this chamber did not look so horrible as the dens of the Prefettura, now that the shutters were opened, yet, when Poerio was its inmate, want of air and light must have made it dreadfully sad and unhealthy.

We entered No. 7. It was like that we had just

left ; but at the foot of a Madonna, which is painted on the wall opposite the entrance, a few words have been scratched by the unfortunate prisoner who inhabited it. It is a short sentence ; but it tells eloquently enough the despair of him who traced it :—" *Vergine Imma-colata, liberate quest' uomo innocente.*" Another no less sad inscription may be read hard by : it is an appeal to the Mother of our Lord, and a more general pro-test of innocence :—" *Vergine Santissima, ajutate l'inno-cenza : 20 Marzo,* 1860."

" Who was the inmate of this prison ?" asked I of the gaoler.

" He was a gentleman who had been arrested," an-swered the man, " on a charge of having taken a pro-minent part in the demonstration of the 6th of June, 1859—the day on which the news of the victory of Magenta arrived. He was shut up for eleven months, although he was never examined by the Judge ; and his wife, being confined at the time, died of grief."

We proceeded on our survey, and entered No. 8. Here, amongst many memoranda scratched on its walls, are two of special note. The first is signed by Guglielmo Martinese, of Lecce, and tells us that the poor man had been " *Sepolto vivo per quattro mesi in questo carcere.*" These eight words—" Buried alive during four months in this prison"—are more elo-quent in their simplicity than the writings of genius. Close to this inscription is the second to which I have alluded. It has not been signed by its writer, but it tells plainly enough the moral torture which the unfortunate man had suffered. The sentence runs thus:—" *Oh, possa la morte ricongiungermi alla mia diletta Madre che mi attende in cielo : mio Dio, ho troppo, troppo sofferto !*"

We now entered another cell, or rather a stone box. The priest Saro was confined in that horrible contrivance of barbarity for more than a year, although the roof is so low as not to admit of an upright posture. The only crime which the Albanian priest was charged with was that of being a distant relation of Agesilao Milano, who attempted the life of Ferdinand II. After his release from prison, the poor man could not use his legs for nearly a month, so stiff and benumbed had they become through total want of exercise. Hard by, there is another cell where Dramis, also a relative of Milano, had been confined for many months. Nero and other tyrants of old were more humane in causing their victims to be devoured by wild beasts in the circus.

Utterly sick at heart with our visit, so suggestive of the miseries to which honest men had been subjected, we were preparing to leave the gallery, when the gaoler, entering one of the cells, said to me, "Here is the place where Signor Pandola was imprisoned only a few months ago."

" What was he imprisoned for?" asked I.

" Really," replied the gaoler, " I was never able to make out. They say that the Director of the Police could not bear him, for he is very tall, and, emerging from the crowd when there was a demonstration in the Toledo, his presence was naturally noticed."

I could not help smiling at this candid confession of the official, which graphically portrayed the system

of arbitrary tyranny characterizing the government
of the Bourbons.

We supposed we had now seen all the prisons of
Santa Maria Apparente ; but on descending the staircase, the gaoler ordered one of his attendants to open
a heavy door screened by the gate of the principal entrance. The order was executed, and we proceeded
through a subterranean gallery which in former times
must have led to the summer cells of the convent.
It was a sort of cavern hewn in the rock on which the
building stands. Although the gaoler at first denied
that political prisoners had been kept there, yet, on
Lord Llanover pressing the question, he answered
that he would not swear that it had not been used as a
prison. Traces of its having been inhabited were
besides too apparent to leave any doubt on the subject. Having, moreover, asked my friend Colonel
Pace, he assured me that some of the Calabrian
prisoners had been kept there for many months.

I shall not dwell upon the system which prevailed
during the trial and subsequent condemnation of
Poerio, Spaventa, Settembrini, and their friends, nor
on the moral tortures which were inflicted on Pace, Co-
sentini, Ricca, and the other one hundred and seventy-
six patriots who were tried at Cosenza in 1852. Both
Mr. Gladstone and Lord Llanover have exhausted the
subject in their remarkable letters. It was a system of
moral and physical torture, the narration of which,
making due allowance for modern civilization, would
recall all that has been written about the Bastille, the
oubliettes of Louis XI., and the *tane* of Ezzelino da
Romano. During the course of the trials—that is to

say, even when the prisoners had not as yet been found guilty by the Judges—the regulations were still more severe than those which prevailed in the place of confinement after the sentence was pronounced. Not that at Procida, at the Ergastolo of Santo Stefano, at Monte Sarchio, or at the other prisons of the kingdom, the punishment was officially mitigated, but that, owing to the great corruption which prevailed amongst the turnkeys and prison inspectors, it was not difficult to procure certain comforts by means of money. Newspapers, books, and letters were allowed to reach the desolate prisoners, if they paid for the luxury. This system was carried to such an extent that even messages from Mazzini could make their way into the Ergastolo. It was simply a question of price. A letter from a relation or a friend cost one piastre; a missive from Mazzini, or from some other political exile, was taxed by the keeper of the prison according to its importance. If, at the time of Pisacane's expedition, Spaventa and Settembrini had wished to escape, they could have done so with comparative facility, for the keepers of the Ergastolo had been bribed by the patriots led by Avvocato Libertini, who organized the expedition in which the chivalrous Pisacane lost his life.

On leaving Santa Maria Apparente, we went to see the prisons of Castel Sant' Elmo, which were no less horrible than those which I have described. And yet, according to the opinion expressed by a turnkey to a correspondent of the *Times*, they were a paradise when compared with those of Sicily. How, then, could we wonder that Providence had at last smitten the son of the man who had used such instruments against his fellow-creatures? Sooner or later, iniquity receives the reward it has earned; and it is expressly stated in Holy Writ, that God has made the son responsible for the wickedness of the father.

CHAPTER IX.

THE TWO ARMIES.

THE organization of the army was Garibaldi's first
occupation after his arrival in Naples. Volunteers
were constantly pouring in from Genoa and Leghorn;
and the irregular forces of Calabria and Basilicata
which had followed our march were drilled at Naples
and Salerno, and sent to the front as soon as they
were sufficiently trained for military service. The
Calabrese formed a division 10,000 strong, under

Baron Stocco; the contingent from Basilicata, a brigade of 2200 men, under Brigadier Corte. With the addition of these forces, Garibaldi, towards the middle of September, was able to occupy the positions before Capua with an army of 37,000. On the other side of the Volturno, Francis II. mustered an army of about 40,000 soldiers, among whom was a fine body of cavalry, from 7000 to 8000 in number. The events which had taken place in Sicily and Calabria, together with an order of the day addressed by Francis II. to the remainder of his army, in which he freed it from the oath of allegiance, led the Dictator to believe that the Royal troops were unwilling to fight any longer for a Sovereign who had so abruptly left his capital. In this opinion Garibaldi was still further confirmed by a report that the Royal troops were in a complete state of disorganization, partly owing to want of confidence in their leaders, partly to the liberal and national ideas which were gaining ground amongst the more enlightened officers of the artillery. To work upon these elements of dissolution, and to avoid, if possible, a fratricidal war, Garibaldi, on the 10th of September, addressed the following proclamation to the Royal army :—

"If you do not disdain Garibaldi for your companion in arms, he only desires to fight by your side the enemies of your country. Truce, then, to discord— the chronic misfortune of our land. Italy, trampling on the fragments of her chains, points to the North : the path of honour is towards the last lurking-place of tyrants. I promise you nothing more than to make you fight.   G. GARIBALDI."

As subsequent events proved, these stirring words were not destined to be listened to; for, as soon as the supporters of Francis II. had recovered from their first shock, they showed a determination to defend the line of the Volturno, and the two fortresses on whose ramparts the Bourbon flag still waved.

Towards the middle of September, Garibaldi had permanently established his head-quarters in the magnificent palace of Caserta, the summer residence of Royalty, whence Ferdinand II. had been called by the Supreme Judge to settle the heavy accounts of his tyrannic rule. The first care of the Dictator on arriving at Caserta was to distribute his forces so as to be in a position to repel any attack which might be made by the Royalists against his line, and to be at the same time able to cross the Volturno, and assume the offensive. The two extreme points of the line occupied by the army of Francis II. leaned on the one side towards the Mediterranean, and on the other towards the Apennines, extending from point to point a distance of about thirty miles. The rear was protected by the frontier of the Papal States, and strongly supported by the fortress of Gaeta. Its front was covered by the course of the Volturno, a deep, muddy river, very difficult to ford. Capua (which has been a fortress ever since the year 1200, and which was enlarged by Vauban, and more recently by a Russian officer in 1855) is flanked on three sides by the Volturno, and forms in itself an important *tête-du-pont*. An army holding it can debouch from the one to the other bank without much difficulty. Screened by the line of the Volturno, and enabled to obtain provisions and ammunition by sea from Gaeta, and by land from the road to Velletri, Francis II. was in a condition to hold his ground until the hoped-for Austrian and Papal reinforcements should arrive to help him. Being master of so strong a position, he could threaten Naples at any moment; for, by a bold march of twelve hours, his army could easily reach it.

To avoid this danger, and to check any offensive movement of the Royalists, Garibaldi occupied the towns of Maddaloni, Caserta, San Leucio, Sant' Angelo, and Santa Maria, leaving to the National Guard the task of garrisoning the capital. These positions form a powerful line of defence against any adversary menacing Naples from the left bank of the Volturno. Indeed, an army which, having crossed that river, should venture to advance on the capital without previously forcing the enemy's line at Santa Maria, would be obliged to execute a flank march between the sea on its right, and the opposing forces on its left. If, on the contrary, the enemy should cross the Volturno in the vicinity of Ponte di Valle, and march on Naples by the road to Maddaloni, the army occupying Santa Maria, Sant' Angelo, and Maddaloni could concentrate itself at Caserta, and fall upon the rear of the approaching columns. It is therefore easy to see that the positions which Garibaldi occupied enabled him to cover the capital in case of his adversary assuming the offensive.

From the 10th to the 19th of September, there had been scarcely any engagements deserving the name of actions. The skirmishers of both armies now and then kept up a brisk fire, at one of the wings or at the centre; but these proceedings always ended with but few casualties on either side, and the Royalists were invariably worsted. Until the 19th, the camp of the Dictator looked more like what I had seen at Faro than a place which might at any moment become the field of a bloody struggle.

Garibaldi, on occupying the Royal Palace of Caserta, took up his quarters in an apartment formerly inhabited by the gentlemen of the Royal household. He slept in a small room facing the large square of the palace; while his Staff, and I, who was attached to it, were heaped together in four rooms, in each of which were five or six beds. In the middle of this suite of rooms, there was a sort of hall, in which the offices of the Staff were established. At night, however, mattresses were laid upon its floor, and these formed the beds of the body-guard, who were armed with long spears, and whose duty it was to keep order amongst the crowd of petitioners regularly besieging the head-quarters from daybreak until night. At three o'clock, Garibaldi got up, as was his habit, attended to the business of the State, consulted with the Ministry, and received his numerous visitors, from the noble down to the humblest petitioner. I remember one morning a poor woman being prevented by the body-guard from entering the room of the General, who was then occupied with the chief of the Staff. The woman, whose husband had been arrested at Naples on the previous evening, was weeping and making so much noise that her lamentations reached the ears of

Garibaldi. On a sudden, he made his appearance in the ante-room, asking what was the matter. The poor woman rushed to him, crying out, "*O, mio marito, O, mio marito, rendetemelo, Eccellenza.*" No sooner had Garibaldi made out what she meant, than he granted her request, intimating at the same time to his guard that the poorer the people were who wanted to speak to him, the sooner they should be admitted.

Affairs of State having been despatched, Garibaldi and his Staff used to go to the front, either by railway or on horseback. Once arrived at Sant' Angelo, hard work began for our legs. The General taking the lead, we ascended the steep and rocky slope of the mountain facing the Volturno, from the top of which the eye could command the whole of the Neapolitan camp, and see the very ramparts of Capua. It was from that eminence, on which he had established a battery, that Garibaldi studied the ground he had to operate upon. At noon, a modest breakfast was generally served, and we did not return to Caserta until the evening, when we dined.

Foreign tourists were constantly visiting Garibaldi at that time. They had no difficulty in getting at him, for almost everybody was at liberty to join the Staff of the General, and survey the line. There were, of course, a good many English, and these were perhaps the most welcome guests at the General's head-quarters. One day, whilst we were standing on the top of Sant' Angelo, the Hon. Mr. Calthorpe made his appearance with some friends, at a moment when shells and shot were falling amongst us with a precision that did great honour to the skill of the Neapolitan gunners in the opposite battery. On other days, Captain Keith Fraser, of the Life Guards, Mr. Arthur Russell, or Mr. Augustus Craven, joined us in our dangerous excursions; on others, again, we were honoured with the company of Viscount Pevensey or Mr. Allen Bathurst. Even English ladies visited us every now and then at Sant' Angelo and Caserta. All these tourists met with the most cordial reception at our head-quarters, where they stopped even for some days, and became guests of the General's table.

On the 14th of September, Garibaldi was obliged to leave Caserta, being suddenly called to Palermo on account of the quarrel to which allusion has already been made, and which led to the resignation of Depretis, the Pro-Dictator of Sicily. The command of the army was in the meanwhile entrusted to Türr, who, a few days afterwards, decided on making a strong demonstration against Capua, in order to effect a diversion whilst crossing the Volturno higher up. Although Garibaldi had by that time come back from Palermo, he left to this Hungarian officer the honour of leading the army in the first action fought since we arrived in Naples. On the 17th, Türr sent a detachment of three hundred men to Campobasso, with orders to cross the Calore, a branch of the Volturno, at a small hamlet called Amorosi. Thence, this detachment was to descend the mountains which overhang the town of Cajazzo. The movement was successful as far as the crossing of the Calore went; but Cajazzo was occupied by a Neapolitan brigade and a battery of artillery, and the three hundred Garibaldians were obliged to wait for reinforcements. Another body of three hundred men was sent as a support on the night of the 19th, under the command of Major Cattabene, who was ordered to attack Cajazzo next morning, and try to carry it.

With the object of facilitating this attack on the enemy's left wing, Türr, as I have already stated, directed that a *reconnaissance* in force should be made against the whole of the Neapolitan line, together with a feint on Capua from Santa Maria. About four o'clock on the 20th, Colonel Spangaro advanced with two battalions from Aversa in the direction of La Foresta, to menace Capua at its south-western angle. At the same time, Colonel Rüstow, of General Milbitz's division, marched from Santa Maria, at the head of six battalions and two guns, towards the front of the fortress. General Eber had to sweep with his brigade the road from Santa Maria to Sant' Angelo, drive the Neapolitans into Capua, and, if possible, skirt the mountain range of Sant' Angelo, and effect his junction with Secchi's brigade, which had been ordered to threaten the ford by which the Volturno is passed in front of Cajazzo.

It was Brigadier Rüstow's party which first opened fire. His columns, having reached the outskirts of the open space in front of Capua, the Milanese Cacciatori were directed to skirmish, and support the action. Two battalions of De Giorgi's regiment formed the right wing of this corps, Colonel Coppi's regiment the left; whilst Rüstow was in the centre, with General La Masa's brigade on the main road as a reserve.

These troops thus disposed, took up a position about 3000 yards from the fortress, and, being screened by the bushes and trees of the surrounding woods, opened fire against the Royalists posted outside Capua. As soon as the enemy became aware of this threatening movement, they recalled a part of their troops from the left bank of the Volturno, which they were at that time guarding. They were thus enabled to concentrate more than 8000 men, partly in a sort of entrenched camp which they had formed in front of the fortress, partly on the road leading to La Foresta. The action had already commenced when Colonel Spangaro debouched from the last-named place, and began to attack the Neapolitans on their extreme right.

On the preceding night, having heard from some of General Türr's Staff that there would be an action, I hastened to Santa Maria. A party of English amateurs, amongst whom were Mr. Evelyn Ashley, Colonel Baker, of the 10th Hussars, Mr. Edwin James, Mr. Lenox Conyngham, Mr. Adam Smith, and a few others, accompanied me. By the time we arrived at Santa Maria, the action had begun, both in the front and on the extreme right of our line. Although my own horses had been taken to Santa Maria during the night, such was the confusion which prevailed in the town when we arrived, that they could not be found, nor could I get any for my companions, as I had promised to do. After a great deal of trouble, and much negotiation with the Sindaco, I succeeded in securing some donkeys for my friends, on which ignoble chargers they rode to the battle. Ultimately, how-

ever, they were compelled to abandon them, and trust
to their own legs, with the exception of Colonel
Baker, who had been fortunate enough to obtain a
horse at Naples.

At the distance of about two English miles from
Santa Maria, the road which leads to Capua turns
suddenly to the right, running between a plantation
of mulberry trees on that side, and a woody country on
the left. When we debouched from the turning of the
road, we found Rüstow's brigade fighting hard against
the masses of Neapolitans, who, judging from appearances, were able to work their artillery with considerable effect. The fire kept up, both by the batteries
of the Neapolitan entrenched camp and the more
powerful artillery on the ramparts of Capua, was
so brisk that grapeshot and shells were dropping
everywhere like hail in a northern storm. The
main road, by which the Garibaldian reserve was to
be brought up, was also swept by the heavy guns of
Capua.

It was then about ten o'clock, and we had had no
breakfast. A Capuchin convent was near at hand, and,
as some of our party were complaining loudly (the excitement adding to their appetite), I proposed to knock
at the door, and see whether it would be opened.
Although the convent had been deserted by its
inmates, the brother cook had been left behind to
watch the pantry and the cellar. At first we experienced some difficulty in making him admit that he
could give us some raw ham and eggs; but at last
the sight of a piastre brought him to his senses. He
asked half an hour to prepare the meal, and went his

way to the kitchen. Whilst engaged in the exercise of his culinary talents, we decided to spend the half hour in taking a survey of the building. That the Capuchin convent stood within two hundred yards of the cemetery of Capua, then occupied by a company of Rüstow's troops, we had seen before entering it. But what we did not know was, that the walls were within range of the fortress guns. Of this fact, however, we became soon aware ; for, having ascended on to the roof, we were saluted by the round-shot of the Neapolitans. Great was the commotion amongst our party ; and a rush down-stairs followed as speedily as possible. In the confusion which naturally arose from this unexpected incident, some of my friends lost their way down, and, instead of taking the gallery leading to the staircase, turned to the left towards a room where the monks kept their cups, coffee pots, and tin trays.

" Now," said I to Mr Ashley, " let us test the steadiness of our companions' nerves."

At the same time I took up a large tin tray near at hand, and, flinging it on the floor with great violence, it made such a thundering noise that some of our party firmly believed it was the explosion of a shell, and went away perfectly convinced that they had had a very narrow escape.

A more serious incident, however, awaited us. We had left the convent, and had regained the main road of Santa Maria, just as Major Laporta's battalion made a bold rush against the Neapolitans, which was repulsed by a terrific cannonade. This was exciting enough, and we were anxious to get a-head as speedily as possible. Mr. Ashley, Mr. Conyingham, and Mr. Vizitelly took a by-road, and Mr. James and I jumped into a *carrozzella* which chanced to be passing. Another of our party, Mr. William Smith, was desirous of getting into the carriage, and I was trying to make a little room for him, when a round-shot swept away the foot-board of the *carrozzella*. The projectile passed so close, that the mere concussion of the air threw Mr Smith into the ditch at the side of the highway.

Whilst this episode was occurring on the road to Capua, the Garibaldians were fighting against the most disproportioned odds. La Masa had been ordered to bring up his reserve, to cover the retreat which had now become necessary. Colonel Coppi had been killed, and there were many wounded and dead on both sides. The backward movement had scarcely begun, when the enemy's cavalry was seen to start at full gallop; but its ardour was soon checked by the resolution of La Masa's brigade. The advancing of the Neapolitan Hussars, however, created a panic; and the drivers of the *carrozzelle*, waiting on the road to carry the wounded to the hospital of Santa Maria, screamed out *"Fui, fui!"* ("Flight, flight!")

The feint on Capua, though not in all respects badly managed, had been uselessly protracted for five hours, when there was no chance of turning it to any advantage. Colonel Rüstow lost two hundred men under a strong fortress, which could not have been taken by a *coup de main*, and consequently without any excuse whatever. He ought on his own responsibility to have retired at least two hours before, and contented himself with diverting a part of the Neapolitan forces from the Volturno, and keeping them in check. The mistake was not the only one made by General Türr. His main point had been to cross the river, and occupy the strong position of Cajazzo; and so far, so good. In presence of the advancing column of Major Cattabene, the enemy had abandoned the town, which the Garibaldians were thus enabled to occupy. But the troops commanded by Cattabene were not numerous enough to hold a position four miles distant from the river which divided them from their base of operations, and which was besides difficult to ford. There were no bridges, no *têtes du pont*, no means whatever for insuring the communication of those six hundred Garibaldians with the main body of their army. This error soon produced its unavoidable consequences; for, two days after Cattabene occupied Cajazzo, he was attacked by an overwhelming force, and, although he held out for many hours, was twice wounded, and lost half of his men, he was at length compelled to yield, and was taken prisoner to Capua. Had it not been for the courage of Major Cattabene and Captain Castellini, the whole of the Garibaldians at Cajazzo would have perished. Seeing that further resistance was totally impossible, the second of these officers was ordered by the Major to take to the other side of the Volturno the men who were able to walk— an order which he at once executed, not, however, without losing many of them, who were drowned in crossing the river.

In the defence of Cajazzo, almost all the children who formed the so-called Company of the Adolescenti perished, defending the barricade which had been erected in the town. The reader may remember that this corps was commanded at Modena by my brother. The youths were great favourites of Garibaldi; for, being unconcerned about danger, as boys generally are, they were as daring as the best and most experienced troops. At the first tidings of Garibaldi's success in Sicily, the greater number of the boys left their military school one after another, and joined the General in Southern Italy. Captain Camuncali was appointed their commander, and they formed part of the column sent to Cajazzo. These children—for the oldest of them had scarcely attained the age of fifteen, fought like lions for five hours. The retreat having been decided upon, they were ordered to form their ranks, and march out of the town; but, on a sudden, a battery which the Neapolitans had concealed in a hollow of the hill opened fire upon them at a distance of two hundred yards. Grape and shot poured mercilessly through their already thinned columns, and only a score of them were left.

On arriving at Santa Maria, my friends and myself experienced the usual difficulty in obtaining dinner, many of the inhabitants of the town having fled in terror, and the Garibaldians having already made a clean sweep of several shops and kitchens. However, after much delay, we got what we wanted, and subsequently rode in state into Aversa, attended by an escort of National Guards, who wished to show all honour to Mr. Ashley, as being a connexion of Lord Palmerston. The party now consisted only of Mr. Ashley, the Marquis Monterrenno, and myself; Messrs.

James, Smith, and Conyngham having disappeared, under circumstances which for a time excited grave fears for their safety. On our return to Naples, however, we were glad to find the first-named comfortably in bed, and the others enjoying their supper at the Vittoria.

Whilst Garibaldi was besieging Capua, great events were occurring in Central Italy. As I have mentioned at the end of the preceding chapter, Cialdini crossed the frontier of the Papal States early on the 11th of September, and, acting in accordance with the advice which the Emperor had given him at Chambéry— " Whatever you do, do it quickly "—pushed forward with so much energy and success that in six days he was able to address the following despatch to General Cucchiari :—

" Osimo, Sept. 18.

" This morning, at ten o'clock, General Lamoricière attacked my extreme positions on the counterfort which extends from Castelfidardo, by Crocetta, to the sea. All the prisoners affirm that he had with him 11,000 men and 14 pieces of artillery, having reinforced the troops at Foligno with all that he had at Terni, Oscali, and elsewhere. He supported his attack by a sortie of 4000 men from the garrison of Ancona. These troops assailed us in a really furious manner. The combat was short, but violent and bloody. We had to storm several positions successively, and, after a simulated surrender, the defenders of these positions assassinated our soldiers with poniards. Several of the wounded stabbed our men as they were coming up to succour them. The results of the day are as

R 2

follows :—We have prevented the junction of Lamoricière's corps with the garrison; we have taken 600
prisoners, among whom are 30 officers, some of them
of high rank; we have also taken six pieces of artillery, and among them those given by Charles Albert
to Pope Pius IX. in 1848; a great many ammunition-
waggons and baggage-waggons, one flag, an infinity
of arms, and many knapsacks left behind by the routed
men.   All the enemy's wounded, including General de
Pimodan, who led the attacking column, are in my
power, as also a considerable number of dead.   The
column which sallied forth from Ancona was compelled to retreat; but I have hopes that I shall capture
a large part of it this night.   Prisoners and deserters
are coming in every moment in great numbers.   The
fleet has arrived, and is opening fire upon Ancona.

> "CIALDINI, the General Commanding
> the 4th *Corps d'Armée.*"

The sudden change in the policy of the French
Emperor, which at that time surprised Europe, had
been brought about by causes not generally known in
England; and it is necessary that I should here explain
the facts as they were related in Italy at the time. In
a former chapter, mention has been made of the French
exile, Colonel Charras, having been offered by Dr. Bertani and his friends the command of the division which
was intended for the invasion of the Papal States.
Although the negotiations between Charras (who was
then in Switzerland) and his Republican Italian
friends were carried on with great secrecy, they were
not unknown to Cavour.   He saw at once the advan-

tage he could derive by hinting to the Emperor that the French Colonel, at the head of a Republican force organized by Bertani, would be a sort of defiance to the Napoleonic rule, and that the invasion of the Papal States by such an army would be the first step towards more decided revolutionary action, and would produce dangerous effects, not only to Italy, but possibly to France itself. Farini and Cialdini were sent to Chambéry by Cavour to impress on Louis Napoleon's mind that if he did not allow Piedmont to cross the Papal frontiers at once, the army of the Revolution would do so in a few days. The Emperor was evidently convinced of the force of the Italian Premier's argument, and consented. Bertani was withheld from carrying out his plan, and the Sardinians, as I have said, prepared to strike a blow which was to annihilate the army organized by Monsignor de Merode with much pains and at the cost of a large sum of money. ·

Lamoricière and his mercenaries, beaten at Castelfidardo, retired upon Ancona, but only to capitulate eleven days later. After the fall of that fortress, the Sardinians pursued their march towards the Abruzzi, in order to effect a junction with the Garibaldian army.

Although the action fought on the 19th on the Volturno led to no important result, it proved that the Garibaldians had attained such a degree of organization as enabled them to meet their adversary in the open field. Reinforcements were sent to the front from Naples and Salerno, and were drafted into the different divisions as they arrived.

Towards the end of September, Garibaldi was therefore able to muster an army of about 35,000 men, 5000 of whom were at the hospital, while a still larger number could only be regarded as stragglers, or as persons occupied in the different branches of the military administration. The actual force in line was consequently not more than from 22,000 to 24,000 men, 10,900 of whom were Calabrese, Basilicatans, and Sicilians. The knowledge Garibaldi had acquired of the ground on which he might be called at any moment to apply his military genius led him to occupy a succession of positions which formed, as it were, the cord of the bow-shaped line held by the Neapolitans. The advantage of the Garibaldians was evident. In order to communicate with their positions, from one extremity to the other, they had only to follow a straight line, whilst their adversaries were compelled to trace a semicircle. The extreme left of Garibaldi's army rested on Aversa. Brigadier Corte, with 800 men of Basilicata, occupied that town, together with Vico Pantano and the line of Lagni Regii, a canal which runs parallel with the Volturno. The village of San Tamaro was held by Malenchini's brigade, composed of 1400 Tuscans and some Calabrians, with two howitzers. General Milbitz, who had succeeded Cosenz in the command of the sixteenth division, was at Santa Maria with 2700 men of Sprovieri's and Langè's regiments, 1300 of La Masa's brigade, besides 112 Genoese carabineers, 37 French (the remains of De Flotte's company), 69 Hungarian Hussars, and five field guns. Medici, on the right, occupied Sant' Angelo with Dunne's brigade (1600 strong), 1200 men of Simo-

netta's brigade, 700 of Spangaro's brigade, and 450 of
Vacchieri's regiment; 40 Engineers, under Colonel
Bordone, 400 Calabrese under Colonel Pace, and eight
guns.   General Sacchi was at San Leucio with 2200
men and two guns.   Bixio guarded the town of Maddaloni and the passes of Ponte di Valle with a whole
division, numbering 3400, including 1500 Calabrese
and five guns.   To connect these positions, Türr's and
Stocco's divisions, mustering about 7000 men with
thirteen guns, occupied Caserta, Caserta-Vecchia, and
Castel Morone, under the command of General Sirtori,
and at the same time formed the reserve.   The Guides
of Colonel Missori and the Hussars of Carissimi were
either distributed amongst the different divisions or
were posted at Caserta, where Garibaldi's head-quarters
were established.   Such were the positions held by
our army at the end of September.   On the 27th of
that month, the subjoined Order of the Day announced
to the army the victory of Castelfidardo :—

"Caserta, Sept. 27.

"Our brethren of the Italian army, commanded by
the gallant General Cialdini, have combated the
enemies of Italy, and conquered.

"The army of Lamoricière has been defeated by
those valiant men.   All the provinces enslaved by the
Pope are free.   Ancona is ours.

"The valiant soldiers of the Army of the North
have passed the frontier, and are on Neapolitan soil :
we shall soon have the good fortune to grasp their
victorious hands.

"G. GARIBALDI."

The victory gained by General Cialdini over Lamoricière, and his crossing of the Neapolitan frontier, was
not only a great political, but also a great military
event.   The advance of Victor Emmanuel's army in
the rear of the Neapolitans deprived the latter of the
advantages which they had previously obtained from
the line of the Volturno.   The Bourbonists had therefore no other alternative than to try the fortune of
arms, and assume the offensive against Garibaldi.
Francis II. was quite aware that, if he could succeed
in routing the Garibaldians, and reoccupying Naples,
diplomacy would arrest the march of the Piedmontese,
and thus restore him to the throne of his forefathers.
He accordingly held a council of war at Capua, in
which it was decided that on the 1st of October,
his birthday, the whole of his army should be concentrated between Capua and Cajazzo, should cross the
Volturno at different points, and, falling upon the
Garibaldians with 40,000 men, should, if possible, cut
through their line, and march on the capital.   In ful-
filment of this plan, the Neapolitan army completed
its preliminary arrangements, and was ready for
action.

About five o'clock P.M. of the 30th of September,
I left Sant' Angelo, and was riding towards Santa
Maria with Colonel Simonetta, when on a sudden we
heard behind us a brisk fire of musketry in the direction of the Volturno.   We turned our horses, and, at a
little distance from Sant' Angelo, saw the enemy's skirmishers drawn up in a long row, and slowly advancing
on the left bank of the river, so as to reconnoitre.
Medici's troops opened fire in reply ; but at dusk both

combatants retired to their camps. I therefore returned to Caserta, where I found Garibaldi and his Staff in expectation of the events which were ripening for the next day.

Though wounded and taken prisoner at the beginning of the battle of the 1st October, many episodes of that memorable action passed so immediately under my observation that, before I begin the narrative of my personal adventures, I will give a short account of it.

The plan adopted by the Generals of Francis II. at the Council of War held at Capua, although too complicated, might have proved successful had the officers who were to execute it been experienced in the practical application of military knowledge, and capable of inspiring confidence in their troops. Excepting a few, the Neapolitan Generals had never seen anything of actual war, nor had the soldiers ever heard the roar of artillery, save at reviews and peaceful manœuvres. They were besides too demoralized, and had too little confidence in their officers, to conquer an army which, though not strictly organized, was composed of volunteers convinced of the righteousness of their cause, and commanded by a great and popular leader. The position of Sant' Angelo, which was the key of the Garibaldian line, was besides defended by Medici, a General who in 1849, at Rome, held the Vascello against the French with a handful of men, and proved himself almost unequalled in defending entrenched positions.

The plan of the Neapolitan attack may be thus briefly summed up :—to debouch from Capua with

24,000 men; to attack the positions of Santa Maria and Sant' Angelo, endeavouring to break through the centre of Garibaldi's line ; and to sever Medici's troops from those of Milbitz ; whilst the remainder of their army was to cross the Volturno above Capua at different points, and attack Bixio at Ponte di Valle and Maddaloni.   Supposing the plan to be successful so far, both the Neapolitan corps were to effect their junction, and march together on Naples.   But to carry out this scheme it was necessary to surmount and conquer a succession of hilly positions, very strong in themselves, and defended by men like Medici and Bixio.   Another difficulty with which the army of Francis II. was obliged to contend arose from the inequality of the ground whereon their left wing had to manœuvre, and which rendered the artillery and cavalry almost useless.

That the reader may the better understand the battle I am about to describe, I will commence by giving a short sketch of the position of Capua, and of the country by which it is surrounded.   The fortress stands at the foot of a ridge, running towards the left of the town, and which may be called a prolongation of the Abruzzi chain.   The Volturno, springing from the inland mountains, runs in the opposite direction towards the Tyrrhenian Sea, into which it falls.   On the left bank of the river rises another chain of lofty hills, thus forming a narrow valley, in the middle of which flows the Volturno.   This chain of hills is skirted by a road leading from Santa Maria, passing the foot of Mount Tifata (on whose declivity stands the village of Sant' Angelo), and then running almost parallel with the Volturno, till it reaches the ferry of Formicola, by which the river may be crossed opposite to the town of Cajazzo. From the ferry, the road bends to the right between the mountain defile leading to San Leucio and Caserta. On the left bank of the Volturno, besides this road, there are many mountain tracks, through which, when once the river has been crossed, Ponte di Valle and Maddaloni can be equally reached. The town of Santa Maria, the last one that the traveller passes when he goes by railway from Naples to Capua, is situated in a large plain, which from the western side of those mountains extends itself more or less widely as far as the capital of the kingdom. The distance from Santa Maria to Capua is about three English miles, and the road proceeds almost parallel with the railway. The canal of Lagni Regii runs towards the sea, side by side with the Volturno, threading the country which lies between the towns of Aversa and Santa Maria.

The principal attack of the enemy, which was directed against Garibaldi's line between Santa Maria and Sant'Angelo, being protected by powerful artillery, was vigorously executed, both along the road from Capua to Santa Maria, and from the same city to Sant' Angelo. A Neapolitan regiment of General Colonna's brigade had at daybreak crossed the Volturno near the ferry of Triflisco, and cut through Medici's outposts, advancing almost unnoticed by the wood of San Vito towards the heights of San Nicola. Thus, at about four o'clock in the morning, not only were the outposts of Milbitz and Medici

driven back along the whole line, but even some of
their entrenchments were stormed and carried by the
Neapolitans. Indeed, the latter were so far successful, that at four they had crossed the road running
from Santa Maria to Sant' Angelo, had ascended
Mount Tifata, and advanced towards the village of
San Prisco. They had besides obtained possession of
the barricade in front of Casa Bruciata (which was
defended by Dunne's brigade), and of the battery which
Garibaldi had erected at the foot of Sant' Angelo.
On the left, Milbitz had to fight hard to repulse
the attacks directed against the battery of the railway and the barricade of Porta Capua. Malenchini's
brigade was also vigorously assailed in front of the
railway, and for a time lost ground, being unable to
cope with the overwhelming forces that were brought
against it.

At the commencement of the action, I left the
head-quarters of Caserta with Garibaldi, and arrived
by rail at Santa Maria, at which time victory seemed
to have abandoned our gallant army. Although the
Dictator at once perceived the gravity of the situation
in which both the left and centre were placed, that
sort of intuition which forms the principal characteristic of his military genius told him that the
enemy must have attacked our extreme right with
equal ardour, in order to pass the line of Ponte di
Valle and Maddaloni, defended by Bixio. So just
was this opinion that, a few minutes after our arrival
at Santa Maria, intelligence came from Caserta that the
last-named General was in fact already engaged with
a column of Bavarians and Neapolitans, 7000 strong.

Garibaldi telegraphed to General Sirtori, Chief of the Staff, to have Eber's brigade, and the rest of the reserve under Türr, in readiness—the first to support Bixio, if need were, the second to march in the direction of Capua. No troops, however, except Assanti's brigade, were to be marched on to the field of battle until the success of Bixio had been ascertained. Giving other orders to Milbitz, the General started in a carriage for Sant' Angelo, and we followed him in other conveyances, not knowing that the Neapolitans had already passed the road we were traversing, and had driven back the weak chain of Medici's outposts. We had hardly reached the last of those little bridges which span the sunken ways leading towards Capua, when the 10th battalion of Neapolitan sharpshooters opened fire against our carriages at a distance of about fifty yards. In a moment, we found ourselves amidst a shower of balls. One of the horses of Garibaldi's carriage fell dead, and the coachman of the *carrozzella* in which Missori and I were seated was killed by our side. We thereupon jumped out, drawing our swords, and waiting for the orders of the General. Fortunately, the Neapolitans, instead of rushing at us, were suddenly stopped by the fire which one of Medici's companies had opened upon them. This unexpected help allowed Garibaldi and his Staff to cross the fields, and follow a path skirting the heights of Tifata, by which the village of Sant' Angelo could be reached. Although the episode I have just narrated nearly proved fatal to the Dictator and ourselves, it was in some respects providential. If, instead of being stopped,

we had been allowed to proceed on our drive to Sant'
Angelo, we might have arrived at the outskirts of
that village at the moment when the Neapolitans had
just carried our battery, and were in possession of the
road from which we had to debouch. With that good
fortune which seems to have made him the man of
Fate, Garibaldi succeeded in reaching the upper part
of Sant' Angelo, which Medici was defending inch by
inch against an overpowering force. Excepting myself
and Captain Paverini, who sprained his foot in jumping
from the carriage, not one of Garibaldi's Staff was
missing.

Ascending the lofty hill which overhangs Sant'
Angelo, Garibaldi was able to comprehend, in all its
details, the dangerous position of his army. He saw
that the communication with Santa Maria had been
absolutely cut off; that Medici was completely outflanked by the Neapolitan right wing, which, pushing
on from Capua along the watercourses, had crossed the
Volturno, gained the heights of Tifata, and was now
descending to attack Sant' Angelo in the rear. The
defenders of that position were therefore entirely
surrounded; for the Neapolitans, having possession
of the heights of Tifata, had severed the communication between Sacchi's brigade (which was occupying San Leucio, and rallying the corps of Bixio) and
that of Medici, and had at the same time isolated the
reserve at Caserta. To reopen his communications on
this side was Garibaldi's first object. He accordingly
ordered the Genoese carabineers and two mountain
guns to ascend the heights above those occupied by
the enemy, and drive them back towards the plain.

This was soon done. In the meanwhile, Medici was holding on in front of Sant' Angelo, thwarting by his coolness, and by the obstinacy of his troops, all the attempts of the enemy to carry it. The fight lasted there four hours; but at length a bayonet charge, led by Garibaldi himself, compelled the Neapolitans to retire, and prevented their attaining the object of their main attack.

They had not been more successful at Santa Maria. Although the attack on that point could not be considered the principal one, their columns had by eight o'clock so far advanced as to threaten the town of Santa Maria itself. General Milbitz soon perceived that the Neapolitan troops were not equal to carrying a position which he had so carefully fortified. He therefore allowed the Bourbonic General Afant de Rivera to deploy his columns right and left in a crescent line, and, when he thought they had spread sufficiently to be outflanked, sent an order to Malenchini to assume the offensive, and attack their right. Malenchini, who with his Tuscan brigade had already sustained a hard fight in defending the battery of the railway, fell unexpectedly upon one of the enemy's regiments, and routed it in less than an hour. To pursue his first success, Malenchini sent his aide-de-camp, Prince Buttera (one of the present Secretaries of the Italian Legation in London), to ask Milbitz for reinforcements. These soon arrived, and the extreme right of the enemy was compelled to fall back on the centre, spreading confusion amongst the reserve which Francis II. and General Rettucci, the acting Commander-in-Chief, were sending up in support of the troops who were engaged in attempting to carry the railway battery. The columns of the Neapolitan left, since the early part of the morning, had been successful. Excepting a farm-house, from which the gallant French company could not be dislodged, they had penetrated far enough to occupy all the houses in the outskirts of Santa Maria, from Porta Capua to the remains of the Roman Amphitheatre.

The success obtained by Malenchini on the left, and the failure of General Barbalunga to carry Sant' Angelo, convinced Rettucci that his first attack was unsuccessful. He therefore brought up a part of the reserve, gathered his scattered forces, and prepared to reassume the offensive. But by that time Assanti's brigade had come up from Caserta, and had been sent by Milbitz towards Sant' Angelo, in order that it might attack the Neapolitans in flank, and thus reopen the communication between that village and Santa Maria. Supported by Colonel Pace's regiment, Assanti started with Borghese's and Fazzioli's regiments, and cleared the road as far as the bridge. The Neapolitans, however, fell back all along their line, only to reassume the offensive with still greater vigour. Attack after attack was renewed, both on the battery of the railway and on Porta Capua, under the orders of the King himself; but they were as constantly defeated. Shells burst by hundreds over Santa Maria, and grape and shot swept away the Garibaldians by scores. Their magazine of Porta Capua exploded, spreading death amongst the gunners and infantry who defended the barricade; but they were replaced by fresh troops, who went forward to meet the advancing columns of the Neapolitans, and took two of their guns before they had time to assault the half-destroyed battery. It was at this moment that a party of sailors belonging to her Britannic Majesty's ship *Renown*, who were on shore, went to Santa Maria. While these men were looking on at Porta Capua, some Garibaldians came up, dragging the two captured guns. These stuck fast about two hundred yards from Porta Capua; on which an Englishman among the Garibaldians asked the sailors to " bear a hand." Blue-jackets never shrink from helping the soldiers of liberty; and the two guns were accordingly brought in by them.

Many sanguinary struggles took place at Santa Maria during the day; but they were gallantly repulsed by the Garibaldians under Milbitz. It now became evident to the Neapolitan General-in-Chief that a final and more determined attack against the town was necessary. Bringing up fresh columns, and unlimbering the field-batteries commanded by General Negri within three hundred yards of the walls, Rettucci commenced a last struggle along the front of Santa Maria. To support this attack, he ordered Palmieri to advance with 3000 horsemen towards the right of the railway line, and charge the Garibaldians who were defending the open space between the town and the station. Santa Maria was surrounded by a hedge of fire, and Palmieri's cavalry charged right and left, almost into the railway battery. But the Garibaldians flung back the assaulting squadrons with such determination that Palmieri was unable to rally them, and was obliged to fall back on Capua.

Garibaldi and Medici at Sant' Angelo, Assanti on the road to Santa Maria, and Bixio at Ponte di Valle and Maddaloni, had, in the meanwhile, been equally successful.   Aided by the Calabrese of the gallant Colonel Pace, the first two repulsed the repeated attacks of General Barbalunga, and definitively repossessed themselves of the battery, which had been taken and retaken twice.   By two o'clock, Assanti's brigade had reopened the communications between Sant' Angelo and Santa Maria.   A part of the Neapolitan column which attacked Bixio had wasted precious time in capturing Castel Morone, bravely defended by Majors Bronzetti and Mirri ; whilst the rest attacked Ponte di Valle, but without displaying that unity of action which is absolutely necessary in war.   Bixio's division was composed of Eberhart's brigade, occupying the northern summits of Monte Longano, and that of Colonel Spinazzi, posted on Villa Gualtieri.   He had besides two battalions of Dezza's brigade on the heights of Monte Caro to the left, and Fabrizzi's column near San Michele, as a reserve.   With this force he completely routed the enemy by noon, thus enabling Türr to send Eber's brigade to Santa Maria, where Garibaldi himself had by this time arrived, his presence being no longer necessary at Sant' Angelo, of the safety of which he had satisfied himself.

It was now half-past two, and a general advance was ordered.   Eber marched out of Porta Capua, and broke through the Neapolitan masses ; whilst, to create a diversion, Milano's brigade was sent out by Porta Sant' Angelo.   General Eber's brigade was formed of Sicilians, and scarcely numbered two hundred men ; but a squadron of sixty-nine Hungarian Hussars was attached to it. What Eber had been ordered to accomplish with this small force was, to march through the columns of the enemy, and retake the Capuchin convent and the cemetery of Capua, which had been occupied by the enemy since the morning. The enterprise was difficult enough ; for, though the appearance of Milano's brigade on the field through which runs the road to Sant' Angelo naturally attracted a part of the Neapolitan army in that direction, they were numerous enough to show themselves in force on both points. As soon as Eber's brigade came in sight, it was received by a tremendous volley of artillery, which would have cut short the advance of even more highly-trained troops. The Hungarian Hussars, however, had got sight of three squadrons of Dragoons and two guns, which seemed disposed to contest their passage. In a moment, those sixty-nine heroes dashed at the Dragoons, routed them, and captured the guns. This gallant act struck Eber's Sicilians with such admiration, that, without numbering the enemy, they charged him at the point of the bayonet, carried the convent and the cemetery, and drove back the Royal Guards, which Francis II. was himself commanding at the time. The Neapolitans now began to fly towards Capua, that they might place themselves under the protection of its guns : they had lost the battle.

It appears that, after the failure of the repeated attacks made by General Barbalunga on Sant' Angelo, the Commander-in-Chief contemplated a last effort in that quarter, and determined to send fresh troops

s 2

to carry the village, which, as I have said, was
the key of Garibaldi's positions ; but, intelligence
having reached him that a strong body of Garibaldians
was advancing by the roads of Carditello and San
Tamaro, he thought it prudent to abandon his design.
This body of men was but the small brigade of Corte,
which had been ordered to defend the line formed by
the canal of Lagni Regii. Brigadier Corte concentrated
his men along the left bank of that canal, and by
noon had pushed strong reconnoitring parties on the
road leading towards the two above-named villages.
The sudden appearance of these troops, which the
Neapolitan generals, owing to their inexperience, regarded as a much larger force, paralyzed their movements during the day, and deterred Rettucci from
making any further attempts.

The success of General Eber decided the action.
Beaten along the whole of their line, the Neapolitans
hastily retreated towards Capua, spreading panic
among their comrades in the rear. From the open
camp which faces the fortress where I had been brought
a prisoner (under circumstances which I shall hereafter relate), I could witness the confusion which prevailed in their army. Garibaldi, with about 11,000
men, had resisted 30,000 Neapolitans, massed in the
comparatively short line from San Tamaro to Sant'
Angelo, and had routed them as soon as his reserve,
scarcely numbering 5000, reached the field of
battle. The Garibaldians had thus won the day by
themselves ; for the report then spread in Europe,
and still believed, that the Piedmontese arrived in
time to help them, is totally unfounded. It is true

that a battalion of Sardinian Bersaglieri was sent by the Marquis Villamarina on the evening of the 1st; but it did not reach the field of battle until the action was over. Garibaldi's success was followed up by Bixio on the 2nd of October, when he captured 5000 of those Bavarians and Neapolitans whom he had beaten the previous day, and who had in vain attempted to recross the Volturno.

The loss sustained by the Neapolitans on the 1st of October may be reckoned at 2500 killed and wounded, and 500 prisoners. The Garibaldians had 1280 *hors de combat*, and 700 prisoners and missing. Among the killed were Colonel Brocchi and Major Romarino; among the wounded, General Milbitz, Colonels Dunne, Longo, Corrao, and Winkler; Majors Cattaneo, Boldrini, Guastalla, Croff, Borelli, and Strambio. The Garibaldians captured nine guns, four of which were taken by the troops of Bixio. It would be difficult to name the Garibaldian divisions which distinguished themselves most on the 1st of October. The deeds performed by the brigade of Simonetta at Sant' Angelo were, however, especially remarked by Garibaldi. Bronzetti, who was killed at Castel Morone, fell like the heroes of old, uttering the cry—" The warriors of liberty never surrender!" The firmness of Medici and the bravery of Bixio were equal to their well-earned reputation. Milbitz stood firm as a rock at Santa Maria, and General Avezzana did more than his duty. With his spirited attack, Eber completed the defeat of Francis II.; and Brigadier Corte, by his well-combined manœuvres, showed great knowledge of tactics at Lagni Regii.

The French company held out at the insulated farm in front of Capua from the beginning of the battle to the end. The troops led by Brigadier Dunne, Colonel Dowling, and Major Windham, also fought gallantly at the barricade of Casa Bruciata. Colonel Pace's Calabrese and Assanti's brigade had their share in the victory of the day. Missori, Stagnetti, Canzio, Caldesi, and Guastalla distinguished themselves greatly, together with Colonel Bruzzesi and Major Nullo of the Guides. As for Garibaldi, he was everywhere, with victory always by his side.

Such is an outline of the Battle of the Volturno. Any Englishman who may be desirous of perusing a more detailed account should consult the excellent works of Captain Forbes and Brigadier Rüstow on Garibaldi's campaign. Although I may say that I keenly felt the effects of that battle, I had the misfortune to witness it from the side of the enemy, into whose hands I had fallen since its beginning. How I got there, the reader will learn in the ensuing chapter.

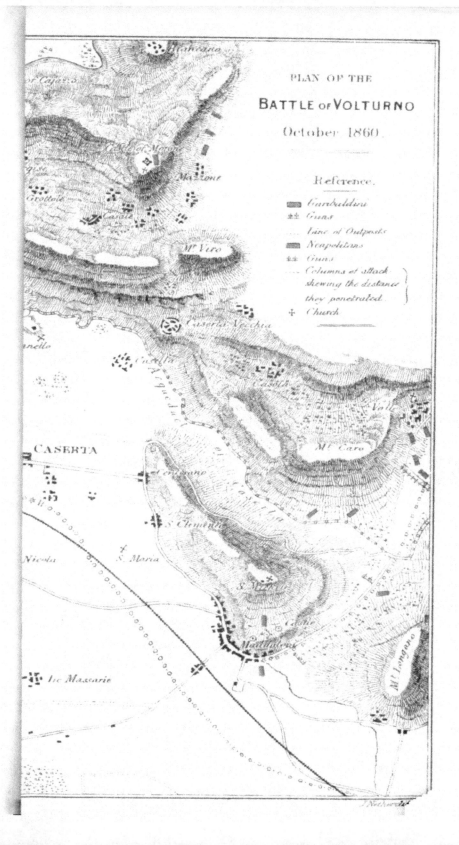

PLAN OF THE

BATTLE OF VOLTURNO

October 1860.

Reference.

Garibaldini

Guns

Line of Outposts

Neapolitans

Guns

Columns of attack
shewing the distance
they penetrated.

Church

CHAPTER X.

MY IMPRISONMENT.

A dangerous Drive—Garibaldi and his Staff in peril—A Comrade
in distress—I am taken Prisoner—Brutality of the Neapolitan Soldiers—A dying Neapolitan Officer—The Neapolitan
Camp—I am brought into the Presence of one of the Royal
Princes—A dangerous Promenade through Capua—The Citadel
of Capua—We start for Gaeta—The Village of Sant' Agata—
The Camp of the Garigliano—New Dangers—Gaeta—Our
Prison—An interested Offer of Don Antonio—The Casemate
of Gaeta—Dreadful condition of the Garibaldian Soldiers at
Gaeta—The Governor of the Castle—I am taken ill—An
obnoxious Number of the *Journal des Débats*—Abuse of Eng-
land—My last Interview with General Viale—How I was set
free — My Return to Garibaldi's Head-quarters — Victor
Emmanuel crosses the Neapolitan Frontier — The British
Legion before Capua — Reactionary Movement at Isernia—
Military Operations of the Piedmontese—Cialdini's Victories
—Victor Emmanuel at Calvi—His Interview with Garibaldi—
French Threats—Bombardment of Capua—Surrender of the
City.

MEILHAN has said—"*La vanité se mêlé dans tout.*"
This sentence would dissuade me from bringing myself personally before the reader in a more marked
manner, were it not that the relation I am about to
make, affords a vivid illustration of the evils of the
Bourbonic government.

As I have stated in the last chapter, having been
informed at Caserta, on the evening of the 30th Sep-

tember, that the Royal troops were likely to attack us on the following morning, I followed Garibaldi's Staff, which left the city at four o'clock, A.M. Before retiring to rest, I told my servant to have my saddle-horse ready by five o'clock at Santa Maria; but, on arriving there, neither horse nor servant could be found, owing to the confusion prevailing in the town, which was already attacked by the Royal army. Colonel Missori kindly offered me a place in his carriage, and we set out, closely following the *char-à-banc* of Garibaldi, towards Sant' Angelo. We were driving at a good speed when, on reaching a small bridge crossing the main road, the carriages were suddenly fired at by a Neapolitan battalion, which, having repulsed the thin line of our outposts, had so far advanced on the road we were pursuing as to discharge their rifles at a distance of sixty yards. The coachmen put their horses into a gallop; but the balls came flying so quickly that one of the horses of Garibaldi's carriage fell dead, and the coachman of that on which I was seated shared the same fate. And, indeed, being at his side on the box, I should have been killed in his stead had I not turned my head to speak to Missori when the poor fellow was struck. The moment was critical enough, and our position extremely difficult. Left to ourselves, almost without any escort (for the twelve Guides commanded by Major Nullo could scarcely have helped us, surrounded as they were by the Neapolitans rushing along the road), we had no other alternative than to jump out of the carriage. Garibaldi therefore set the example, and we followed him into the ditch on our right.

Major Paverini, one of Garibaldi's orderly officers, had by this time been severely hurt in the leg; and another officer was slightly wounded in the shoulder. Major Nullo, seeing that he could not help us, bravely ordered his Guides to gallop in the direction of Sant' Angelo, making his way through the enemy's columns, though not without leaving some of his men either dead or wounded on the road. The Neapolitan sharpshooters had now advanced close to the ditch, and it was clear that their intention was to surround us. Garibaldi, calm and composed as he always is, drew his sword, and told us to be ready to charge the enemy, and fight for our lives. Happily, a company of General Medici's men, coming from Sant' Angelo, perceived our danger, and hastened to the rescue. On their appearance, Garibaldi ordered them to open fire against the Neapolitans, and to keep them in check— a proceeding which stopped our enemies at once, and enabled Garibaldi and his Staff to escape across the fields, and reach the village of Sant' Angelo, then held by Medici.

I at first followed my companions; but, seeing that Major Paverini could scarcely walk, I thought it my duty to help him until we had reached a farm-house near at hand, from which I intended to walk to Sant' Angelo by a path over the hills. I had pretty nearly succeeded in executing my project, when I was suddenly stopped by three shepherds, who, knowing that I was surrounded by the Neapolitans, summoned me, in the name of his Sicilian Majesty, to surrender. However, they were not aware that I was in possession of a good Adams' revolver, a weapon which never

fails.   Self-defence gave me the right to use it, and I
did so.   Having lodged a bullet in the leg of one of
the ruffians, the other two took to their heels.   I
thought myself for the moment so safe that I stopped
to take a survey of the surrounding country.   I saw
masses of Neapolitans coming up from the camp
of Capua in a circular line, their fire literally covering
the plain.   Right and left, the batteries of Sant'
Angelo and Santa Maria were spreading death ; and
away towards the front, at the barricade of Casa Bruciata, Brigadier Dunne and Major Windham were
making almost incredible efforts to oppose the advancing columns of the enemy.

Whilst I was looking at that fratricidal fight, I
was suddenly roused by a loud shout, followed by a
volley of musketry.   The sharp whistle of balls, and
the flash of hundreds of muskets, left no doubt that a
party of Neapolitans were coming up the hill behind.
Instantly perceiving my danger, I moved from the
place ; but the next moment I was surrounded by the
enemy's riflemen, who, as I mentioned in the preceding
chapter, had turned Mount Tifata since the morning.
There was nothing to be done—I was a prisoner
without hope of escape.   But it seemed as if the
Neapolitans preferred to have me dead ; for, although
I was walking towards them, they kept firing at me,
and a bullet slightly wounded my left leg.   I fell, and
the men came up, surrounded me, and took my money,
my watch, and part of my clothes.   My watch was
positively appropriated by the officer in command,
though it was afterwards restored by the express
orders of the King.   One man struck me on the head ;

another gave me so heavy a blow on the shoulders that, although it was a bright day, I appeared to see all the stars in the heavens. Had not one of the officers come up, they would certainly have murdered me. I was a Garibaldian, they said, and they wanted to revenge the imaginary assassinations of their comrades.

The captain having ordered me to follow the column, I was obliged to do so, although I could scarcely walk. I begged him to send me to Capua at once; but he would not. "I am ordered to go up the hill," he said, "and I cannot detach any of my men; besides, were I to abandon you, my soldiers would assuredly kill you. Follow me as well as you can."

I shall always remember the pain I suffered during those four long hours. About twenty Garibaldians had also been taken prisoners by the sharpshooters into whose hands I had fallen. They, like myself, had been forced to exchange part of their clothes for the coat and cap of the Neapolitans, and, thus dressed, we were ordered to march at the front of the sharpshooters. "You will thus have a chance of being killed by your own comrades," said a rabid Sicilian sergeant to me when I remarked that such was not the manner in which prisoners ought to be treated.

The marching column we were preceding by a few yards was constantly fighting with Garibaldi's Bersaglieri; men fell dead around us, and the scene was one of the most distressing that can be imagined. The Neapolitans, however, proceeded very carefully, as men who were more earnest to spare their lives

than to perform their duty. Instead of heading them,
the officers kept in the rear, perpetually shouting out,
"Avanti, avanti!" but never setting the example.
It is not to be wondered at if the soldiers, instead of
obeying the order, scorned their officers, and abused
them roundly, calling them cowards, and worse. At
about half-past ten o'clock, one of the lieutenants of the
party—the only brave officer of the column—was struck
by two balls, and fell mortally wounded at my side.
He was a fine young fellow of about one-and-twenty. I
hastened to assist him, and implored the captain to
allow me to dress his wounds with my handkerchief.
The captain refused, in spite of the entreaties of his
wounded comrade, who begged me not to abandon
him. I offered to give my word of honour that I
would present myself at the Neapolitan camp as soon
as I had brought the poor fellow to Garibaldi's ambu-
lance, which was near at hand. All was of no avail.
The wounded officer was hoisted on the shoulders of
two privates, who, ten minutes afterwards, threw him
into a ditch, and left him.

I could no longer think of myself. Death and
misery were around me, and I was almost heart-
broken at witnessing such a scene. My companions
and I felt the horror of the thought that at any
moment we might perish under the bullets of our
friends, who, owing to the dress we had been compelled to assume, were unable to distinguish us from
the enemy. After many hours of anxiety, however,
we at length reached the Neapolitan camp before
Capua. My leg was by that time so swollen that two
of my fellow-prisoners were obliged to support me, as

I was almost unable to move. We had scarcely made our appearance at the farm-house at which were established the head-quarters of General Rettucci, when we fell in with a party of Neapolitan officers on horseback, coming from the road to Santa Maria. They were making their way with great difficulty through the retiring masses of their soldiers; every one being anxious to get under cover of the guns of Capua as fast as possible. A scene of the utmost confusion prevailed in the camp. Soldiers of all arms were running about pell-mell, shouting and screaming, amidst upset guns and commissariat carriages; now calling to their assistance all the Madonnas and saints they could think of, now abusing their officers, and loudly exclaiming, "Treason! treason!" The officers themselves were standing in groups in a state of hopeless incompetence; and the very horses seemed to partake of the prevalent dejection, and to confess with their drooping heads the utter ruin of the Bourbon cause.

The cavalcade I have mentioned had by this time reached the yard of the farm-house where we had halted. A young superior officer was riding in front of the party. A little man, about fifty years of age, with grey hair carefully smoothed down over the temples and back of the head, was riding at his left side. Other general officers followed them; and all were proceeding towards the head-quarters. On passing close to us, the officer who rode at the front stopped, and inquired who we were. We answered that we were Garibaldian prisoners. As, before reaching the Neapolitan camp, our own clothes had been re-

stored to us, the attention of the Neapolitan officer
was attracted by the Indian cap I wore. He therefore
asked who I was, and what rank I held in the Garibaldian army. I replied, that, although an Italian by
birth, I was a naturalized English subject, and that I
did not belong to the army of Garibaldi, but was only
a newspaper correspondent; on which, the officer broke
out in an angry voice, saying—

" What has the King of Naples done to the English
people that you should be so anxious to join his
enemy ?"

" I do not know, sir," answered I ; " but I repeat
that I am only a newspaper correspondent, whom
Garibaldi has allowed to follow his Staff. You have
no right to keep me a prisoner, and I hope the King
will send me back to Santa Maria."

" No, no," answered the officer ; " you will be taken
with your companions to Capua, where you will be
made to learn not to mix yourself up with things
which do not concern you."

One of the Generals, on hearing my declaration,
said in a tone of exasperation, that I should pay for
all the " calumnies" the English press had spread
against the Neapolitan army. At this unwarrantable
accusation I lost patience, and protested against the
treatment to which I had been subjected, telling the
General that I had been knocked down by his soldiers, and that one of the officers had taken my watch.
My indignation was roused to such a pitch that I
hardly knew what I said. I must, however, have
allowed myself to utter some hard words; for I was
warned to moderate my language, as I was in the

presence of one of the Royal Princes. "Very well," answered I; "be it so, for he will then know that amongst his Majesty's troops there are wretches who disgrace the uniform they wear."

Whilst I was thus speaking with the Neapolitan General, an officer came up and ordered me and my companions to follow him to Capua. We were marched between two rows of soldiers, and soon entered the gate of the town, amidst the brutal insults of a frantic population. They wanted us to cry out, "Long live Francis II. !"—a thing which all declined to do. A rabid barber, who was standing on the threshold of his shop, seized hold of his razor, and, rushing at me, seemed quite disposed to cut my throat, shouting out, in a wild voice, "Capitano, damene uno!" ("Captain, let me have one of the fellows!") Men, women, and children were throwing stones and all sorts of dirty projectiles at us; soldiers were trying to cut us down with their swords, or kill us with their bayonets. Had it not been for our escort, not one of us would have reached the prison to which we were being conveyed. But we at last crossed the drawbridge of the citadel, and were safe.

Once within its walls, we were kindly treated by the officers, who frankly told us that they deplored the fratricidal contest then staining the soil of Italy with Italian blood. They added that military honour alone induced them to fight against their brethren; and one young artillery officer (Captain Negri) said that they had been deceived by Francis II., who had not kept his promise of releasing them from their oath of allegiance. More than one pressed our hands as those of brothers.

Whilst this scene was going on within the citadel, the guns were roaring outside. Wounded men were constantly brought in, and the countenances of these soldiers confirmed our first impression that the day had gone against the Royal army. This increased our danger; for the soldiers, in the fury of their exasperation, wanted to murder us. In their eyes we were Garibaldians, belonging to the army which had beaten them. Our guard, however, was doubled, and we prepared to pass the night—a long night, full of anguish. It is sad enough to see passing before our eyes the dismal incidents of war, even when the enemy is composed of strangers to our blood, our language, and our traditions. But when the struggle is between members of the same family— children of the same great mother—men whose community of tongue should link them in the bonds of love, instead of only enabling them to understand each other's curses—the misery is indeed something beyond expression. Such was the misery I had to endure that night, surrounded by my dead and dying countrymen in the citadel of Capua.

Next morning, we were told that an order had come from the King to remove us to Gaeta. I asked leave to say good-bye to my wounded companions at the hospital—a request which was granted. . I there saw Major Cattabene and his noble comrades on their beds of sorrow, and learnt that the Queen had visited them two days before, evincing great commiseration for their misfortunes. In the evening, at eight o'clock, six carts were waiting for us, and we started with eighty-five of Garibaldi's soldiers. An escort, formed of a battalion of infantry and a squadron of Hussars, accompanied us. We marched the whole of the night, and at daybreak arrived at the village of Sant' Agatha. The people—a population of savages in human form—were waiting for us. As our *cortége* approached, we were received with the most horrible howlings, and with a shower of stones. However, we were safely taken to the gendarmerie barracks. Some of my companions and I were so ill that we sank helplessly on the ground, and could not move for hours. Thus we passed the day, thinking of the fifteen miles we had to perform before reaching our destination, and feeling as if existence itself were a weary and feverish dream. At night we started again, with the same escort of cavalry and infantry. The officer who commanded the latter was a Count Ruiz, a noble-minded man; and we soon looked upon him as our best friend. Captain Ruiz told us that at midnight we should pass through the camp of the Garigliano, a military position which defends the road leading to the Abruzzi, and at which 12,000 Neapolitan troops had been posted, to check the advancing march of the Piedmontese. At this announcement, new dangers rose before us; for we did not know how far we might be in peril from the ferocity of our fresh enemies. About midnight, a sudden turning of the road revealed to us the bivouac fires of the Neapolitan army. The night was dark, the country flat; and the outline of the distant mountains extended itself on our right. Near at hand, enormous fires had been

made, which cast a vivid glare over the surrounding
objects.   Here and there, groups of soldiers, wrapped
in their large white cloaks, could be seen moving
about the camp.   The shining helmets of the Dragoons, the picturesque caps of the Lancers, and the
shakos of the infantry, stood out distinct and full in
the red glimmer of the flames ; and the steady tread
of feet, varied occasionally by the deep but quiet
utterance of the watchword, added to the solemnity
of that wild and striking scene.

Our *cortége* having come in sight, a loud cry of " The
Garibaldian prisoners ! the Garibaldian prisoners !"
was suddenly heard from one end of the camp to the
other, accompanied by dreadful execrations.   The
soldiers left their bivouac fires to meet us, and some of
them brandished the burning stakes about our heads.
We all thought our last hour had come, and that we
were going to be burnt alive.

" Let us die like Christians !" exclaimed one of our
companions, the chaplain of a Milanese battalion, who
had been taken prisoner at Castel Morone ; and he
began to sing aloud the prayers for the dying.   The
pious summons of the minister of God was answered
with the unanimous cry, " Yes, let us die like Christians, and like the soldiers of liberty !   Long live
Italy ! Long live Garibaldi !"

But Captain Ruiz had promised to protect us, and
he nobly kept his word.   Charging right and left, he
kept in check the infuriated soldiery, and ordered the
drivers of the carts to proceed faster.   A quarter of
an hour afterwards, we had passed the camp, and were
delivered out of the hands of our bloodthirsty foes.

At daybreak we came in sight of Gaeta, and entered the gate of the castle, upon which we seemed to read the famous verse of Dante :—

Lasciate ogni speranza, voi ch'entrate.
(All hope abandon, ye who enter here.)

We were then desired to leave the carts in which we had been conveyed, and the commanding officer handed us over to our gaoler, having first counted us, as if we had been a herd of sheep. The iron gate was closed, and we were pent up in a low, dirty den, not dissimilar to those I have already described, and which have been so graphically portrayed by Lord Llanover in his well-known letters. As for us officers— for my companions and I were considered as officers of Garibaldi, and were treated accordingly—we were shown into a square, ill-ventilated room, without furniture, and so damp that the walls were green and mouldy. The stench, moreover, was dreadful. All the indignation of a man who thinks himself wronged found expression on my lips, and I strongly inveighed against the barbarity of locking us up in so filthy a place. My boldness gave courage to my companions, and we all protested. Don Antonio—for such was the name of the aged sergeant who fulfilled the duty of gaoler—coolly rubbed his hands, took his handkerchief out of his pocket, wiped his mouth, and, producing his snuff-box, offered me a pinch, saying, " I have no better room to offer you, Signorini ; but I am sure you will find yourselves comfortable when Tobia has brought some straw mattresses."

We insisted, however, on seeing the superior officer

T 2

in charge of the castle.   The lieutenant, in whose
custody we were placed, was accordingly sent for, and
two more decent rooms were found.   We were twenty-
four in number ; but, on arriving at the new rooms,
we discovered six others—Garibaldian officers who had
been made prisoners at Cajazzo.   All our furniture
consisted of a rough table, and a mattress stuffed with
old and half-rotten straw.   Don Antonio told us that
the King allowed us thirty *grani* * a-day, upon which
we were obliged to subsist.   Tobia was also presented
to us, as the steward of the prison, together with two
galley-slaves, who were to perform the menial duty of
assistants.   In those rooms, scarcely large enough
to accommodate four persons, Field-Marshal Viale,
the governor of the castle, had decided that we should
be confined—to sleep, to cook, to eat—in a word, to
live.

In these days, prisoners of war are so well treated
that, except for the loss of their liberty, they may bear
their fate without complaint.   But the Neapolitan
Government, in this as in many other respects, refused
to adopt the principles of modern civilization. Not only
were we treated like galley-slaves, and deprived of all
physical comforts, but even books were denied us. We
were obliged to cook our own dinners by turns, and to
make what Don Antonio and Tobia called our beds.
The amount of water at our disposal was but scanty,
and in a few days the state of the prison became
almost intolerable.   Such was the stench, such the
suffocating heat, that continuous sleep was out of

* A *grano* is four-tenths of a penny.

the question, and the torment of gnats and of other insects was so great that, on rising from our couches, we found ourselves reduced to a miserable condition. Had we been in possession of money, we could have bribed the gaolers and turnkeys; but his Sicilian Majesty's soldiers had taken good care to relieve us of the trouble of keeping accounts and dispensing cash.

One evening, as I was walking up and down, Don Antonio, who called me "il Signor Inglese," came into the room, and requested me to follow him on to the platform of the castle. I did so, and he then abruptly said :—

"I am really pained, sir, to see you in such a condition, and am willing to do something for you."

"Thanks," answered I, believing that Don Antonio was a good man, who really meant what he said; "but in what way can you help me?"

"Well, sir," pursued the gaoler, "there is the English Vice-Consul here; he has asked about you, and I have no doubt he will be disposed to lend you some money. Money, sir, is an indispensable article in places like this, and with a well-filled purse I can procure you a great many things, such as good wine, fruit, and even paper to write on, if you like."

I saw at once that all Don Antonio wanted was to get money out of my pocket, in case I should be able to borrow some; and I therefore declined the offer, saying that, as I was unknown to the Vice-Consul, he would in all probability object to become my banker. This reply must have given Don Antonio a very poor idea of my resources. From that day, he took no further notice of me, and his pretended kindness was lavished entirely upon a Garibaldian lieutenant, who, having been fortunate enough to conceal his money in his boots, had saved it from the rapacious hands of the soldiery.

A few days afterwards, when eight new prisoners came in, we were removed to the upper story of the castle, and confined in a sort of casemate, which in 1849 had been the place of durance of two Neapolitan officers, Signor Delle Francie and Signor Longo, who fought on the side of the insurgents in Sicily. It was a spacious gallery, commanding a view of the sea on the right side of the famous hill called Torre d'Orlando. We were locked up all day, except for half an hour after dinner, during which we were allowed to promenade on the terrace of the castle. As for our living, full ten of the thirty *grani* granted by his Majesty were absorbed by Tobia, and by the two convicts —one of whom had murdered his intimate friend— who were charged to buy our provisions. But what was this compared with the condition of the poor soldiers of Garibaldi? They were obliged to live upon five *grani*, were confined in a horribly close dungeon, and were compelled to sleep on a bed of rotten straw, which had been already used by all the prisoners for two or three months before. The consequence was that half the men were taken ill the day following their arrival, and in two days more they were nearly starved. On our remonstrating, General Viale answered that he could do nothing, as he knew that food and straw were wanting in the place—an assertion which, at the fall of Gaeta, proved to be

totally false. Such was the condition in which prisoners
of war were kept by Francis II.; such was the treatment of soldiers and officers who had always been
kind to the Neapolitan prisoners taken in Sicily and
Calabria.

On my arrival at Gaeta, I again protested against
my imprisonment. I said to General Viale that I had
been taken as a simple spectator; that I did not hold
any commission in Garibaldi's army; and that I was
an English subject—in consideration of which I asked
to be allowed to write to the representative of Queen
Victoria at Naples. General Viale and General Ferrari seemed to admit that I could only be regarded
as a tourist, and even the King, to whom they
applied, took the same view of the case; but by the
Ministers, who were then consulted, the point was
decided against me—mainly on the suggestion of Don
Antonio Ulloa, the Minister of the Interior. I was
told, however, that I could write to Mr. Elliot, and I
did so; but, as I discovered on my subsequent arrival
at Naples, my letter, and those I had addressed to my
friends, Mr. Percy French and Mr. Conyngham, had
never been forwarded.

One morning—it was the 7th of October—as I was
standing at my window, enjoying the bright sunshine
and the merry notes of the birds singing in the trees
planted about the batteries, I was suddenly taken ill,
and fell senseless on the pavement of the prison. The
doctor was sent for, and at once declared that the
scanty prison allowance was not enough to support
me. One of my companions—the lieutenant who had
saved his money—came to my help, and asked to be

allowed to buy for me more substantial food.   This
excellent man was a baker from Bologna, named Paggi,
who had left his family as a volunteer, and had risen
to the rank of lieutenant, owing to the courage he
had shown in the action of the 19th, and at the affair
of Cajazzo.

Next day I was attacked by fever.   My illness
seemed to increase my courage, and I asked to be
brought into the presence of General Viale.   Following his advice, I wrote a statement of my case, which
he promised to present to the King, giving me at the
same time some hope of a speedy deliverance.   Nevertheless, my deliverance did not come, and my days
passed more wearily than ever, now that I had to bear
the additional burden of sickness and fever.   I began,
moreover, to find that I was the subject of some
strange and contradictory reports.   From the convicts
who served us, I learned that I was suspected of being
a Muratist agent; and a fellow-prisoner of mine told
me that he had heard a Neapolitan captain say that I
had been sent to Garibaldi by Lord Palmerston, to
persuade the Dictator to cede Sicily to England.
Knowing with what a stupid Government I had to
deal, these absurd suspicions (which under other circumstances would have made me laugh) were not calculated to dispel my fears that Francis II. and his
Ministers would bring me before a court-martial,
have me summarily judged, and get rid of me as
Ferdinand II. got rid of the unfortunate brothers
Bandiera.

Two days after the interview I had had with General
Viale, I was suddenly summoned to his presence.

Although ill, I went down, and, on entering the General's room, he handed to me a *Journal des Débats*, in which my name was mentioned together with that of the Hon. Evelyn Ashley. The General told me, in an angry voice, that the letter in the French paper plainly proved that I had led the soldiers of Garibaldi on the 19th of September, and that I had better admit at once that I had been sent on a secret mission to Garibaldi by the English Government.

" How can you believe for a moment," said I, " that Lord Palmerston would send a foreigner on so delicate an errand ?"

" Oh, we have proofs of the intrigues of the noble Lord," replied General Viale ; " and we believe that your presence on the battle-field of the 19th, with his Lordship's relative and secretary, was by no means accidental, as you pretend."

It was of no avail for me to point out that the letter in the *Journal des Débats* was anonymous, and that the only thing I had done on the 19th was to stop the *carrozzelle* sent to take away the wounded. General Viale continually repeated that I was an agent of the English Government, and that I should be treated accordingly. Seeing that reasoning powers had not been granted to the General, I once more protested against my captivity, and told him that I had a firm faith in my adopted Government, which would make the dignity of the British nation respected in my case, as it had done in the case of the *Cagliari*.

" Well, we shall see," answered General Viale, dismissing me from his presence. " The English Government is in the habit of bullying everybody ; but

in your case it will not have time to do so, I assure
you."

The reader may easily imagine the state of my
mind after I returned to prison. Absorbed by grief,
and utterly depressed in body and mind, I nevertheless
summoned up all my courage to meet with dignity
the fate which seemed to await me. The ensuing
day, however, passed without any new incident, and
my good friend, Paggi, urged me to look forward to a
speedy release from captivity. His words were so reassuring that hope was suddenly revived within me.
I rose from my bed, and wrote some letters to my
friends in England, which, by means of a piastre given
by Paggi to Don Antonio, were forwarded to the
General for transmission; and, having thus done all I
could to secure my safety, I rested with a greater
degree of tranquillity than I had felt for some days.

On the following Friday, I was summoned anew to
the presence of the General, where, for the first time,
I met a Signor Materasso, the English Consular
Agent at Gaeta. This gentleman had not been idle.
On hearing that an English subject was amongst the
prisoners, he sent word to Mr. Elliot, who did all
he could to get me released. Although it had been
already decided at Gaeta that I should be sent to
Trieste, and handed over to the Austrian authorities,
the kind interference of Lord John Russell and Mr.
Elliot prevented the Neapolitan Government putting
this project into execution; and there is no doubt that
I owed to them my deliverance after the lapse of two
weeks. I was not without aid from other quarters,
however; for, immediately on hearing of my misfor-

tune, Garibaldi sent a *parlementaire* to General Rettucci, asking him if he were disposed to exchange me with two Neapolitan colonels captured on the 2nd of October at Maddaloni. The King declined, and it was then that the action of the English Government began. On the arrival of Mr. Elliot's despatch, a council of Ministers was summoned to consider my case (a circumstance which I cannot but regard as a great honour for a humble newspaper correspondent), and it was at once decided to grant my liberation.

After conveying to me this news, General Viale handed me over to the English Consular agent, to whom he delivered a despatch addressed to Mr. Elliot, in which, as I was told, there was an autograph letter of Francis II. to the Queen of England. As soon as I was dismissed from the presence of the General, I returned to the castle, to impart the consolation of a free man to those who still remained in prison. My companions had all some commission to give me, and all wanted to be remembered to Garibaldi. It was a sad interview; but at last I left the castle, and went with Signor Materasso to see the Minister Ulloa, who was to furnish me with the necessary pass to get out of the fortress. This individual—once a Liberal—was at that time the most influential counsellor of Francis II., and felt the greatest animosity against England. He had taken it into his head that, on the 1st of October, Rear-Admiral Mundy, on hearing that artillerymen were wanted at Garibaldi's camp, had sent a party of " blue-jackets" to assist the Italian patriots.

" Sir," he said to me, " this is no less than an

armed interference——a breach of neutrality—and we have already denounced it to Europe."

Signor Materasso hastened to say that he knew how the affair had happened, and explained to the Minister (as I have already explained to the reader in a previous chapter) that some sailors of the *Renown*, being on leave at Santa Maria, had helped the Garibaldians to mount a gun. But Ulloa, apparently not satisfied with this account, still persisted in denouncing " la perfide Albion." For my part, I had only one object in view——namely, to secure the pass. This, however, was refused by the Minister, and I should in all probability have remained at Gaeta for many days, had it not been for the kindness of Count Perponcher, the Prussian Minister at the Court of Francis II., who smoothed matters, and enabled me to get out of the fortress, and go to Borgo di Gaeta, where Signor Materasso lived. In the house of this gentleman I was treated in the kindest manner. Signor Bonomi, the chemist of the *borgo*, was sent for, and I was attended to as if I had been one of the family. On the morning of the 14th of October, the French man-of-war, *La Mouette*, came into harbour. Signor Materasso asked the captain to take me to Naples, which he consented to do ; and on the evening of that day I had the inexpressible pleasure of making my appearance at Garibaldi's headquarters, where I was greeted by my friends as one risen from the tomb.

Here I must stop. I have already written too much about my personal adventures ; but, before proceeding to more important events, the reader must allow me to make an observation. Perhaps there may be some who will think it strange that I, an Italian, should have renounced my nationality, and made myself a British subject. Had I been born in any province of Italy ruled by one of those Princes who, wrongly or rightly, were called national, I should never have asked to become the citizen of another country. But, when I emigrated to England, I was an Austrian subject, and in exchanging the citizenship of the foreign oppressors of my country for that of free and liberal England, I thought I could do so without repudiating my character as an Italian. When Venetia is united to the Italian kingdom — and let us hope, for the future peace of Europe, that that day is not far distant—I shall become *de facto* the subject of Victor Emmanuel, without, however, forgetting the generous hospitality which England has extended to me, and to many of my fellow-sufferers, in her classic land of liberty.

I may now resume my narrative of Garibaldi's campaign.

The battle on the Volturno, and the advance of Victor Emmanuel's army on the Garigliano, had irretrievably decided the fate of Southern Italy, and of the Bourbonic dynasty. The first had been gained by the valour of the Italian volunteers, without any help from the Sardinian regular forces ; the second seemed rather a triumphal progress than a contest between two fighting armies. The success of the Piedmontese in Umbria and the Marches enabled Victor Emmanuel on the 4th of October to issue the following proclamation, which was to be considered as his Majesty's manifesto with respect to farther operations in Southern Italy :—

"SOLDIERS !—I am satisfied with you, because you are worthy of Italy. By arms you have vanquished your enemies, and, by conduct, the calumniators of the Italian name.

"The mercenaries whom I set free will speak of you in foreign countries, after having learnt that God recompenses those who serve him, and not those who oppress peoples and despise the rights of nations.

"We must establish a strong Italian monarchy on the liberty of the people, who will aid us with order and concord. The National army will increase more and more the glory which during eight centuries has shone on the Cross of Savoy.

"Soldiers ! I take the command. It would cost me too much not to be foremost wherever there may be danger."

On the 11th of October, the future King of Italy first set foot on Neapolitan territory, and on the previous day the Dictator—nay, the conqueror—of the Two Sicilies kept his word by calling the people of Southern Italy to vote, by universal suffrage, on the 21st of that month, for or against the annexation of Naples and Sicily to the Northern Kingdom. At the same time, he thus announced the crossing of the frontier by the Italian army—an event which, in his mind, ought to have dispelled all party dissensions :—

"TO THE CITIZENS OF NAPLES.—To-morrow, Victor Emmanuel, King of Italy, the elect of the nation, will break down the frontier which has divided us for so many centuries from the rest of our country, and, listening to the unanimous voice of this brave people, will appear among us.

" Let us worthily receive the sent of Providence, and scatter in his path, as the pledge of our redemption and our affection, the flowers of concord—to him so grateful, to us so necessary.

" No more political colours, no more parties, no more discords ! Italy one (as the people of this metropolis wisely determine), and the King Galantuomo, are the eternal symbols of our regeneration, and of the grandeur and prosperity of the country.

" G. GARIBALDI."

The position of the Neapolitan army had now become desperate. Kept in check by Garibaldi on the Volturno, and assailed in his rear by the Piedmontese, Francis II. could only concentrate his scattered forces on the Garigliano, and, leaning on Gaeta, try a last effort, if not to save his kingdom, at least to retrieve the honour of his demoralized troops. To secure this result, he set vigorously to work, and to a certain extent succeeded, by maintaining himself as long as he could in his last stronghold. The Commander-in-Chief of the Neapolitan army ordered the main body to retire from Capua, leaving in that fortress a garrison of 12,000 men, to prevent, if possible, the junction of the Garibaldians with the Sardinians. But it was easy to foresee that this attempt would be a failure, and the progress of events proved once more the inequality of the contending armies.

A few days after my return to Garibaldi's head-
quarters, the Sardinian Royal Brigade came up from
Naples, and occupied the position of Casa Bruciata,
which, on the 1st of October, had been valiantly defended by Dunne's brigade. The English regiment,
commanded by Colonel Peard, was also sent to the
outposts towards the right, where it was attacked in
great force by the Neapolitans. The Colonel placed
one company in support of the battery in the centre
of the position, and pushed forward another to occupy
a farmhouse in the front; at the same time sending
out two to the left, and two to support the advanced
body from the first battalion. Hearing a smart fire
in front, he went in person to the farm where the
tenth was posted, and, ordering up three more from
the second battalion, advanced two companies *in
catena.*

The fire continuing heavy, and the Bersaglieri on
the hill appearing pressed, Peard ordered the second *in
catena* to support them, and advanced two companies
to occupy the line which the tenth and seventh had
held.

The gallant Colonel went forward with his troops,
accompanied by Lord Seymour. The men advanced
in admirable order, and opened fire with great precision. At this time, Peard had to deplore the loss
of Mr. Tucker, the interpreter of the brigade, who
fell in advance of the line of skirmishers. The enemy
being in great force, Peard ordered his adjutant to
return, and procure reinforcements; and Nos. 4 and 5
were brought up to the front. The fire was exces-
sively severe; but, united to the Bersaglieri, the

British Legion was enabled, not only to resist, but to drive back the Neapolitans within their lines, with great loss. The brigade had two killed and eight wounded, without mentioning contusions. All the men, however, though raw levies, totally unaccustomed to stand fire, behaved with conspicuous gallantry, and retired with all the steadiness of veterans.

This was the only action in which the British Legion was engaged during Garibaldi's campaign in Southern Italy. It were greatly to be wished that the conduct of these Englishmen had been in all respects equal to their courage in action; but I am sorry to say that in some instances, and especially at Santa Maria, the men behaved badly—so much so that Garibaldi himself, although a great admirer of the British nation, is reported to have said that, if he could succeed in getting rid of the English volunteers, he would never have them again. .

While the Sardinians were advancing, and while skirmishes were daily occurring on the Volturno, a reactionary movement suddenly broke out at Isernia. Garibaldi instantaneously despatched to that mountainous district Colonel Nullo, Major Caldesi, and Captain Mario, with 800 men. The attempt to crush the demonstration, however, failed for a time. Attacked by a large body of Neapolitans, and hunted by the armed peasantry, the Garibaldians were partly massacred, partly dispersed. It was on that occasion that a young volunteer from Mantua, Pilade Mori, having fallen into the hands of the Bourbonic peasantry, was burnt alive in the square of Isernia. The soldier attending Major Caldesi was destined to a no less agonizing death; for his limbs were torn from his body, cut into pieces, and divided among the savage supporters of Francis II. Caldesi himself was frequently in imminent danger of being taken and killed; and he and a companion of his, named Mingoni, owed their lives to the speed of their horses. It was the last effort of Bourbonic reaction at that time; for the Piedmontese were fast advancing towards the Garigliano. A Sardinian division, under General de Sonnaz, landed at Manfredonia on the 14th of October, and marched on Maddaloni, while at the same time the main body of the Sardinian army, divided into two columns, was pushing on from the Abruzzi towards Capua, despite the opposition of the Neapolitan Generals, Scotti and Klepi de la Grange. Beaten at Macerone by Cialdini, and thwarted in their attempt to contend the pass of the mountains which slope down towards the plain of the Garigliano, the Neapolitans were compelled to fall back on Gaeta, and place that river between them and the advancing columns of the Sardinians.

On the 25th of October, General Salzano went to see Cialdini, in order to negotiate an armistice. Cialdini had been ordered by Victor Emmanuel to explain to Salzano how hopeless was the position of the Neapolitan army, and how far better it would be to come to an honourable arrangement. Salzano, however, declared that the troops of his Royal master were determined to fight as long as there was a battalion left; and he then went back to his headquarters at Sessa. In the meanwhile, Garibaldi, who had concentrated at Calvi the whole of the forces he had brought from Sant' Angelo two days before, sent Colonel Missori to convey his respects to Victor Emmanuel at Teano, and inform him of his arrival. The King received Missori most affectionately, and complimented him on his gallant exploits at Melazzo. Victor Emmanuel, who was surrounded by his Staff, evinced great interest in the army of Garibaldi, and asked Missori several questions about its organization. He then questioned the young officer as to how many Garibaldians, under Colonel Nullo and Major Caldesi, had returned to the camp from the Abruzzi expedition. On hearing that, out of 800 who had started from Caserta, only half had come back, the King told Missori that they had been mostly massacred by the armed peasantry of the country. "I have the official proofs in my possession," added his Majesty, "that at Isernia even the women subjected those poor young fellows to the most cruel tortures. One of them was burnt to death; three others were mutilated in the most horrible manner." Here his Majesty mentioned details inexpressibly shocking.

It was agreed that the King should meet Garibaldi next day at the foot of a hill called Santa Maria della Croce, and that he should review Eber's brigade and Bixio's division, which had followed the Dictator. At eight o'clock on Friday morning, accordingly, our soldiers were drawn up in good order, and, although in rags, did not make a bad show. When the King made his appearance, followed by his Staff, Garibaldi advanced to meet him. It was a singular sight. The elegant and splendid uniforms of the Piedmontese officers contrasted with the coarse garb of the Garibal-

dians.   The General himself wore his wide-awake, a
plain red flannel shirt, half covered by his American
grey cloak, and a pair of black trousers.   At his side
hung his famous English sword, which had done such
service at Calatafimi and Melazzo——a sword worth all
the embroidered uniforms in the world.

The two great leaders of Italian unity cordially
shook hands, and I could see by their faces that that
action was the expression of a true sentiment of
affection on Garibaldi's part, and of the greatest
admiration on the part of the King.   The respective Staffs halted at a little distance, and listened in
breathless expectation for the conversation of those
warriors.   The King complimented the General by
saying that without his daring expedition the unity
of Italy would not have been a reality for ten years
to come.   "It may be, Sire," answered Garibaldi;
"but I could not have attempted my expedition had not
Victor Emmanuel been the most noble and generous
of Kings."

When the King and Garibaldi appeared in front of
the patriot columns, the enthusiastic cries of 12,000
men saluted them.   It was touching to see those
ragged fellows forget the miseries of a harassing campaign in greeting the two men who personified the
cause of their country.   Victor Emmanuel seemed to
be extremely gratified with his reception; and when
the soldiers cried out, "Long live the King of Italy!"
he never failed to answer, "Long live Garibaldi!
Long live his army!"

The review being over, Garibaldi and Victor Emmanuel rode together towards Bellona, the two Staffs

following them at a distance of twenty yards. The King had decided to go and inspect the positions of Sant' Angelo and Cajazzo, and to have a near view of Capua; and Garibaldi accompanied him as far as Carmigliano, a ride of nearly an hour. They talked freely on the situation of the country, and Garibaldi did not lose the opportunity of defending the policy he had followed after his arrival at Naples. On parting from Victor Emmanuel, the Dictator said to one of his Generals, " I did not shrink from telling the King that he is surrounded by a set of men who are not the warmest friends of Italy. I tried to persuade him that what has been said about the influence which Mazzini and his friends exercised over me is a mere calumny. ' How could I have insisted upon sending Mazzini into exile, when he has done so much for Italian unity?' said I to Victor Emmanuel; and his Majesty agreed that I was right."

At this meeting, it was agreed that Garibaldi's army should return to Sant' Angelo and besiege Capua, as the King had troops enough to offer battle to the Neapolitans on the right bank of the Garigliano. This order gave some offence to the Garibaldians, who felt that injustice was done them. "Why," said the soldiers, " it seems as if the Piedmontese were ashamed of us; as if they did not want to associate with us. It is true we are not so handsomely clothed as they are; but we have fought hard for six months, and as gallantly as they did." The Garibaldians may perhaps have misinterpreted the meaning of the King; but in my opinion it would have been better to have had the two Garibaldian divisions on the Garigliano, so that they might have fought by the side of the Royal army, instead of sending them back to besiege the fortress of Capua.

The subsequent military operations of the Piedmontese army on the plains of Garigliano were one continuous victory. The numerous earthworks which the Neapolitans had thrown up all round the remains of the Roman amphitheatre, marking the site of the ancient city of Minturnæ, were easily stormed by the far-famed Bersaglieri; the Garigliano was crossed, and the main body of Francis II.'s army was driven back to Gaeta, in spite of the threats of the French Admiral then stationed in the Gulf. Barbier de Tinan not only refused to recognise the blockade officially notified by Sardinia, but went so far as to tell the Sardinian Admiral, Persano, that he would open fire against his ships if he attacked the rear of the Neapolitan army, then in full retreat on Mola di Gaeta. In this respect, however, the French officer exceeded his instructions, and was told so by his Government. Persano, who is now at the head of the Italian Admiralty, received this insolent intimation with a dignified composure, answering that even if the French fleet fired upon his vessels he would remain passive, and not repel the attack. He did not, however, suffer himself to be deterred from his duty by the menaces of Barbier de Tinan. When the hour of action came, the Marquis Persano shelled the retiring forces of the Neapolitans, and was not hindered by the French.

The success of Cialdini and Fanti on the Garigliano brought to a close the resistance of the garrison of Capua; and that town, having been bombarded by

General Morozzo della Rocca for forty-eight hours, capitulated on the 2nd of November. It was at six o'clock A.M., on the 1st, that the Sardinian batteries of Carditello and Sant' Angelo opened fire against the fortress; and Victor Emmanuel himself came up from Sessa to witness the bombardment.

On that morning, as I was standing at the door of General della Rocca's head-quarters, with Captain Keith Fraser (who since my deliverance from Gaeta had been my constant companion in following Garibaldi's operations), a carriage drove into the yard of the house. What was our surprise on seeing the Marquis of Downshire, with the whole of his family, who had arrived at Santa Maria in order to view the battle-field of the Volturno! Although both the Marchioness and her daughter were of the party, it was arranged that we should take our unexpected visitors to the front, and to our batteries at Sant' Angelo. We therefore started for the last-named place, together with Captain Farquhar, of her Majesty's ship *Hannibal*, and Major Earl. Ascending the steep hill of Sant' Angelo, we directed our steps towards the mountains of Tifata; but the Neapolitan gunners of Capua, getting sight of our party, began to throw shells in our direction. The incident was rather unpleasant, considering that we had two ladies with us; but their courage did not fail them, and happily no accident occurred.

On returning to Santa Maria, we witnessed the first shells thrown from the battery of Carditello into the fortress. Victor Emmanuel had arrived by this time, and the work of destruction began on both sides. When the fire was opened from our batteries, the expression of the King's face betrayed the pain he felt at seeing an Italian city fired on by Italian guns. "This is a sad scene," said he to General della Rocca; "it breaks my heart to think that we are sending death and destruction into an Italian town. Let us trust that the cries of those helpless inhabitants will induce General de Cornet to surrender."

The hope expressed by the King was to be accomplished sooner than we anticipated; for two days had barèly elapsed ere we were enabled to make our entry into Capua, which yielded almost without conditions.

It was a month since I had been escorted into that town as a prisoner, walking through its streets amid the threats of an infuriated crowd. On the 3rd of November, I entered it with the Staff of the conqueror. The very mob which wanted to murder me and my Garibaldian companions on the 1st of October was then shouting out, "Long live our liberators!" The very barber who would have cut my throat, had it not been for the Neapolitan officer of the escort, was foremost amongst those enthusiastic bystanders. Having been recognised by some Garibaldians, the ruffian received such a lesson as, I have no doubt, will teach him moderation for the rest of his days. I was passing through the principal street of the town, when I fell in with the Neapolitan captain who had been the commander of our guard whilst in the citadel. He had become the staunchest of patriots since the capitulation of the city, though a few weeks before I had heard him call Garibaldi a brigand, and Victor Emmanuel a scoundrel.

"Holloa, captain!" said I, stopping my horse, "I

am glad to see that you have changed your opinions, and that you are in a fair way of becoming a good Italian patriot."

"Changed my opinions!" echoed he, turning pale. "I can assure you that in my heart I was even then a good patriot ; only that——"

"Yes," interrupted I, "you were then afraid of expressing your sentiments, and are not so now. Is not that true?"

"Just so," answered he, "and I hope you will recommend me to the Sardinian General, who, I trust, will give me a commission as Major."

"They are almost all of the same debased stuff," observed one of General della Rocca's officers, who had listened to our short conversation. The remark was too true ; for this captain was but a type of the men with whom he associated, and of whose moral degradation he partook.

CHAPTER XI.

NAPLES UNDER THE NEW RULE.

The Dictatorial Authority draws to a close—Garibaldi's Opinion on the Pope—Meeting of the King and Garibaldi at Santa Maria—Victor Emmanuel's Entry into Naples—Which is the King?—Final Interview of Garibaldi with the King—Errors of the Garibaldians and of the Piedmontese Government—A Retrospect of the Political situation of Southern Italy—Garibaldi's Plan on entering Naples—His Antipathy to the French Emperor—Antagonism of Cavour—Garibaldi's Farewell to his Army—Last Hours of Garibaldi at Naples—Departure for Caprera—The new Court—Farini's Government—Its Difficulties—The Martyrs of Freedom—The Camorra—Anecdotes illustrating the Camorra—The Duke of Cajanello's Trial—Letter of Francis II.—Sir James Lacaita—Baron Poerio's Advice—An Economical Question—Condition of the Rural Population in Southern Italy—Suggested Remedies for Existing Evils.

POLITICAL affairs were about to enter a new phase in Southern Italy. The Plebiscite had already determined, by 1,303,064 votes to 10,312, that the Bourbons should cease for ever to be the rulers of a country they had so long misgoverned, and that the Neapolitan provinces should be annexed to the rest of free Italy. The task of Garibaldi was accomplished; his programme was faithfully fulfilled. Before, however, leaving the soil he had conquered, the General had a duty to perform—that of distributing the medals to the remainder of those thousand heroes who, six months before, had ventured with him on the daring exploit of delivering Sicily. In so doing, he did not forget the brave Hungarian Legion which hastened to join him on the first tidings of his victories. To those gallant warriors, Garibaldi gave the national colours at Naples on the 1st of November. The ceremony was surrounded with all the pomp which the feasts of liberty deserve. It will perhaps not be out of place to record here the speech made by the General on that occasion, for it conveys an idea of his opinions on a question of vast importance to Italy— the temporal power of the Pope. In transcribing this address, I shall make no comments of my own, further than to observe that the severe judgment passed by the conqueror of the Two Sicilies upon the Pope as a temporal sovereign is, in the minds of nine-tenths of Italians, justified both by past and contemporary events. The General spoke as follows:—

" This is a memorable day for us, for it cements the alliance of two nations, and establishes the fraternity of the people. To-day you have destroyed that principle of egotism which has kept the nations separated, and thus has facilitated the servitude of all. The people with whom you have fraternized to-day have the same enemies who threaten you. Your cause is theirs, and theirs is yours.

" But, before fighting against this external enemy, you have internal enemies to beat down ; and I will tell you that the chief of them is the Pope. If I have acquired any merit with you, it is that of telling you the truth frankly and without a veil. In using this privilege, 'I tell you that your chief enemy is the Pope.

"I am a Christian as you are; yes, I am of that religion which has broken the bonds of slavery, and has proclaimed the freedom of men. The Pope, who oppresses his subjects, and is an enemy of Italian independence, is no Christian; he denies the very principle of Christianity; he is Antichrist.

"This truth you must spread among those who are near to you; for it is only when all Italians shall be thoroughly convinced of the fact, that Italy will be really free and united."

On the 7th of November Victor Emmanuel made his solemn entry into Naples. The day was rainy, the air dark, and a damp southerly wind came from the sea towards the city, spreading gloom upon her fair bay, from Promontorium Minervæ to Cape Misenum. On that day I followed Garibaldi's Staff to Santa Maria, where the General was to meet the King, and enter the capital in his company. It was then that Garibaldi had to decide whether he would remain at Naples, or go back to his island of Caprera. The interview was of the most cordial kind. Neither Farini nor General Fanti was present; for the King knew that Garibaldi entertained an insurmountable antipathy to those two advisers of the Sardinian Crown.

Having arrived at the station, the King entered the Royal carriage, with Garibaldi at his left side, and the Marquis Pallavicini and Signor Mordini (the two Pro-Dictators of Southern Italy) in front. In spite of the rainy weather, an immense crowd thronged the streets, from the station of Capua to the Royal Palace. Enthusiastic shoutings, and the usual eccentric Neapolitan gesticulations, were the main features of that popular demonstration. A stranger, however, would probably have been induced to ask which of the two personages seated in that carriage was the King. Not that *evvivas* for the hero of Palestro were wanting; but those with which the Neapolitans greeted the name of Garibaldi—the man who, to their minds, had almost dethroned San Januarius—were undoubtedly more numerous. Had Victor Emmanuel been as proud and envious as many kings are, he would have had reason to regret entering Naples for the first time by the side of so popular a companion.

After the official reception at the Palace, Victor Emmanuel remained with Garibaldi to discuss the political condition of the country he had added to his dominions, and to try once more to persuade him to remain at Naples, and aid in the government of Southern Italy. Already, a few days before, Cialdini had had an interview with Garibaldi at Santa Maria, at which he tried to bring about a reconciliation between him and Count Cavour. The gallant General, however, did not succeed in his endeavour. Garibaldi asked that he should be appointed for three years Governor of Southern Italy, with almost dictatorial powers; that the decrees he had signed during his Dictatorship should be respected, in so far as they did not oppose the constitutional laws of the country; and that the rank conferred by him upon his companions in arms should be recognised by the new Government. The first of these demands was peremptorily refused,

and perhaps not without reason, on the plea that it
was altogether unconstitutional; the second and third,
the Ministers of the King were only disposed to grant
upon certain conditions.

In his interview with the King at the Royal Palace,
Garibaldi renewed his application, and could not be
persuaded to desist from it.   It is even stated that on
this occasion the General said to Victor Emmanuel,
" Get rid of Cavour, and allow me to march on Rome ;"
to which the King is reported to have answered, " I
will not get rid of my Premier, and you shall not go
to Rome."   Victor Emmanuel having himself failed
to bring about the reconciliation which he desired so
much, there remained nothing for Garibaldi but to
leave Naples.

We need not seek far for the causes which brought
about this split. Errors were unquestionably committed
on both sides ; but they were only the natural consequences of those angry feelings which actuated the
two parties.   Garibaldi and his advisers, on the one
hand, showed a systematic antipathy to the Ministers
of the King; but, on the other hand, it must be admitted that the latter had done all they could to
increase, nay, to justify, that unfriendly feeling. They
had sent, both to Sicily and Naples, the very men who
had always been considered by Garibaldi as his personal enemies.   They had not even spared the Liberator the humiliation of despatching to Sicily La Farina
—a man whom Garibaldi had previously banished
from Palermo. Nor was this all. To regulate the
future destinies of the Southern army, a Piedmontese
General was chosen, who had always been the greatest

adversary of the volunteers, and the bitterest foe of Garibaldi. These wrongs the advisers of Victor Emmanuel tried to justify on the ground that they were but the necessary results of the Dictator's mis-government, whose disastrous effects it was their duty to check by all the means at their disposal. I must in truth acknowledge that, both in the civil and military administration of the Dictator, gross errors, and even fatal faults, were committed. I have not hesitated to point them out elsewhere; and there were certain acts of Garibaldi's officials, especially as regards the squandering of public money, and the making of questionable military appointments, which cannot be defended even by the warmest admirers of the Dictator. But some degree of responsibility for these mistakes must fall upon the Piedmontese Ministers themselves. When Garibaldi entered Naples, they could have averted a great many evils, had they listened to the suggestion of the patriots who wanted to bring about an understanding between the two parties, and who proposed to the Ministers the name of a states-man who would have been accepted by Garibaldi. The better to explain how this might have been effected, I will here narrate an incident which occurred on the day of our entry into Naples.

On the arrival of Cavaliere Gallenga in the capital of Southern Italy, about four or five hours before Garibaldi's entry into the city—viz., in September, 1860—he (Gallenga) received a visit from Lord Llan-over, who had a letter of introduction to him. His Lordship asked Gallenga's opinion with respect to current events; and the latter, thinking he had gained a sufficient insight into the state of parties at Naples, communicated his views very freely to his Lordship. At that time, as I have said before, the " Party of Order " and the " Party of Action" were struggling for mastery over the mind of Garibaldi; and, from what Gallenga had seen at Lagonegro, Auletta, Eboli, and Salerno, he readily and correctly inferred that Bertani and his friends had got the upper hand. Dr. Tommasi and Professor Piria, it will be recollected, had been received with little favour by the General at Sala, in spite of his personal friendship for them; and Garibaldi, who was far from apprehending the check he was soon to suffer at Capua, talked very confidently about leaving Gaeta on his left, and marching straight from Naples to Rome. He was sure the French Emperor had a " tail of straw" (*una coda di paglia*)— an expression from which it was apparent that the hero, still flushed with his wonderful and somewhat too easy success, had again given himself up to those sanguine notions with which Mazzini had so blindly and obstinately deluded himself in 1849—viz., that any liberal movement on a large scale would induce the French nation, and especially that Republican opposition which was crushed by the *coup d'état*, to declare themselves against the Emperor Napoleon, overthrow his government, and espouse the cause of freedom all over the world. Under these circumstances, Cavaliere Gallenga foresaw that the rule of Garibaldi at Naples would be neither more nor less than that of Bertani; and although the Dictator, on the very day of his arrival, endeavoured to bring the Party of Order and the Party of Action to a compromise, and to make peace between them—going even so far as to constitute a Ministry mostly belonging to the former party—still, it soon became apparent that the Ministry had no real power, and that the actual sovereign of Naples was the Secretary of State, Bertani. Fully convinced that Garibaldi, with all the cares of an unfinished war on his hands, had no leisure to bestow a thought on the civil government of Naples, and that, even if he had had the time, he had not the practical ability for so arduous a task, Gallenga thought it highly desirable that some one enjoying the confidence of the King and of Count Cavour should be sent from Turin to administer the affairs of the distracted southern kingdom. As, however, Gallenga perceived that Garibaldi was almost the idol of Naples, it seemed to him a necessity that the men commissioned to rule the country in the King's name should be acceptable to the Liberator. Everybody was well aware at the time that Cavour, Farini, Minghetti, La Farina, Fanti, and all the men who had given their vote for the detested cession of Nice, were looked upon by Garibaldi with feelings little short of abhorrence. Gallenga had heard enough in Garibaldi's camp to feel sure that the General entertained a deep-rooted, though erroneous, conviction that Cavour had done all in his power, either to prevent or frustrate at its outset the expedition to the South, and even to cause it to miscarry after it had met with the astonishing successes of Calatafimi and Palermo. Any man coming to take the reins of government at Naples in Cavour's name, especially if he were a known friend of the Premier, ran the risk of being received as an

enemy by Garibaldi, who was persuaded by his pre-
judiced advisers that Cavour meant to reap all the
benefit of an enterprise which he had done his utmost
to oppose.

After laying before Lord Llanover the state of
affairs as he saw it, Gallenga told his visitor that the
only wise measure, in his opinion, would have been
for the King's Government to send a neutral person to
Naples : some one who might seem to be commissioned
by the King himself, not by Cavour (as Garibaldi never
spoke of the King without feelings of the most enthusiastic loyalty)—some one who might even appear to
be on no very friendly terms with Cavour, who had
been in opposition to him on important matters, and
especially on that most delicate of subjects, the surrender of Italian territory to France.   Such a person,
Gallenga believed, was Rattazzi, who, together with
all " the Third Party," had abstained from voting on
the Savoy and Nice question, and who had been
ousted from power by Cavour, only a few months
previously.   Gallenga therefore suggested that Rattazzi, Capriolo, Berti, and their friends, should come
in the King's name to lend their aid to Garibaldi
in the serious task of carrying on the civil government ; for he believed that, if they obtained a warm
reception from Garibaldi, their popularity with the
Neapolitans would be at once assured, and they would
be enabled to counteract the Party of Action, which
had begun to create some uneasiness amongst the
thinking classes, both in the Southern Provinces and
throughout the Peninsula.

Lord Llanover seemed rather favourably impressed

with this suggestion, and said that he would talk
about it with Mr. Elliot, who would probably communicate with Sir James Hudson, through whom the
plan might reach Count Cavour.   I have myself reason
to believe that the Premier heard of Gallenga's proposal ; and that Rattazzi, to whom the same scheme
had been suggested from other quarters, would willingly
have undertaken the mission, had not Cavour (who,
misled by the Party of Order, mismanaged the
affairs of Naples) determined from the very outset to
crush the Party of Action.   He was so bent on this
design, that he would hear of no compromise ; and
when at last a statesman was sent to take from Garibaldi's hand the reins of the Neapolitan Government,
choice was made of Farini—a man, as I have before
remarked, whose antecedents had made him highly
distasteful to the Liberator.   To disoblige Garibaldi,
and induce him to quit Naples, was a very easy task ;
for that brave and good man is always ready to exhibit any amount of self-denial and self-sacrifice ; but
it was not equally easy to win the good-will of the
Neapolitans, whose best feelings were wounded by
having the most notorious enemies of their beloved
idol set to rule over them in succession.   This political mistake of Count Cavour we have not outlived
yet.   Had he at that time accepted the suggestion of Signor Gallenga, a great many misfortunes
might have been averted, and the question of Southern Italy would have been brought to a speedy
and satisfactory close.   But the great Italian statesman was led astray by the erroneous views of those
Neapolitan exiles who wanted to govern their native

provinces, though totally ignorant of the real wants of the South. Inflated with vanity, and full of antipathy to their political adversaries, they thought themselves able to govern the State, whilst they did but increase the difficulties by which the Government was already surrounded.

When Garibaldi became aware that the question at issue was a mere struggle for power, he could not do otherwise than oppose the entreaties of the King, and leave the country he had so heroically freed from its oppressors. This he did on the 9th of November, after bidding farewell to his companions-in-arms, in the stirring address here annexed :—

" We must consider the period which is just drawing to a conclusion as almost the last stage of our national resurrection, and must prepare ourselves to finish worthily the marvellous design of the Elect of twenty generations, the completion of which Providence has reserved for this fortunate age.

" Yes, young men ! Italy owes to you an undertaking which has merited the applause of the universe. You have conquered, and you will conquer still, because you are prepared for the tactics that decide the fate of battles. You are worthy of the men who pierced the serried ranks of a Macedonian phalanx, and who contended, not in vain, with the proud conquerors of Asia. To this wonderful page in our country's history, another more glorious still will be added, and the slave shall show at last to his free brethren a sharpened sword, forged from the links of his fetters. To arms, then, all of you ! all of you ! and the oppressors and the mighty will disappear like dust. You, too, women, cast away all cowards from your embraces ; they will give you only cowards for children ; and you, who are the daughters of the land of beauty, must bear children who are noble and brave. Let timid *doctrinaires* depart from among us, to carry their servility and their miserable fears elsewhere. This people is its own master. It wishes to be the brother of other people, but to look on the insolent with a proud glance : not to grovel before them, imploring its own freedom. It will no longer follow in the trail of men whose hearts are foul. No! no! no! Providence has presented Italy with Victor Emmanuel. Every Italian should rally round him. By the side of Victor Emmanuel every quarrel should be forgotten, all rancour should disappear. Once more I repeat my battle-cry :—' To arms, all—all of you !' If March, 1861, does not find 1,000,000 of Italians in arms, then alas for liberty, alas for the life of Italy ! Ah, no! far be from me a thought which I loathe like poison. March, 1861, or, if need be, February, will find us all at our posts—Italians of Calatafimi, Palermo, Ancona, Volturno, Castelfidardo, and Isernia ; and with us every man of this land who is not a coward or a slave. Let all of us, rallying round the glorious hero of Palestro, give the last blow to the crumbling edifice of tyranny. Receive, then, my gallant young volunteers, at the honoured conclusion of ten battles, one word of farewell from me. I utter that word with the deepest affection, and from the very bottom of my heart. To-day I am obliged to retire, but for a few days only. The hour of battle will find me with you again, by the side of the

champions of Italian liberty. Let those only return
to their homes who are called by the imperative
duties which they owe to their families, and those
who by their glorious wounds have deserved the gratitude of their country. These, indeed, will serve
Italy in their homes by their counsel, by the very
aspect of the noble wounds which adorn their noble
and youthful brows. Apart from these, let all others
remain to guard our glorious banners. We shall meet
again before long, to march together to the redemption
of our brethren who are still the slaves of the
stranger. We shall meet again before long, and
march together to new triumphs.

" G. GARIBALDI."

I shall never forget the last hour I passed at the
Hôtel d'Angleterre, where the man who had added to
the Italian crown 9,000,000 of people had taken up
his quarters since he had left the King. Missori,
Canzio, Stagnetti, Deideri, Basso, Caldesi, and a few
others of his officers, were with him—the faithful
companions of his bright day, the steadfast friends of
his hour of obscurity. The General had retired to
bed at his usual hour, and we agreed to pass the
night in the ante-room of his apartment, and there
await the day—the sad day of separation. At dawn
of the 9th, Garibaldi rose, and made his appearance in
the hall just at the moment when his private secretary, Captain Basso, was telling us that all the money
which the recent Dictator of the richest provinces of
Italy had at his disposal was thirty pounds, saved by
him (Basso), by the exercise of great economy, during
the campaign. When Garibaldi was informed of the

low state of his private treasury, he said with a smile :
—"Do not be anxious, Basso; we have at Caprera
plenty of wood and corn, which we will send to
Maddalena for sale."

Before leaving Naples, the General went on board
the *Hannibal*, to pay a last visit to his friend, Admiral
Mundy, whose guns rendered him the honours due to
a General.

"Look, Arrivabene!" exclaimed one of his officers,
as we set foot on the ladder of the *Hannibal*. "England is more just to the General than Italy is grateful !"

An hour afterwards, Garibaldi was on board the
Washington, which was to take him to Caprera. He
bade us farewell in his soft, clear voice, and turning
to Colonel Trecchi, handed him a despatch for the
King. It contained his resignation of the rank of
"Generale d'Armata" and of the Knighthood of the
Grand Collar of the Annunciation, which had been
conferred on him. A few minutes later, the *Washington* was steaming fast towards the distant rock which
forms the elbow of the Strait of Moneta—the solitary
rock of Caprera—carrying on board the man who, after
having conquered a kingdom, was leaving it as poor
as when he wandered in exile through the forests
of South America. In justice to the King, however,
I must not forget to state that Garibaldi was repeatedly offered rewards and distinctions, all of which
—with that lofty sense of honour and self-abnegation
which in him is carried almost to too great an extent
—he refused to accept.

The Royal Palace of Naples, so long the abode of

tyranny, had at last become the dwelling of a liberal Sovereign; its halls, which only three months before were involved in gloom, were now resounding with the joyful animation usually attending popular monarchs. Although the conflict of the opposing armies had not yet ceased under the walls of Gaeta, official receptions, gay parties, and popular festivals were constantly taking place in the Neapolitan metropolis. In the early days of his arrival, Victor Emmanuel willingly subjected himself to the tiresome ceremonials to which the deities of this lower world are condemned. The King, however, is not endowed by nature with those qualities which are almost necessary to a sovereign. Court etiquette and incessant official receptions do not agree with his rough and vigorous tastes. He is a sort of Nimrod, to whom the free air of the country, the hard chase across mountains and marshes, are indispensable. To the great popularity which surrounds him personally, and to his duty as Chief of the State, he may sacrifice his quiet, unobtrusive life for a week; but when the week is over, he must return to more congenial ways. This love of simple habits would increase the popularity of a northern prince, but cannot fail to have a contrary effect in a southern land. The Neapolitans are fond of amusement and all kinds of display, and like to see in their rulers the same predilections; consequently, Victor Emmanuel could not in the long run be a very popular King. "We admire him," they said, "because he is our 'Re galantuomo,' the champion of the national cause; but we should like him better were he to show himself more."

It may seem an exaggeration, but I firmly believe that one of the causes which just then quenched the enthusiasm evinced by the Neapolitans for their new Sovereign is to be found in the fact that, a few days after his arrival in the capital, he scarcely showed himself at all. It is true that since 1848 the Bourbonic princes were not much more prodigal of their presence; but the indifference with which they were looked upon by the Neapolitans testified to the ill effects of their reserved and distrustful manners. Ferdinand II. was hated and feared; and, where these sentiments follow the steps of monarchs, the less they appear in public the better. Such, however, was not the case with Victor Emmanuel, and he ought to have been more careful to keep up the popularity which surrounded him during the first days of his sojourn at Naples, by submitting to the exigencies of the situation. This he has wisely done during his recent visit.

On the departure of the King, the hard burden of the government fell upon Farini. Whether the fatigue he had undergone during the nine months when he ruled over the population of the Æmilia had exhausted him, or whether he had now a more difficult task to perform, the fact is that Farini's mission in Southern Italy turned out a complete failure. He chose for his advisers men who did not enjoy the confidence of the people; the very men who had obstinately opposed the hero of the day, the great warrior whose influence had increased in proportion to the wrongs which, according to the general opinion, had been inflicted upon him. It is certainly not my intention to underrate the diffi-

culties surrounding the newly-established National Government. They were undoubtedly great, and could
be traced to the Bourbon system of rule, which even
now clings to many of the departments. From the
highest class to the lowest, demoralization, in its most
hideous forms, had struck its roots into the very foun-
dations of society. Dignity and self-respect were not
to be found, as a rule, either among the aristocracy, or
in the classes lower down. With a few honourable
exceptions, the new rulers were surrounded by a host
of minor officials, who, from a vicious predisposition
or from habit, sold their connivance to those who,
having violated the laws, were willing and able to
pay for impunity. Under the former *régime*, bribery
had been practised to such a frightful extent that
almost every official could be bought. Even amongst
the most intimate attendants of Ferdinand II.
and his son, men were to be found who, for a
money consideration, would have obtained for the
persons they patronized—or, rather, who patronized
them — any concession of public works, any employment or pension, or who would have secured for
them impunity for the most lawless actions. When
a prisoner at Gaeta, I was told that a General, in
whom Ferdinand II. placed his entire confidence, had
a daughter who was charged with the execution of
these dishonest transactions. The moral standard,
indeed, was no higher amongst the greater number of
the Liberals. In that party, men like Poerio, Settembrini, Massari, Spaventa, Pace, Nicotera, Piria,
Stocco, Tommasi, and some others, were rather the exceptions than the rule. I remember that one day, under

Farini's lieutenancy, I was at the Palace, talking with Count Visconti-Venosta, when the porter came into the room, and said to him that a deputation from the "martyrs of freedom" was in the hall, and wanted to be presented to Farini.

"What do you mean by 'martyrs of freedom?'" asked my friend of the porter.

"Excellency," answered the man, "they are the patriots who were either imprisoned or persecuted under the Bourbons."

Visconti thought that the deputation merely wanted to pay its respects to Farini, and ordered that it should be ushered into the Governor-General's presence. This was soon done; and the deputies were received with all that courtesy which characterizes Farini when he is in good-humour.

"What can I do for you, gentlemen?" asked the Viceregent.

"The martyrs whose messengers we are," answered the martyr spokesman, "request places in the Government—every man a place; but a lucrative one, and without delay."

The Lieutenant of his Italian Majesty seemed to acknowledge the justice of their claims, supposing them to be true sufferers from political causes; and he therefore promised to take their case into consideration, but at the same time pleaded the difficulty of finding room for so many applicants, however deserving they might be.

Thereupon, as if all the martyrs living and dead, not only of the Kingdom of Naples, but of all Italy, were assembled in the room, there arose a chorus of voices, shouting, "Bread! Bread! We are all starving!"

Farini, though wondering how starving stomachs could support such excellent lungs, drew out a purse, half in pity, half in disgust, and flung it among the crowd of supplicants, saying :—

"If it is only bread you want, take this !"

I witnessed the incident from the door of the room; and it was revolting to see how the miserable wretches, changing at once from candidates for office into down-right beggars, clutched at the purse, tore it from each other's hands, and seized upon the few Napoleons it contained, squabbling and snatching, as if oblivious of the absent martyrs, who were probably as hungry as themselves, but who assuredly never had their share of Farini's liberality.

The reader must not think that the individuals who were the actors in this shameful episode were persons belonging to the riff-raff of society. On the contrary, they all belonged to the well-to-do classes, and were lawyers, physicians, and engineers, who, since the grant of a constitution by Francis II., had either returned from exile, or had been released from prison, or from the police *surveillance*.

To increase still more the difficulty of governing the country, Farini, and at a later period his successors, the Commendatore Nigra, Count San Martino, and General Cialdini, had to deal with a powerful and well-organized society, commonly known under the name of "the Camorra." This famous association, in spite of the strenuous exertions made by the present Government, has not as yet been extirpated; and some account of its constitution and objects may be acceptable. There is at Naples a class of ruffians, addicted traditionally to all descriptions of crime, and exercising, ever since the Spanish domination, an intolerable pressure on the population of the city and the neighbouring provinces, infusing its poisonous influence amongst the poorest classes of the community, and working its way even into the prison establishments. This society is composed of a set of wretches consisting of liberated convicts and minor officials, but more particularly of persons connected with the police and with the prisons, those being preferred who are gifted with great physical strength, or who possess influence among the lower orders. These villains set a price on every one's head, or impose contributions on those who, to avert threats of violence, are disposed to pay them according to the degree of immunity that may be granted. The Camorristi, caring little for the public force (the inaction or connivance of which, under the Bourbonic Government, they purchased), ruled Naples to their own ends, and without any check. They paid no Custom-house duties, showed no respect for the most sacred rights, and used the property of the citizens as they pleased. Prisoners were obliged by them to buy with hard cash protection from annoyance and injury. Even the Bourbonic Government, although not remarkable for public virtue or spirit, disdained to tolerate so frightful a social evil. At various times, the principal Camorristi were arrested, and summarily dispatched to the penitentiary island of Ponza.

Such was the state of things when, in June, 1860,

free institutions being established, the Camorristi, by that natural reaction which is always the consequence of absolute government, were set at liberty. Not long afterwards, however, the Government perceived the imprudence of allowing the presence of such ruffians. The Camorristi, under the pretext of being friends of liberty, and adverse to the Bourbons, gave themselves up once more to all the bad instincts and perverse habits of their body. Francis II. thought to effect a remedy by bringing many of them, and especially the chiefs, into the lower ranks of the police; leaving thus a sad inheritance to future governments. But as might easily have been foreseen, the remedy was worse than the disease; the Camorristi became bolder as they advanced in their evil path under the shelter of official authority. They smuggled, and protected smugglers; they violated all moral laws; they robbed openly; they used thieves as their instruments, and committed deeds of blood, which remained unpunished, owing to the cowardliness of the witnesses, who would not depose against them, for fear of their lives. The evil increased to such a degree that the public feeling was at last aroused, and demanded with one voice some guarantee of security. What the Bourbonic Government would probably have failed in effecting, even had it remained in power, the new rulers have to a certain extent brought to pass. Farini and Nigra comprehended the necessity of a measure which would free the city of so dangerous an element; and they ordered the arrest of the most desperate of the Camorristi.

This bold act naturally gave great offence to the

persons concerned. On the night of the 21st November, 1860, the Prefecture of Police was besieged
by the dependents of the imprisoned Camorristi, who,
it was supposed, were still kept in that place—a fact
which strikingly shows to what an extent the audacity
of this association was sometimes carried.

When, under the Government of Commendatore
Nigra, I went to the prison of Santa Maria Apparente,
to visit the Duke of Cajanello—of whose political trial
I shall have an opportunity of speaking hereafter—I
was enabled to judge how powerful was the organization of the Camorristi. Every Sunday, the Duke,
who had been allowed to take his walk in the lobby
of the prison, in company with a mob of thieves and
assassins, was addressed with the greatest respect by
the chief of the Camorra, who would say to him :—
" Eccellenza, this week you have been fined such and
such a sum." The amount was generally from twenty
to thirty piastres, which the Duke was obliged to
disburse in order to live in peace. Had he dared to
denounce the Camorristi to the inspector of the prison,
he would in all probability have been murdered.

One day, two individuals, who had the appearance
of workmen, presented themselves to the porter of a
mansion at Chiaja, carrying a piano.

" Is Marquis X. at home ?" asked the men.

" No ; he has gone into the country this morning,"
answered the porter.

The workmen expressed annoyance at this, but
said that if any of the servants were within, they
would carry the piano upstairs, as they were acting
under the Marquis's orders. The porter replied that all

the servants were out ; but he gave the men the key of
the apartment for which the instrument was designed,
and showed them up. The piano was placed in the
room, and the two carriers left. In the evening, an
inmate of the house went downstairs, and asked the
door-keeper whether the Marquis had returned from
the country. On being answered that he would not
arrive until the next day, he said that he had heard
persons moving about in the Marquis's private apartment. The two then went upstairs, and found a pack
of thieves at work. One of the servants of the
Marquis was a Camorrista ; he had told his associates
that nobody would be in his master's apartment
during that night, and they had placed in the piano
one of their comrades, who had afterward let in the
robbers.

I will here briefly advert to the trial of the Duke of
Cajanello under Commendatore Nigra's Administration—a trial which was more than once referred to
in both the English Houses of Parliament.

The Duke of Cajanello had always been considered
a Liberal by Ferdinand II., and for this reason was
never liked by him. However, shortly before Francis
II. fell from power, he sent him as a sort of Ambassador
to the French Emperor at Chambéry. On returning
to Naples after the retreat of the King to Gaeta,
the Duke of Cajanello kept aloof from public matters,
neither approving nor disapproving of the new system.
The Minister of Police, Silvio Spaventa, had, however,
reason to believe that the Duke was conspiring. In
this opinion he was strengthened by some information
communicated to him by one Pastore, formerly a

Major in the Garibaldian army, and who told the Minister that a Bourbonic agent, of the name of Litrà, whom he had known at Capua, had written to him, offering money if he would join his party. Litrà had also engaged him to go to Rome, and see the King. On hearing this, Spaventa advised Pastore to accept the offer at once, and try to discover the plans of the conspirators. The Major went to Rome, spoke to the King, and came back to Naples, bringing a Royal letter addressed to the Duke of Cajanello. The letter was of course opened, and, though it was not signed, an official inspection showed that it was in the handwriting of Francis II. I have reason to believe that it ran thus :—

" DEAR DUKE,

"I have received yours, and I thank you for the interest you take in the good cause. The bearer of this is a friend of ours, and you may trust him, as he has been presented by a person devoted to me, and whom you will see by following the instructions of the bearer."

When Spaventa had read this letter, a question arose as to whether it would be better to keep it, and arrest the Duke at once, or to have it delivered, first making an authentic copy. The second course was adopted, and Major Pastore was instructed to take the original to Cajanello. The person whom the Duke was asked to see was Litrà, who had on the same day arrived on board the French steamer *Carmel* from Civita Vecchia. According to Commendatore Spaventa,

Cajanello, although showing but little confidence in Pastore, went on board the French vessel, and had a long conversation with Francis II.'s agent. The question whether the Duke was to be arrested was now brought before the Council of Ministers. Commendatore Nigra was of opinion that, as the original letter was not found in Cajanello's possession, there was no ground for arresting him, but that he should be kept under the strict watch of the police. This view, however, was not shared by the majority of the Council, and Cajanello was consequently arrested. An indictment was laid against him for conspiracy, and he was kept in prison for nearly a year; though he constantly denied, and still denies, having received the letter of the King.

The man who chiefly directed the proceedings against the Duke was the notorious Avvocato Tofano, President of the Criminal Court of Naples. I say " notorious," for he had scarcely begun the trial when a search in the police archives of Naples brought to light papers from which it appeared that, whilst in exile, he had been in communication with the Ambassador of Ferdinand II. at Turin, and had, if not betrayed his political friends, at least passed severe censure upon them, and lowered his character as a patriot by soliciting favours from the King who had banished him. So much for the morality of the man to whom the proceedings against the Duke had been assigned.

Of the trial itself, little need be said. Count Cavour observed more than once that it had been foolishly got up in spite of the opposition of Nigra, who, with the uprightness of his character, saw that it was at once a political mistake and an act of oppression. But what could Nigra do with colleagues who so readily forgot the first principles of freedom ? He tried to persuade them that legal proof against the Duke could never be obtained ; but in vain. Equally ineffectual were the arguments set forth by Sir James Lacaita (formerly private secretary to Mr. Gladstone, and an English knight, though an Italian by birth and family), who wrote a letter to the Minister Minghetti at Turin, urging him to have the scandalous affair brought to an end. Commendatore Minghetti was no more successful than Count Cavour had been, and the Duke of Cajanello was only set free in November, 1861, when every Italian of sound political judgment had disapproved of the unlawful proceeding.

The question at issue is, not whether the Duke did or did not actually receive Francis II.'s letter, and act according to the instructions it contained, but whether the original itself could be produced in court. This the Government was unable to do ; and the imprisonment was therefore illegal. Although an honest and clever Minister, Silvio Spaventa is still persuaded that he was right in bringing the Duke before the criminal court of his country. Surely the well-known recommendation of Talleyrand to his dependents — " *Surtout, pas de zèle*"—was not invented for Neapolitan officials, either Liberals or Reactionists.

The rule of Nigra succeeded the short Administration of Farini. The first advice which Baron Poerio thought proper to give to the young statesman who, out of devotion to Cavour, had consented to conduct the affairs of the distracted Southern

Kingdom, was to the effect that he should take for Minister of the Interior the famous Don Liborio Romano—the most popular man, according to the Baron, to be found in the country. Nobody feels more respect for the venerable Poerio than myself. His misfortunes, and the nobleness with which he bore them, entitle him to the admiration of every Italian. But I am nevertheless bound to say that the advice he gave, both to Count Cavour and to Nigra, was to some extent the cause of increased difficulties to the Government of Victor Emmanuel.

Another evil which checked the development of the Southern Provinces was, that everybody was anxious to get employment from the Government, as a means of providing for his wants with little trouble. In the Northern and Central parts of the Peninsula, the individual depends generally upon his own energy, and tries to get a livelihood by manual industry, commerce, or the liberal professions. In Southern Italy, on the contrary, all must come from the Government. Is there a lamp-post to be removed, or a street to be swept? The first thought which occurs to the mind of a Neapolitan is, " Let us apply to the Intendente; let us see what the Government will do." Nepotism, or the habit of patronising one's relatives and friends when one has got into power, was carried out at Naples to such a frightful extent under the Bourbons, and during the early period of the Liberal Government under Garibaldi and Liborio Romano, that a Neapolitan Minister or Secretary-General could get all his most distant relatives and friends employed, to the great detriment of the Treasury.

To these numerous difficulties was added another, of still greater importance, which has its origin in the economical condition of the country. It is a sad, but nevertheless a true remark, that to Northern Italy the provinces of the South are what, in former times, Ireland was to England. Ireland, with an intelligent, active, and courageous population—with a fertile soil and numerous mines—with ports opened to commerce, and great natural advantages—was for many years in a chronic state of famine and anarchy. The palliatives applied by different statesmen were of no avail. The mounted constabulary, the millions allotted to public works and charitable purposes, were without effect; and no approach was made towards rescuing Ireland from this state of misery until the English Parliament had the courage to pass a law for the sale of encumbered estates. A somewhat similar evil still exists in the worn-out body of the Neapolitan community. A half-feudal, half-clerical mode of dividing property exists in the Southern kingdom, and concentrates the greater part of the land in the hands of a few persons, devoid of ability and power to develope its riches. In a country where such a system is maintained, agriculture can never be carried on otherwise than imperfectly; the rural population must remain ignorant, disorderly, and fonder of theft and violence than of a useful life. "Let a peasant be a landowner, and he will be honest," rightly says Stuart Mill. Not long ago, Ireland was divided into a few great properties, belonging to the families of the aristocracy and gentry, who lived in England, where they spent the income derived from Irish soil, without caring to improve their estates, which indeed they often impoverished. It may be objected that the land in England and Scotland is well cultivated, and yet is not divided into small properties; but may not this depend on the superior wealth which Great Britain derives from her commerce? And is it not notorious that the agricultural population of this island is far from being either very prosperous or very highly civilized? Without great capital, large estates can never be successfully cultivated; whilst on small ones the labour of the owner's family represents, if not the whole, the major portion of that which is required.

In Southern Italy, the greater part of the land belongs to the communes, to the crown, to the religious corporations, or to the families of the feudal aristocracy. The minor landowners are only a small number. This is the main cause why agriculture languishes in spite of the beauty of the climate and the fertility of the soil, and why the country population is poor and given to brigandage. In speaking of the Campagna of Rome, Niebuhr says :—

" Wherever you find landowners who cultivate their own land, or small proprietors, industry and honesty are also found. I am of opinion that he who would employ a large capital in creating small properties would put a stop to the brigandage which desolates these districts."

On the land belonging to the communes, the inhabitants have the right of feeding their sheep and cutting wood. The first herd which arrives gets the best chance, and the consequence is that the grass is eaten up even before it has time to grow to a proper height. With such a system, the fertility of the *beni comunali*

is exhausted, and its woods devastated. The properties belonging to the religious communities and to
the Crown are cultivated as land generally is by
those who have no direct interest in its improvement.
These large estates are generally let to poor
tenants, who cannot command the required capital to
work them well, and who make as much money as
they can by cutting down every tree, and only culti-
vating a third of the area, to save expense. With
a few exceptions, the same may be said of the land
belonging to the Neapolitan aristocracy. In many
cases, families possessing thousands of acres have been
reduced almost to poverty in less than half a century,
only because their land has never been effectually cultivated, and the taxes and interest on mortgages have
consumed the value of the land itself.

If the Italian Government understood this question,
it would boldly face the evil by dividing a part of the
conventual and communal properties into small lots,
distributing them among the population of the different districts, in proportion to the wants of families, and
making the holders pay a moderate annual rent for a
certain number of years, after which the land should
belong absolutely to the tenant. In this way, the rural
population of Southern Italy would be brought to those
steady and industrious habits which distinguish the
people of Lombardy, Piedmont, Tuscany, and Romagna.
The banditti would soon be turned into laborious
peasants, and the great scourge of brigandage would
be got rid of for ever.

Were I writing this book in Italian, I should hesitate about taking in hand this delicate argument. My

countrymen would undoubtedly say that my theory is difficult of application, and that it is only a dream. But, for my part, I respect theories which have been suggested by such men as Adam Smith, Sismondi, Niebuhr, and Stuart Mill, and which have been tested and approved by actual experience.

CHAPTER XII.

NAPLES IN 1860.

Mendicity at Naples—Organized bands of Beggars—*Intra muros* Beggars—*Extra muros* Beggars—The Workhouse of Naples —Laws and Regulations—The Post-Office at Naples—Siege of Gaeta—Mola and Castellone—Preparations for the Investment of the Fortress — Working Parties — Northern and Southern Italians—Difficulties of the Siege—Siege Operations of the French in 1806—The Fortress of Gaeta in our Days— French Policy—Attack of the Sardinian Navy upon Gaeta— General Cialdini — Sketch of Cialdini's Military Career — Cialdini as General and Statesman—Brigands and Brigandage —Stories of Brigands in Southern Italy—A Marquis acting as a Brigand—Prince Carignan and his Councillors—Disturbance at an Infant School at Naples—San Januarius—Education the Hope of the Future.

FROM the moment a traveller enters the port of Naples, one thing strikes him with ever-recurring pertinacity, and thrusts itself before his eyes even ere he lands. It is mendicity. Mendicity is the scourge of Naples; a harpy, like that of Virgil, which spoils everything — which stands between you and the sun, and casts a gloomy shade in full mid-day. I hope the evil has by this time been abated; but, when I was last at Naples, mendicity awaited the traveller even in the boat which conveyed him to the Mole; for the boatman, after being paid the price fixed by the tariff, asked for drinking money. It awaited him on the Mole: the Custom-house officer who mounted guard, with his gun in one hand, begged with the other. It awaited him at the Custom-house: the porter who took his luggage to the hotel asked for something beyond his legitimate fee. From the Custom-house to the hotel, the stranger passed literally between two hedges of beggars. One showed him the stump of his arm, another his withered leg; all being more or less afflicted with disease or malformations distressing to witness. One called him "Excellency," another "General," another "Highness." This crowd of mendicants pressed upon him, on his right, on his left, before him and behind him. However well he might have been forearmed against the danger, pity would at last seize him, and he would finish by distributing two or three *carlini*. From that moment he was lost.

The news immediately spreads that a "Milordo Inglese" has disembarked—that he gives alms—and that he lodges at the Crocelle, or at the Vittoria. In the innocence of his soul, the newly-arrived traveller is ignorant of all this. He has been told so often to see Naples and then die, that, as soon as he has reached the hotel, and plunged his face and hands into fresh water, he opens his window to look at the beautiful view which is before him—the Gulf, Capri, Posilippo, Vesuvius. He sees all this, and a cry of admiration escapes him. But at the same moment, in all the notes of the scale, in all kinds of intonation, he hears, "Excellency—General—Highness! we are dying of hunger—we are dying of hunger!"

He looks down, attracted by the noise, and sees no longer the five or six beggars to whom he has given some trifle in coming to the hotel; but a band of beggars—a troop of beggars—a very army of beggars —who are all endeavouring to exhibit their misfortunes.

The heart of the traveller is touched: he throws to the miserable creatures all the change he has, and shuts the window. Thenceforth he is condemned to look at the port, at Capri, Posilippo, and Vesuvius, through his window-panes; he dares not open the window again.

He rings the bell, and asks the waiter what he can do to get rid of this eighth plague—a plague unknown to Pharaoh.

"You have probably given them some money," says the waiter, philosophically.

"Certainly," replies the traveller.

"Then, Excellency, there is no remedy," rejoins the waiter, in the tone of a man who has made up his mind to another's martyrdom.

An idea suggests itself to the traveller.

"Order a carriage; I am going out, only I wish to get into it in the court-yard, and not at the door."

The waiter bows, and leaves the room without replying. Ten minutes afterwards, he comes up again, saying, "The carriage is ready, Excellency."

His Excellency goes down: the beggars, however, have made an irruption into the court-yard, and he is obliged to pass through the midst of them, and to push them forcibly aside ere he can reach his carriage. Hardly is he seated before he shouts with all the strength of his lungs—"Quick, coachman, quick !"

The coachman hesitates : some of the beggars are too close to the horses ; some are before the pole, some before the wheels.   At last, however, he starts.   His Excellency hears cries, groans, lamentations ; no one has been touched, but every one appears to have been frightfully hurt.   As long as the carriage rolls along a plain or descends a hill, there is rest ; the beggars know that in those situations his Excellency has the advantage of them ; but at the first ascent they are waiting for him.   From the distance he perceives them in two rows—one on each side of the street—leaning against the wall, or seated ; all immovable, talking of their affairs until he arrives within ten steps of them. Then the two lines join and encircle the carriage, and his torments recommence.

They stick close to the carriage all the time the horses are obliged to walk ; and the coachman, who is himself a beggar of another kind, will keep the beasts walking as long a time as possible, so as not to injure his colleagues : in fact, he will only put them into a trot when his complicity would become too evident.

A little girl runs after the carriage, and throws into it a yellow flower which has a horrid odour. She, too, is a beggar.   If the traveller does not fling back the flower, she will be sure to throw him one every time he passes, and some day, when she meets him walking, she will present him her account.

A Capuchin jumps on the carriage steps, shaking his bag.   He too is a beggar.   He begs for the souls in purgatory.   If his Excellency gives him anything, he is off without even saying "Thank you:" if he does not, he excommunicates him in the name of our Lord.

On reaching the Toledo, where the carriage is obliged to fall into the rank, a man nearly as well-dressed as the traveller speaks to him, putting his hand to his hat, and bowing ; his Excellency touches *his* hat, and returns the bow. Some words pass between them, and then the traveller discovers that his interlocutor is a beggar like the rest, with only this difference—that he begs in a black coat and cravat, or, if he does not actually beg, at least finds something to solicit.

Should his Excellency stop before a café to take an ice, or at a shop to buy some trifle, he probably gets out of the vehicle quietly enough ; but, in returning to his carriage, he finds it literally stuck fast, hemmed in by women, old men, and children—like a ship in the ice in the midst of the Polar Seas. He imagines that, on leaving Naples, he will escape this annoyance. Half distracted, he cries, "To Pozzuoli!" Alas! mendicity outside the city is even better organized than within. The fellow who runs after him to sell antiquities—the one who insists upon conducting him to the baths of Nero—he who goes before him into the temple of Diana at Baiæ —all are beggars. This man who almost loses his breath in running after the carriage as soon as he sees it, and who leads two peasants who dance the Tarantella—he too is a beggar. This other, who strokes and pats your dog, if you happen to have one —he also is a beggar : he will ask you for something for having patted your dog !

This goes on day after day.   At the end of a fortnight, the traveller's patience is exhausted, and he
is almost tempted to say, " It is not ' see Naples, and
die,'—but rather die than again see Naples."

From this sketch of mendicity at Naples, the reader
will perhaps infer that there do not exist any charitable institutions in which the poor can obtain shelter
and food.   This, however, is not the case.   No city in
Italy is better provided in this respect than Naples.
The well-known " Ospizio de' Poveri," or, in other
words, the Central Workhouse, has an annual income of
nearly 300,000 ducats.   Four thousand poor can be
accommodated within this spacious establishment,
which, had it been well administered, would have
rivalled the best of England and France.   But under
the Bourbons the income of the " Ospizio de' Poveri,"
instead of being distributed amongst the poor, went
to swell the purses of the administrators, or was bestowed on the *protégés* of Mazza, or of some other
Director of Police.   Not one-third of it was really
employed to relieve the needy.

There were, indeed, laws against beggary ; but, except in the case of politics, any law in Naples previously to the Revolution could be violated without
danger.   Such being the case, the natural bent of the
Neapolitan to avoid work, and to live in the open air,
remained without a check, and beggars multiplied to a
fearful extent, organizing themselves into regular
bands, and forming almost a State within the State.
To this great evil, both Nigra and Count San Martino
tried to oppose a barrier, by calling into active existence the old decrees, and adding to them new ones. A

police constabulary was organized, and when I left Naples, in June, 1861, things had taken a turn which bade fair to effect very favourable results.

The difficulties with which the new rulers of Southern Italy had to contend, increased every day. Complete disorganization prevailed in the administration of the city and the provinces; and the new officials, sent either from Lombardy or Piedmont to take into their hands the reins of public affairs, had scarcely set to work before they were disheartened. To give an illustration of the confusion which prevailed in one of the branches of the administration— the Post-office—I will relate a circumstance which happened to Sir James Lacaita towards the end of 1860. That gentleman arrived at Naples in the beginning of December, and was astonished at not receiving letters from his friends in England. Every day he went regularly to the Post-office himself, and the answer was, "No letters." At last one day he went with the determination to look himself into the box marked with the letter " L." His inspection soon led to the discovery of a dozen letters which had been lying there since the 10th of the month. When the chief clerk was appealed to, to explain the circumstance, he merely said it could be a matter of no importance whether a man received a letter one day or another, provided he got it at last. I have also heard of Garibaldians who, at the period I am speaking of, had not received a single line from their relatives since they left home, although they had been assured by friends who had come to Naples that their families had written regularly once a week. Accusations of similar remissness might be fairly brought against the other branches of the administration.

The siege of Gaeta played so great a part in the later events of the war, that I should very imperfectly execute the task I have undertaken were I not to mention the principal facts connected with it. After the defeat sustained by the Neapolitans on the Garigliano, which led to the loss of Mola di Gaeta, Francis II., morally supported by the presence of the French fleet, decided to make a last stand in the stronghold which remained to him, trusting that Austria would sooner or later come to his rescue. Having chosen those which he considered the best regiments of his army, he shut himself up with about 16,000 men, and prepared for the worst. On their side, the Piedmontese, under the command of General Cialdini, established themselves, towards the end of November, 1860, at Mola, and began the siege.

As I had nothing better to do at Naples, I left that city about the 20th of November, and went to Mola with two of my English friends, Captain Keith Fraser and Mr. George Russell. Mola is a small and dirty town, standing on the road from Naples to Rome, about four miles from the fortress of Gaeta. It is divided into two distinct parts—the lower and the upper; the first of which is called Castellone, the other Mola. Being situated on the shores of the Gulf, amongst picturesque groves of orange and olive trees, its external aspect is very agreeable. The Formiana Villa, the favourite residence of Cicero, stood below the terraces of the hill where the upper part of the modern town has been built, and precisely under the gardens of Villa Caposelle, where General Cialdini established his head-quarters. The main street of the town is parallel with the Gulf, and leads to the road running towards the fortress. At about half a mile from Mola, this road divides into two; one fork following the shore of the sea, the other branching off in the direction of the mountains. The latter is the Via Consolare, leading to Rome. For awhile it skirts the foot of Monte Conca, and then winds up through the defiles of the mountains, at the end of which the town of Itri and its half-ruined castle rise before the eye. From the point at which the main road to Gaeta branches off towards Itri, Monte Conca stands on the left in the direction of the Gulf, screening a narrow valley with its broad flank. Until recently, there were no roads, properly so called; for the paths which skirt the base of the mountain do not deserve that name. Following the foot of Monte Conca, the traveller reaches the two other eminences, called the Cappucini and Monte Sant' Agata, which command the round hill at the bottom of which stands Gaeta. This hill, known under the name of the Torre d'Orlando, forms an integral part of the famous fortress, and enters into its system of defence. Batteries over batteries were thrown up on its flank by Ferdinand II., so that any army stationed there could at one and the same time dominate the narrow defiles of Monte Conca and the shore of the open sea. It was only by silencing these formidable rows of artillery that the right side of the fortress could be approached by a besieging force. But in order to place guns and mortars on the heights of the Cappucini and Monte Sant' Agata, the Piedmontese were obliged to make roads to them; for, as I have said, none existed previously. The execution of this work was confided to General Menabrea, of the Royal Engineers. One of these roads led from the Via Consolare of Itri to the Borgo, where I was taken after my release from Gaeta; the other skirted Monte Conca, and joined the former at the base of Monte Sant' Agata. No one who has not visited that country can judge of the difficulties of this undertaking. The hollow of the valley and the foot of the mountain, along which the two roads were to pass, form a continuous succession of acclivities and declivities, and are obstructed by stones of enormous size. The working of the ground was rendered still more laborious by the rainy season, which had already begun. In consequence of the perpetual wet, the soldiers were obliged to work in the mud; and the soil was so slippery that they could scarcely stand on their feet. The work, however, was performed by parties of soldiers of the Line, who got extra pay to the extent of two *soldi* a day, and a glass of rum besides.

On our arrival at Cialdini's head-quarters, my English companions and I were furnished by the General with the necessary *permis* to inspect the works, and Lieutenant De Renzis, the aid-de-camp of General Menabrea, was to accompany us. We started about noon on the 21st of November, and in an hour reached the place where the soldiers were at their task.

As we were looking at the working parties, Captain De Renzis told us that when they were formed of

Piedmontese or Lombards the work was more quickly done than when the majority of the men belonged to the more southern provinces of the Peninsula. The superiority of the northern element was thereby proved in an unmistakeable manner.

Proceeding on our way, we reached the turning of the road which leads to the isthmus facing the fortress. The Neapolitans in the Philipstadt battery got sight of us, and soon began to fire in our direction. The chemist of Borgo di Gaeta, who had followed our party, had just taken Mr. Russell and Captain Fraser on to the top of the hill hard by, and they were consequently more exposed to the bursting shells than I was. The poor chemist, who could not boast of much courage, began to scream, " Gesù, Gesù ! we are dead!" and, had not my two English friends kept up the spirits of the frightened man, Signor Bonomi would in all probability have died of fear, even had he not been killed by a shell.

When, in making our way back to Mola, we skirted the ill-fated Borgo, shortly doomed to complete destruction, we found it occupied by a battalion of Piedmontese Bersaglieri, who were continually fired at by the guns of the fortress. The Borgo, whose population had emigrated to the neighbouring villages, was already half destroyed by the Neapolitan projectiles.

One day, I followed a captain of the engineers to the Monte Sant'Agata battery, and, on my way back, chanced to pass through the court-yard of a casino, or villa, which had been deserted by the family of the proprietor, a certain Count who had followed the

fortunes of Francis II.   The casino, which stands on
a height opposite the Regina battery, had been abandoned by the Count since the beginning of the siege
—a fact of which the captain and myself were aware.
What, therefore, was our astonishment on hearing the
noise of a hammer coming from the inner part of the
ground floor ! It could not surely have been the
owner, or any of his servants ; they were at Gaeta.
The young officer accordingly hastened to the place,
the gate of which was wide open, and called out,
" Who is there ?"

Presently, two Bersaglieri came up, and the officer
inquired the cause of the hammering.

" Nothing, sir "—(Italians, when found in fault,
never fail to begin their answer with that phrase)—
" Nothing, sir ; we happened to pass here, and have
just been having a look at the casino."

" What then ?" pursued the captain.

" Well, we have broken open the cellar, and have
found some bottles of Capri wine, in which we intend
to drink your health."

On the captain remarking that marauding was
not permitted, the Bersaglieri seemed to think
all objections removed by their promising that, after
having taken away all the bottles they could find,
they would " shut the door of the cellar as it was
before."

Accurately to estimate the work on which the
National forces were now engaged, it should be borne
in mind that the famous siege of Gaeta by the French
under Massena, in 1806, lasted six months. The French
were then almost in the same position as that in

which the Sardinians found themselves during the late operations. The English fleet in 1806 prevented the French vessels from attacking Gaeta by sea, and the besieged fortress was thus provided with stores and ammunition. At the end of January, 1806, Prince Hess of Philipstadt refused to give up Gaeta, and decided to oppose the French General. On the 13th of February, when Massena made his appearance before the place, Prince Hess had a garrison of 2900 regular troops, and 2000 convicts; 174 pieces of artillery defended the fortress, and the Prince could dispose of one frigate, twelve gunboats, and about as many transports. These means of defence were afterwards increased; so that when the town was compelled to capitulate, in the month of July, its garrison amounted to 6200 men, and it had 178 guns, 2 brigs, 3 frigates, and 24 gunboats. Massena began the attack with 4000 men and 29 pieces of artillery; but, these producing no effect, great additions were made within a period of five months. At the end of June, Massena had 134 guns and 12,192 men at his command. During this memorable siege, the French fired against Gaeta 68,700 shots, and the besieged answered with more than 100,000. If such were the difficulties Massena had to encounter when he had only to deal with 178 guns and a garrison 6200 strong, the reader can judge how much greater were those of the Piedmontese in 1861, when he bears in mind that Gaeta was defended by a garrison of 16,000 men, and 800 pieces of artillery, mounted on numerous batteries—a number which was considerably augmented at a later period. I will enumerate the batteries, to give some idea of the strength of the place. There were the Trinity bastion, with five tiers of guns; that of the Queen, with sixty 60-pounders; then those of St. Andrew, of Breccia, of Philipstadt, of Capelletti, and of the citadel, where I was shut up with my fellow-prisoners. Besides these, there were the Annunziata, Favorita, Ferdinanda, San Giuseppe, Santa Maria, Del Porto, Guastaferro, Torrione Francese, Trabacco, Carolina, Duca Calabria, Fico, Conca, Falsa Bracca, Gran Guardia, Poterna, Contro Guardia, and, lastly, four more, called the Trinceramento of Porta di Terra.

The artillery employed by General Cialdini in the siege of Gaeta was of course far superior to that used by Massena in 1806. But, if the attack was thus more powerful, the means of defence were also greater. Military science, and especially artillery, has in our days made such advances that there are but few fortresses in Europe which could stand a properly conducted siege for more than a year. It was during the operations against Gaeta that the powerful gun invented by the Piedmontese General Cavalli was first tried, when it proved to be exceedingly successful. By the use of these formidable guns, the Piedmontese would have compelled the garrison of Gaeta to capitulate at least three months before, had it not been for the French Emperor, who, with that uncertainty which characterizes his actions towards Italy, maintained a continual drag on the siege operations by keeping his fleet anchored in the Gulf while professing a rigid neutrality. When, at the end of January 1861, a sudden change came over the policy of France, and

the fleet was withdrawn, Gaeta was not long in sur-
rendering. The capitulation took place early in February. There were also minor supporters of Francis
II. before Gaeta. Two small Spanish men-of-war had
undertaken to play the part of the Don Quixotes of
the siege by a series of hostile but in reality harmless demonstrations. Their arrogance, however, was
checked by the determined attitude of General Cialdini
and Admiral Persano, who told the Spanish Commodore to keep his officers on board if he did not wish
to see them summarily dealt with.

The Sardinian navy, under the command of Admiral Persano, had already distinguished itself at
Ancona; but since the beginning of the siege of
Gaeta it had no opportunity of going into action
until the 22nd of January. At eight o'clock on the
evening of that day, 2000 Piedmontese were occupied
in throwing up new batteries at the extremity of
the Borgo di Gaeta, where the isthmus begins, when
the besieged opened a tremendous fire upon them.
Naturally enough, the working parties drew back in
the greatest confusion, for shells and shot were
pouring upon them in a shower. The Piedmontese
gunners, overworked as they had been during the
previous days, were at the time asleep, either in the
batteries or in the camp, and about two hours were
required to get them ready for action. At ten
o'clock, however, they opened fire from the battery
of Monte Tortola, which was soon followed by the
other batteries, both of the right and left attack.
The fire became so tremendous and continuous that,
although I was at the time about two miles from the

camp, the house in which I was taking my supper
seemed to tremble.   I hastened back to Mola, and
arrived in time to witness the operations of the Sardinian fleet, which began a little before eleven o'clock.
It was the war steamer *Garibaldi* which, together with
two gunboats, was first sent by Admiral Persano to
attack the sea side of the fortress.   She steamed up
boldly towards the Mole, and, taking a position within
range of the tremendous batteries, began her work of destruction.   The two smaller ships followed her example ;
but in an hour one of them was obliged to draw back,
having been nearly disabled by the fire of the Neapolitans.   It was then about half-past twelve o'clock,
and the fire of the land batteries had reached its
greatest intensity.   Cavalli's guns were throwing their
powerful projectiles from Realto di Castellone—a distance of about three Italian miles—with wonderful
precision.   Scarcely a shot missed its aim, and, from
the place where I stood, I could follow the erratic
yet elegant curves of the shells about to burst on the
besieged city or on its bastions.   The time had come
for the Sardinian Admiral to move in support of the
Garibaldi, and thus begin more serious operations.
Marquis Persano therefore slowly steamed up with the
Charles Albert, the *Maria Adelaide*, the *Victor Emmanuel*,
and two other smaller vessels, in the direction of the
bastions which face the Gulf towards Mola.   As these
three frigates carried guns whose range was greater
than that of the enemy's artillery, Marquis Persano
could safely open fire from the ship he commanded ;
and he inflicted great damage on the Neapolitan battery of the harbour.   But this was not all ; for he soon

steamed up within a distance of a thousand yards, and fired a double broadside in less time than I take to write this sentence. The roar was frightful. A dense cloud of smoke and dust concealed the harbour from the view of the bystanders; but, when the wind had dispersed it, the fact became evident that the guns of the Sardinian vessels had greatly injured the Neapolitan batteries of the port.

The life of a man who watches the operations of a siege is by no means pleasant. One day passes like another, and until the breach is opened, and the assault ordered, there is scarcely anything to observe or chronicle. Had it not been for the goodhumour and courtesy which prevailed at Cialdini's head-quarters, I should not have been able to stand the monotony of Mola di Gaeta longer than a week. The Staff of General Cialdini was composed of excellent officers, brave as lions, and merry as schoolboys. There were Lieutenant-Colonel Piola, Chief of the Staff; Counts Borromeo, Seristori, and Mosti d'Este; Lieutenant Fermi and Captain Pozzolini—most of them belonging to the first families of Italy, and all courteous and jovial companions, who would have done anything to oblige a friend. General Cialdini himself —who has the absurd reputation of being a bloodthirsty man—was exceedingly kind, though strict in regard to military discipline; and altogether my time passed more agreeably than might have been expected.

Cialdini was born in the village of Castelvetro, near Modena, in 1813. His family intended him to be a physician, and he was sent to the University of Parma

with that view.   At the breaking out of the Italian
revolution in 1831, however, Cialdini left the medical
school, and went to Reggio, where he enlisted as a
volunteer in the National bands.   But Austria soon
interfered, as was her habit, and the Italian patriots
were obliged to seek safety in exile.   Cialdini was
one of the last to leave the country.   He went to
Paris, and a year afterwards entered the Foreign
Legion which had been organized with the object of
supporting the cause of Don Pedro in Portugal.
Liberty having triumphed in that country, the young
patriot went to Spain, and took part in the battles
fought by Espartero against the supporters of Don
Carlos.   In 1839, when the treaty of Bergara was
concluded, Cialdini had reached the rank of Captain
in the 18th, or Almanza Regiment.   After the capture of Morella, he was sent to Barcelona ; but, having
been aid-de-camp of the unfortunate General Borso
Carminati, who was shot by order of Espartero, he was
placed on half-pay, and remained out of the army for
a long while under suspicion of being an *exaltado*.
Three years afterwards, however, at the time of the
celebrated *pronunciamentos* against the regency of Espartero, he followed the fortunes of General Narvaez,
who appointed him his first aid-de-camp.   In this
quality he distinguished himself at the taking of
Madrid ; and, to reward his services, Narvaez made him
Lieutenant-Colonel of the Carabineers.   Such was the
opinion which the Spanish General entertained of his
military knowledge, that in 1848 he sent him to Paris
to study the organization of the French gendarmerie.
Cialdini was still in the French capital when the war

between Austria and Sardinia broke out. The young officer hastened to his fatherland, and joined the Papal forces under his friend General Giovanni Durando. Wounded at the battle of Vicenza, he went back to Piedmont soon after the armistice of Milan. But this armistice was only a short truce, and war was again declared by Charles Albert seven months afterwards—a war which was destined to end in the defeat of the Piedmontese at Novara. On that sanguinary day, Cialdini commanded the 14th Regiment of the Line, and distinguished himself very much by holding the position of Biccoca against the whole of the Austrian advanced guard.

During the ten years of respite between the two contending powers of the Italian Peninsula, Cialdini rose gradually to the rank of Lieutenant-General, and in that capacity, as the reader will remember, commanded one of the Sardinian *corps d'armée* in the war of 1859. When military commander at Bologna in 1860, he was chosen by his friend Fanti, then Minister of War, to direct the operations against General Lamoricière, whom he conquered in the battle-field of Castelfidardo; and he was now adding to his brilliant services before the walls of Gaeta.

As a General, Cialdini is undoubtedly one of the best in the Italian army; but the qualities which make him an excellent military leader failed when he was called to play the part of a politician. His character is too impetuous to allow him to judge with calmness the various necessities of the situation when action must give way to reflection and calm judgment. His mission in the Southern Provinces proved a complete failure, and increased the difficulties of Ricasoli's Government in that quarter. It is only fair, however, to add that Cialdini himself admitted that he did not possess the qualities of a statesman. His post is now occupied by a calmer and more experienced politician—the illustrious General Della Marmora, who has succeeded in extricating the Neapolitan provinces from their critical position.

A few remarks may be here appended on the much-talked-of barbarities which, according to the enemies of Italy, Cialdini unnecessarily ordered during his stay at Naples. No doubt, acts were then committed which deserve severe censure; as, for instance, the shooting, without trial, of seven men at Somma, and the burning of the town of Ponte Landolfo. But, without justifying these acts, I beg the reader to consider the position of Cialdini at that time. He was sent to govern the Southern Provinces when the brigandage organized by Francis II. at Rome was ravaging the country to a fearful extent. At Ponte Landolfo, a company of Piedmontese, having fallen into a trap, were mercilessly slaughtered by the population; and at Somma and other places the same had been done with the National Guards. It must be admitted that the retribution was terrible; but these are acts which a General cannot always prevent, however much he may desire it—a truth of which the history of the Indian mutiny furnishes sufficient proofs. If we knew in all their details the means employed by the English army to suppress the Indian rebellion, we should perhaps have to register more than one sad episode not very dissimilar to the tragedy of Ponte Landolfo. That which occurred in India in

1857, took place, although on a smaller scale, in the Southern Provinces of Italy. There, as at Delhi, Cawnpore, and other localities, soldiers, National Guards, and inoffensive travellers have been murdered by the brigands in cold blood. There, as in Oude, villages whose inhabitants were suspected of siding with the Liberals were plundered, devastated, and burned. There too women were dishonoured, and officers and soldiers crucified, roasted alive, or otherwise tortured. Of all the cruelties inflicted by the Sepoys on the English, there is probably not one that has not also been perpetrated, more or less extensively, by the supporters of Francis II. against the subjects of Victor Emmanuel. These atrocities, if they do not justify, at least explain the terrible retribution ordered by the Pinellis, the Fumels, and the Fantonis. It was only the other day that Mr. Wreford, the correspondent of the *Times* at Naples, sent home a striking brigand story ; and the reader will remember how the ten travellers who were stopped near Foggia by Crocco's and Schiavone's band were treated on that occasion. Were the noble lords and honourable gentlemen, who in both Houses of Parliament break lances in support of Francis II., to find themselves in a similar situation, they would in all probability change their opinion upon the subject.

To wind up this dissertation upon brigands and brigandage, I may be permitted to tell a story of my own. Whilst at Mola di Gaeta, I knew the Sindaco, a Signor Spina, who was very kind to me, as well as to Mr. Russell and to Captain Keith Fraser. One morning, the poor man went to Itri on some business. About a mile from that town, he fell in with a band of brigands, who, recognising him as a Liberal, took him into a neighbouring wood; but what happened to him I know not, for he was never heard of again.   A few days afterwards, a party of four Piedmontese Lancers fell into the same hands.   They were all killed, and their heads stuck on their lances at the entrance of the village where they had been captured.

These barbarous deeds were not only performed by ignorant brigands, but were ordered and encouraged by those foreign adventurers who had volunteered to become their leaders.   In the course of last November, the Marquis Alfred de Trazignies, a native of Namur, clad in black, picturesque garments, like a warrior of the famous company of Giovanni Delle Bande Nere, entered San Giovanni Incarico, and ordered his brigands to burn it.   Some Piedmontese soldiers, however, were on their track, and reached the village whilst the young Belgian nobleman was busily engaged in the work of destruction, showing his brigands how the fire could be made to spread from house to house, with his own hands throwing fuel on the flames, and threatening with his revolver the poor women who were seeking safety in flight.   The noble Marquis (who is a nephew of M. de Merode) was seized and shot.   Great, of course, was the indignation of his friends at Rome, who cried out that a murder had been committed.   But would any English General have acted otherwise? Would he have let such a miscreant go free because he was a Marquis? As for the Spanish General, Borges, he too was shot because he was caught whilst fighting against the National forces. From the letters found upon him, it was clear that he was disgusted with the brigandage practised by the defenders of Francis II. In one of these documents he says:—"Crocco is a monster and a villain, whose only thirst is for murder and pillage." This was the opinion which Borges entertained of the man whom Francis II. addressed by the title of "My dear General."

The adversaries of the Italian cause may ask—"Have not the Piedmontese Generals shed blood in their turn?" Again I reply, Yes; and I do not attempt to justify them if they did so without absolute necessity. Blood cries out for blood; retribution follows crime. This is unhappily a truth always apparent in the sad history of humanity. Some very severe measures have no doubt been taken in the Southern provinces; but I repeat that they were provoked by the atrocities of the reactionists, and that exceptional acts of severity must always be judged with reference to those necessities which called them forth.

In any case, there are men who have governed the Southern Provinces without being compelled to leave a train of blood behind them. This may be said with entire truth of Prince Carignan, Farini, Nigra, and Count San Martino. The first left Naples esteemed and blessed by every one; the others may have made political mistakes, but they governed humanely, as General Della Marmora does now.

Prince Carignan, a cousin of Victor Emmanuel, may be taken as a model for princes. Intelligent, self-sacrificing, and charitable, he worthily fulfilled at

Naples the duty which had devolved upon him. Aided by Nigra, and surrounded by able and upright men, such as the Marquis Courtanz, Captain Crespi, Counts Perrone and Cavour (the last-named a nephew of the great statesman), he succeeded in conciliating many opponents of the National Government. The Marquis Courtanz did much in the way of pacification, and was so successful as even to get into the society of the Neapolitan Codini, some of whom he rallied to the cause of Victor Emmanuel. Captain Crespi brought to the councils of Prince Carignan the weight of his knowledge and wisdom. Brave as the blade of his sabre, he is a true type of those warriors whom we find so graphically sketched in the histories of the Middle Ages : he would have been a worthy aid-de-camp to the English Henry V. at Agincourt, or to Emmanuel Philibert at Saint Quintin.

Prince Carignan was either recalled or allowed to resign towards the middle of May, 1861 ; and this was undoubtedly a political mistake. Count San Martino was sent to replace him ; but he too had scarcely begun to see his way through the intricate maze of Neapolitan affairs, when he was withdrawn from his post. The Central Government of Turin continued thus heaping errors upon errors ; and, to crown all, it made the unfortunate experiment of trying whether the sword of a popular General would cut the Gordian knot. Hence the appointment of Cialdini. But to regenerate the Southern provinces of Italy is not the work of a soldier ; it can only be effected by the slow process of education, and by the action of a wise and experienced administrator. Where ignorance and demoralization are so profoundly rooted, violent acts will avail but little in getting rid of them.

At the time General Cialdini was appointed Lieutenant-General of Victor Emmanuel in Southern Italy, an association, organized by that good and charitable lady, Mrs. Craven, had opened an infant school in the vicinity of Chiaia. The best mistresses that could be obtained were secured in Northern Italy; and everything which could promote the welfare of the children was carefully provided. The day for opening the school at length arrived, and the children flocked in; their parents blessing the names of Mrs. Craven and her friends. Matters went on well for a week; but one day it was found necessary to cut the children's hair, for reasons of health and cleanliness. The operation was accordingly performed, and the children were sent home minus their hair. The next morning, a host of women suddenly broke into the school, raving like furies, and with shouts and screams began to assault the mistresses. So serious was the disturbance that the police were obliged to interfere; and, when the intruders were asked the meaning of their conduct, their answers showed the degree of prejudice which darkened their minds.

"We do not want to have our children trampled upon," cried one. "To cut the hair of my Maria, when the May moon is over!" shouted another. "To wash my Agnese! Oh, San Gennaro, what an infamy!" exclaimed a third.

I have mentioned this infant-school incident to show

how far ignorance and superstition can pervert the
minds of human beings. At Naples, these two great
scourges of society show themselves in all sorts of
forms :—at the steps of the altar of San Januarius,
where a band of slatternly women, who pretend to be
the descendants of the saint's family, scream and
shout, pouring forth, now a torrent of blasphemies
and insults, now prayers and supplications, until
the liquefaction of the blood has taken place ; on
the threshold of the fisherman's hut, where the fisherman about to embark will on no account put to sea
should a gust of wind quench the light of the oil
lamp burning before the Madonna of the house ; at
the door of the osteria, where the lazzarone will not
enter if a dog and a cat should fight together ; and so
on with the whole round of southern life.

And yet, strange to say, the Neapolitans are extremely quick, sharp, and intelligent. They are the
only people in Europe who can express to each other
their inmost thoughts by a mere lifting of the eyebrows or a movement of the hand. This abounding
intelligence is often coupled with much goodness of
heart, and with a generosity which only requires to be
led on the right path. Correct ideas of right and wrong
are what is especially wanting in them. Their Greek
origin betrays itself at every moment ; yet they
have in them the elements of good, hard-working
citizens, and useful members of the Italian family
to which they belong. Let their new rulers give
them the education which they need — let them be
taught, more by example than by words, that religion can exist without superstition, and morality

without hypocrisy ; and one day they will assuredly be equal to their Northern brethren.   But to secure this result—a result which deeply concerns the future happiness of Italy—the temple of Janus must be shut, and that of knowledge and social progress opened in its stead.

CHAPTER XIII.

TRAITS OF NEAPOLITAN LIFE.

WHEN foreigners, and more especially Englishmen, speak of Italian nobility, they are accustomed to remark—" In Italy, there are swarms of Dukes, Marquises, and Counts,—but no titles of really aristocratic import—no true nobility in the English sense of the word." I must be permitted to observe that this is altogether a mistake. No doubt during long centuries of trouble and vicissitude a questionable titled class has grown up in Italy side by side with the genuine aristocracy ; but between these orders the line of demarcation is, for all Italians, most distinctly drawn ; and the great Italian names, marking illustrious ancestry and glorious historical traditions, are as rare and as highly esteemed in Italy as are, in this country, the proudest and most ancient of the great English aristocratic houses.

The ancient titles in Italy were a consequence of its greatness during the Middle Ages ; a greatness scarcely perhaps ever surpassed by any other country at any one period.   Venice, Genoa, Florence, Milan, and Naples were then so many centres which might be fairly compared, both for influence and wealth, with several modern States.   The merchant princes of Milan could afford to pay the expenses of Charles VIII. of France, when he was stopped for want of money in the prosecution of that expedition against Naples to which he was invited by the treacherous Ludovico Sforza ; and the Peruzzis and Bardis of Florence, in the fourteenth century, lent large sums of money to many potentates of their time.   The origin of the Italian nobility must therefore be traced as far back as that powerful era.   There is not a Marquis or Count of ancient family who cannot boast some ancestor whose name is closely connected with the history of his country.   When a man calls himself Gradenigo, Faliero, Trivulzio, Sant' Arpino, Massimi, Colonna, Doria, Valenti-Gonzaga, Ricasoli, &c., he cares but little for any title which he may have the right to bear ; his family name tells who he is, and what his forefathers have done.

So much for the genuine Italian nobility.   The questionable owes its origin to the custom, adopted by the foreign monarchs who descended to plunder Italy, of conferring honours upon persons who paid for them.

Charles V., for instance, granted to the Sartoris of
Bologna the right of making three Counts every year.
The Popes made Counts of all those who were elected
Knights of the Golden Spur, and it was customary at
the Roman Court to give the title of Counts Palatine to
the sycophants of Cardinals and prelates.   Even in our
own day almost any man can procure a title either at
Rome or at Monaco, by paying a sufficient sum of
money to the Government, or by buying from a ruined
nobleman a castle or an estate to which the title is
attached.   But in Italy, as elsewhere, the nobility
obtained by such means is considered ridiculous ; and
worthless titles of this kind are more sought after by
foreigners than by the Italians themselves.   As for
the multiplication of titles by their descent to younger
sons, such distinctions have, for Italians, no more
significance than the courtesy titles, or the prefix
"honourable," conferred on the younger sons of noble
houses in England.   These circumstances do not interfere with the position of the real Italian nobles ;
whose lineage and traditions are as ancient and honourable as those of any aristocracy in Europe.

The Neapolitan aristocracy may be divided into
three categories : the feudal, the municipal (which
derived its titles from dignities held either in the
provinces or in the city—dignities then conferring the
right of a *scanno*, or seat, in the Neapolitan Parliament), and, lastly, that which was attached to
high offices at court.

The first is for the most part of Suabian, Anjouan,
or Spanish origin ; the second and third are more exclusively national. In 1800, when titles were abolished,
the names of the families which had borne them were

inscribed in a sort of peerage, called the *Libro d'Oro*; and this, even to the present day, is the recognised authority for testing the nobility of a family. Although the propensity to lavish titles of nobility upon their favourites was one of the main characteristics of the Spanish princes, yet even amongst this class some illustrious names are to be found in the *Libro d'Oro*. Of such are the Davolos, by title Marquises of Pescara and Vasto, by birth descendants of the conqueror of Francis I. at the battle of Pavia; of such also are the Guevaras, Dukes of Bovino, and Counts of Savignano—and many more.

Passing from these titles of foreign origin to the great names of more purely national growth, I may mention, as most distinguished among the Neapolitan aristocracy, the Acquavivas, Dukes d'Atri, and Counts of Conversano; the Aquinos; the Brancaccios; the Capeces; the Caracciolos, divided into many branches, the chief of which are Prince Torella, and the Duke of San Teodoro; the Colonnas, the Orsinis, and the Dorias (the two former belonging to the great Roman family, the latter to the Genoese); the Gaetanis; the Medicis, of Florentine origin; the Pignatellis; the Sanseverinos; the Serras-Monte Santangelo; the Sangros; the Saluzzos; the Filangieris; the Carafas-Policastro; and many others.

The third division of the Neapolitan aristocracy comprises sixteen families—the Folgori, the del Balzo, the Gallone, &c.—entitled to attend the Court without special invitation; that is to say, attached to it by right.

The reader will, I trust, excuse these rather uninteresting details, when I have explained my reasons for giving them. As the adversaries of the Italian cause are daily affirming that almost all the Neapolitan aristocracy have either kept aloof from the court of Victor Emmanuel, or followed Francis II. into exile, it is important that Englishmen should be placed in possession of facts from which they may draw the right conclusion. No doubt there are many representatives of the Neapolitan nobility who have not as yet recognised the government inaugurated by the Plebiscite of October, 1861, and who are re-siding either at Rome or Paris. The number of these families may be fairly reckoned at forty or fifty. Some of them held, and still hold, high dignities at Francis II.'s court, if that can be called a court which has now no official existence; some were employed in diplomacy; some have followed their master with honourable devotion; but the majority have left their native provinces, because in their mind the new Govern-ment is not as yet well organized, and they will in all probability return to Naples when they think the state of the country more settled. The list which the reader will find in the Appendix speaks for itself, and relieves me from the necessity of any further comments. It has been carefully drawn up, and I can vouch for its correctness.

It not unfrequently happens that members of the same family are to be found in the opposite camps. Thus, the Marquis Carracciolo Bella is an ardent sup-porter of the National Government in the Italian Par-liament, though his brother, Prince Torella (one of the most high-minded of the Neapolitan aristocracy), was a Minister of Francis II. after the granting of the Constitution. Duke Cajanello, their brother-in-law, is also—and not without reason—to be found amongst the ranks of those who are not satisfied with the present *régime ;* but I need not here enter into any further details with reference to his position towards the Government, as I have related his story in the previous chapter.

The splendour and wealth of the Neapolitan Barons under the Princes of the House of Suabia, the Anjouan Kings, and the Spanish Viceroys, was so great that, during the Middle Ages and at a later period, they could in this respect rank with any of the aristocracies of Italy. Their opulence often enabled them to perform acts of princely munificence. Thus, Giulio Antonio Acquaviva, Duke of Atri, towards the middle of the fifteenth century, removed the whole population of San Flaviano to the more healthy town of Giulia Nova, which he had founded at his own expense. The income of many of those families is now greatly reduced, and there are not a few noblemen who, although inscribed in the *Libro d' Oro*, have declined almost to the verge of poverty. The Sant' Antimos, Bovinos, San Teodoros, Del Vastos, and Torellas, are, however, to be reckoned amongst those families which are still in possession of large fortunes. The average of their annual incomes may lie between ten and twenty thousand pounds, English.

. During my stay at Naples, that brilliancy and charm for which in former years the fashionable society of the Southern capital was so celebrated, had almost completely disappeared, owing to political events. After the revolution of 1848, the incessant interference of the police rendered social intercourse very difficult, if not utterly impossible. Excepting the *soirées* of the Count of Syracuse, of Lord Holland, of Baron Rothschild, and of Mr. Adolphus Craven, scarcely any house at Naples was regularly opened to society.   The certainty of being placed under the serveillance of spies even within the walls of their own homes, induced the nobility to restrict themselves to the circle of a few intimate friends.   During the epoch to which I am alluding, no one could feel assured that he was beyond the reach of Mazza's police.

In the early days of Francis II.'s reign, the Prince Torella himself was arrested, and ordered to leave the kingdom, although he held the rank of chamberlain, and his loyalty had always made him keep aloof from active political life.   But the police agents of Francis II. knew that he entertained moderate liberal opinions; and in those days that was enough to justify any enormity.

Another member of the Neapolitan aristocracy, Francesco Proto, Duke of Maddaloni, was perpetually, both under the Government of Ferdinand II. and of his son, the object of police persecution. The Duke was an ardent Liberal in 1848, and being returned as a member of the elective Chamber in the Neapolitan Parliament, sat on the benches of the extreme Opposition.   He was compelled to leave his country after the insurrection of the 15th of May, 1848, but was allowed to return to Naples in 1853. Although Duke Proto thus made his peace with King Ferdinand, he was nevertheless threatened with imprisonment and exile more than once, until the arrival of Garibaldi at Naples gave him an opportunity of reentering the ranks of the National party.   Having accepted the appointment of *Ricevitore*, or tax-receiver, offered him by the Dictator, he was looked upon as one of the warmest advocates of annexation to the rest of Italy. The constituents of Cesoria, believing Proto to be the proper man to represent them in the Italian Parliament, elected him deputy, and in that capacity he went to Turin. One day, however, the Duke suddenly startled his colleagues by moving for a Parliamentary inquiry into the affairs of Naples, accompanying his motion by a speech in which he ridiculed the idea of Unity, and gave it as his opinion that the Peninsula must be again divided, and Naples remain a separate monarchy. His remarks on that occasion were so offensive to those members who regarded the annexation of the Southern Provinces to Piedmont as an irrevocable fact, that he found himself under the necessity of resigning his seat in Parliament, and travelling abroad. The reader will by this see how, under the Bourbonic rule, even the weakest and most harmless men were made victims of police persecution.

Soon after the entry of Victor Emmanuel into Naples, some of the more fashionable *salons* began to be opened. That of the Duchess Sant' Arpino — formerly Lady Burghersh — was among the first. Others followed; and it may be said that they all rendered a service to the Government of Victor Emmanuel, by bringing together persons who, but for these reunions, would not have met, in consequence of the difference of their political opinions.

Naples has always been renowned for its distinguished foreign society. There was a time, before the Revolution of 1848, when numerous families, belonging to the English and Russian aristocracy, were in the habit of taking up their winter quarters in that enchanting city, and of opening their apartments to its best society. The receptions of the foreign Faubourg Saint Germain of Naples had, however, almost completely ceased when I was staying there. Only two *salons* were then opened : those of Lady Holland and of Mrs. Craven. The best Neapolitan families—the Sant' Arpinos, the Castellanas, the Bugnanos, &c.—were to be found there regularly, together with many distinguished foreigners. Of this number were the Marchioness of Ely, the Marchioness of Downshire, Mrs. William Russell, &c. Another lady who received was the Marchioness Casanova, who, though belonging to an English family, had married the Marquis Federico, the only member of the Neapolitan aristocracy who, at the breaking out of the national war in 1859, joined the Sardinian army, which he entered as a private soldier— an honourable exception I have great pleasure in mentioning.

Neapolitan fashionable life, however, presents some features less agreeable than receptions. With the Southern aristocracy, duelling is nearly as common as among the students of the German Universities. Any one going to Naples must take the greatest care to avoid all sorts of disputes ; for, in ninety-nine cases out of a hundred, even the most frivolous quarrel ends in a duel. During the year I passed at Naples, a great many were fought. A few cases in point will show the reader how difficult it is in Naples to keep out of mischief, even when not meaning to be offensive to any one.

One day, a Garibaldian officer was walking through the Toledo, when, on passing near the Café dell' Europa, he inadvertently pushed against one of those fire-eating Neapolitans who are always ready to fight. The officer hastened to apologize; but the Neapolitan answered, in a haughty tone—" I do not accept your apology. Here is my card. Please to mention the names and addresses of your seconds." Next morning, a duel took place at Capo di Monte, where both champions were badly wounded by sword-cuts. On another occasion, a friend of mine had gone to a *bal masqué* at the Fondo Theatre with some Piedmontese officers. The ball was dull, and, to make it more lively, the party masked themselves in dominoes, and went down into the pit. Pushed by the crowd, my friend was driven against a young nobleman, who, without any warning, gave him a blow. He immediately went back to his box, divested himself of the domino, and returning into the pit, sent two of his companions to ask the nobleman to apologize; but the latter, whilst asserting that he had not the slightest intention to insult my friend (whom, owing to his disguise, he had not recognised), declined to do so. A duel was therefore arranged for the next morning; and, the result was, that my friend lost one of his fingers, and received a wound on his head besides.

According to Neapolitan custom, when a duel is over, the two principals become intimate friends; and there is a proverb at Naples which says—"As friendly as two men who have fought a duel."

A third story of Neapolitan duelling which I may here introduce is one in which no less noted a man than Alexandre Dumas was concerned. By a dictatorial decree of Garibaldi, that prolific novelist was allowed to inhabit the Royal mansion of Chiatamone, built, according to tradition, on the site of the famous villa of Lucullus. Being an ardent admirer of Garibaldi, Dumas thought proper to become the editor of a newspaper, in which he rather violently opposed the Government of Count Cavour, and denounced what he called its blunders. On a certain morning, whilst I was talking with Mr. Alfred Seymour, Dumas entered my room in great excitement.

" What is the matter with you ?" asked I, on seeing his generally jovial face red with anger.

" The matter," answered he, " is, that the newspaper, *Il Popolo d'Italia*, charges me with having pocketed 40,000 francs, which I am accused of having drawn from the National Treasury, without accounting for their employment."

" Well," said I, " as it cannot be true, I don't see that you have any reason to be so angry."

" What do you mean ?" exclaimed Dumas. " Do you not understand that I am charged with having made use of money which was not my own ? I—the best friend of Garibaldi — I, who made the revolution of Naples—to be accused of such an act !"

" Calm yourself," said Mr. Seymour, " and let us see what is to be done."

" Oh, don't be anxious about that," answered the

French romance-writer. "I have already sent our friend, Count Teleki, to the office of the paper, to challenge its editor. It must be a duel to the death. The ninth article of Chatauvillard's Code of Duels distinctly says—'L'offensé choisit les armes;' and I have chosen the revolver."

"The revolver!" .exclaimed I.

"Yes, the revolver; and we shall shoot at each other till one of us is dead."

This would, indeed, have been a duel *à la Mousquetaire;* but the reader must not be alarmed, for the matter was satisfactorily arranged on the next day. Count Teleki conveyed the challenge to the editor of the *Italia e Popolo;* but there was a gentleman, belonging to the staff of the paper, who took the affair into his own hands, and brought it to a peaceful issue. This was Count Aurelio Saffi, the very personification of all that is good, wise, and noble. He saw that there was no ground for the charge, and had it contradicted on the next day. Thus the quarrel ended, and Dumas is still safe at Chiatamone, busily occupied in writing the Memoirs of Lady Hamilton, and giving dinners to his friends, if not as costly, at any rate as good, as those of the famous Roman Proconsul.

The chance of being shot or run through the body in an "affair of honour" is not the only danger which, in Neapolitan popular opinion, attends on human nature. There is something far worse, because belonging to the supernatural world; viz., the *jettatura,* or "evil eye." It is vulgarly believed that certain individuals can exercise a malignant influence upon

others by a species of witchcraft. There are few people
in the Southern Provinces of Italy who do not believe
in this terrible power. The origin of the superstition,
which finds credit even among educated persons, is not
very clear, although there is no doubt that it was
brought from the East, where it exists to this day. So
great is the faith of the Neapolitans in this terrible influence, that any one who is supposed to be a *jettatore*
is at once avoided, as a man infected with the plague
would be. Nor is this all ; for in many cases the reputation of being a *jettatore* is transmitted from father
to son as a fatal inheritance, and generally the whole
family is included in the ostracism more especially
directed against one of its members. Ferdinand II.
believed so absolutely in the existence of this power,
that he declined to receive all those—even if they
belonged to the aristocracy—who had the reputation
of possessing the "evil eye." A few years after his
accession to the throne, the King gave a ball at
Caserta. All the nobility of the city were invited, with
the exception of a Prince who could claim an invitation
by right. The Master of the Ceremonies having
drawn his Majesty's attention to what he thought
was an accidental oversight, the King answered,
"Oh, I won't have him ; he is a *jettatore.*" The
nobleman, however, had the boldness to press the
case, and the Prince was invited. On making his
appearance in the ball-room, the guests got out of his
way as quickly as they could—a circumstance which
induced Ferdinand II. to show him the greater kindness. Taking him by the arm, he drew his attention
to the large chandelier. Scarcely had the Prince

uttered a word of admiration at its beauty when the chandelier fell from its fastenings, seriously injuring some of the bystanders. From that moment, the poor Prince was not only excluded from Court, but was shunned even by his intimate friends.

Two days before my capture by the Neapolitan troops at the battle of the Volturno, I accepted an invitation to dinner from a famous *jettatore*. On my return to Naples, after being released, all my Southern friends said to me that they did not wonder at my misfortune, as they knew I had been at the house of the gentleman in question. To have the character of a *jettatore* is at Naples equivalent to being placed in the position of a Bravo, or of a *Fante dei Cai*, under the Republic of Venice. The unlucky individual is feared and avoided by all.

Such are the grosser forms of superstition in Naples. But in that land religion itself has a tendency to run into excess. Even stanch Roman Catholics are found to admit that one of the greatest evils of the Neapolitan provinces until recently was the large number of convents. According to a statistical account published by the Italian Government in the month of February, 1861, it appears that at that date there existed in those provinces 1020 establishments for men, containing 13,611 monks and laymen, viz. :—
I. 3055 monks-proprietors ; that is to say, 1924 fathers and 1131 laymen, with a revenue of 3,323,785f. a year.
II. 1657 mendicant friars, with a revenue of 1,232,182f.
III. 8899 absolute mendicants, without revenue, viz. : —5382 fathers and 3517 laymen. The above 4712 monks-proprietors, therefore, enjoyed a revenue of

4,555,697f., which makes an average for each individual of 964f. a year.   The other 8899 lived on the alms of devotees and of the lower classes.   The nunneries in February, 1861, were 276 in number, occupied by 8001 females, of whom 5103 were nuns, and 2898 novices, with a revenue of 4,772,794f., making an average of 596f. for each.

It must be remarked that, at the date of this official document, several monasteries had not sent in a return of their revenues. Judging by approximative estimates, however, the value of the lands belonging to the Neapolitan convents before the publication of the law of the 13th of October, 1861, confirming the Viceregal decree of the 17th of February, amounted to 255,000,000 francs ; and those lands, when they shall have become private property, will be of three times that value.

By the law just alluded to, almost all the religious corporations were abolished, their property was put under the administration of Government officers, and an annual pension was paid to each member in proportion to the revenue possessed by the convent.   In these provisions, however, were not included those religious orders which devote themselves either to public instruction, or to attending the hospitals. When the law of the 13th of October was put into execution in Southern Italy, it undoubtedly created a very bad impression on the people, who are by tradition devoted to conventual institutions.   The nobles are accustomed to look upon the monks as their spiritual advisers, and willingly intrust the education of their daughters to nuns ; in many cases, indeed, looking forward to a convent as the fittest place for at least one of them, who may thus have a chance of becoming abbess. The poorer classes, too, have ever been friendly to the monks ; knowing that, in the hour of distress, they could always get a morsel of bread by knocking at the convent door.   No wonder, therefore, that the edict originally promulgated by Counsellor Mancini should have met with the general disapprobation of the Neapolitan community.   The manner in which it was afterwards acted upon, moreover, was too harsh, and naturally led to the same results which ensued in England when, in the reigns of Henry VIII. and Edward VI., it was sought violently to suppress the mendicant monks.   The embarrassments which this country had to pass through three centuries ago, the Italian National Government has experienced in our days.   The abolition of religious communities is unquestionably wise in principle, for Monachism is out of date in the nineteenth century ; but, at the same time, justice demands that proper care be taken to secure to the monks and nuns an honourable livelihood.   The measures adopted by the Government of Victor Emmanuel were not, perhaps, altogether in accordance with the wants of the dispersed communities ; and from this has arisen much of the opposition and the difficulties which Italy has not yet succeeded in surmounting.   It is easy to turn out from the convents a number of idle fellows ; but, to prevent their becoming dangerous to the Government, they should be offered work and bread.

When the day came for enforcing the law, the religious corporations in the Southern capital and the provinces made no opposition to the taking of an inventory of their property. The Abbess of the Donna Regina convent at Naples was the only person who tried to resist the authorities by refusing to open the gate, which was in consequence broken open by the officers. At the present time, some of the nuns are living at their parents' homes, to which they have returned; some are still domiciled in their former convents, or in others allotted to them. But, on the whole, both nuns and monks are very unfriendly to the new rulers of their country. There have of late been instances of the latter assisting the brigands by furnishing them with provisions, arms, and ammunition. Only a few weeks ago, a British subject, Mr. Bishop (who is not to be confounded with the eminent Dr. Bishop, the best English practitioner at Naples), was arrested at Mola di Gaeta, as the agent of certain reverend fathers who were conspiring against the Italian Government. It would, however, be unfair to say that all the monks of the Neapolitan provinces detest the sway of Victor Emmanuel. There are to be found almost everywhere in Italy liberal priests and monks—men who attend to the duties of their sacred office, and keep aloof from worldly affairs. Amongst these must be reckoned the well-known Benedictine Fathers of Monte Cassino and La Cava, as well as the Teatini and Girolomini of Naples. I have myself known many of the Fathers Girolomini, and especially one, Father Capecelatro, who is a perfect model of piety and charity. The Government ought to take the greatest care to enlist these good priests among its friends; for the influence they exercise

over the common people is immense, and fully deserved.

Quitting these graver subjects, let me endeavour to
give the reader some idea of the externals of Neapolitan life.

The appearance presented by the streets of Naples
at sunrise on a summer morning is at the same time
curious and delightful.   You breathe an air of gentle
warmth, filled with the fragrance of a thousand
flowers, the odour of which is increased by the slow
evaporation of the night dews under the first rays of
the rising sun.   The sky, a bright and glowing azure,
reflects itself in the silvery waves of the bay; whilst,
right and left, the whole of the scenery is beheld
faintly through a luminous mist.   The busy stir of
morning — the going to and fro of the fishermen,
hastening to the beach of Chiaia, where lie the boats
—the bustle of water-carriers, of lazzaroni, of women
hurrying towards the *frutti di mare* market at Santa
Lucia—in short, the lively movements of the lower
population, conversing, in their almost unintelligible
dialect, exchanging warm salutations, asking and
answering questions which nobody is able to understand except themselves — all this makes the early
Neapolitan morning very striking to the stranger.
At the tolling of the bells which call the faithful
to early mass, the Capuchin monk leaves his convent, to collect the offerings of the people, which
he will share with the poor next Friday.   He is
one of the earliest persons to appear in the streets;
but, little by little, the thoroughfares become thronged
with an eager crowd of human beings, horses, and

donkeys. The working population of Pozzuoli and
Portici are fast pouring into the long and bright
Toledo, or directing their steps towards the churches,
whence, after having heard mass and received the
benediction, they proceed slowly towards the place
of their daily work. The liveliness of the scene has
by this time greatly increased ; for the carrozzelle
have begun to appear in the principal streets, and the
noisy drivers have taken up their quarters at those
stands where they hope to have the best chance of
getting customers. In the meanwhile, the girls of
Baiæ, Portici, and other neighbouring villages, are
offering their fruit and flowers in the market.

But here is the corricolo of Resina, coming at a
fearful speed along the road which leads to Pompeii.
The corricolo is a vehicle of classic origin, and, as it is
about to disappear, it requires some special notice at
my hands. Naples is no longer what it was to the
tourist even twenty years ago. It is now comparatively
dull ; at that time, it was a scene of constant gaiety.
What has become of the improvisatore, of the preacher,
and of Punch—those three popular comedians of the
Molo, who engaged in a combat of wit, and delighted
the spectators? What has become of the dancers of
the Tarantella, who, at the sound of the first guitar,
or of the first organ, would spring forward, each
towards the other, to perform, with smiling face and
rounded arms, the national dance? Alas! they have
followed the improvisatore, the preacher, and the Pulci-
nella ; and now the corricolo—the true corricolo—the
primitive corricolo—is in a fair way to share their
fate.

When I speak of the primitive corricolo, I mean that fantastic vehicle which is now only rarely seen in the streets of Naples, like a spectre of past days. I mean that oblong box, painted vermilion, raised high on gigantic wheels, like an American cabriolet, and ornamented with blue and green painted flowers, which do not belong to any Flora of the known world, but purely to the imagination of the artist. The corricolo is dead—or at any rate it has been legally condemned to death, for there is a decree prohibiting carriage-builders from making corricoli. It is with them as with the monks belonging to the suppressed orders: the authorities allow those now existing to die tranquilly of old age—to fall away one by one; but with them the species is to disappear. It is true that it is more than half a century since this law was promulgated; but, though the corricoli are become rare, they have not yet quite vanished. How comes this miracle? the reader may ask. I will explain.

Our neighbours, the French, have a legend about "the knife of Jeannot." This knife is a simple wooden one, bequeathed by a remote ancestor of its present possessor to his great grandfather; by his great grandfather to his grandfather; by his grandfather to his father; by his father to him, who in his turn will leave it to his eldest son. It is a talisman originally bestowed on the family by a fairy; and it brings happiness as long as it remains whole. But, since the day when it came from the hands of the fairy, it has had ten new blades, and ten new handles. No matter! Jeannot believes none the less in the power of his talisman, and, according to him, it is always the same knife which the fairy gave to his ancestor.

This is the history of the corricolo. It is illegal to make new ones; but it is not forbidden to put new wheels to the old boxes, or new boxes to the old wheels. In this way, the corricolo does battle with the decrees of fate; thus it resists, thus it defends itself, and, like Hercules, fights off death.

It is one of those valiant carriages—one of those obstinate machines—which from time to time you see passing, laden with fifteen or eighteen persons, on the roads to Pozzuoli and to Portici. After what I have said, the reader may imagine that the corricolo is a sort of omnibus. This would be a great error. The corricolo is a sort of tilbury, originally intended, like the fabulous car of Apollo, to hold only one person, and to be drawn by one horse, as plainly appears from its double shafts. But civilization, which, according to Rousseau, turns everything from its original purpose, has made the corricolo one of its victims. In the same way that the *Dame aux Camelias* is *traviata*, the corricolo is *traviato*—gone astray. Consequently, instead of being drawn by one horse, it is drawn by two; and, instead of carrying one or two persons at most, it carries eleven at least, and sometimes more than fourteen. And at what pace does it carry them? I have said that the corricolo is Apollo's car, led through the heavens by the Hours. I was mistaken. It is rather the car of Pluto, carrying off Proserpine at a furious gallop, and drawn by two fantastic horses. When it passes, you see nothing but a whirlwind of dust, from the centre of which come shouts and laughter.

One day, between Portici and Resina, a corricolo, going at the frantic rate I have described,
was caught in one of the wheels of the carriage
in which I was seated. I escaped with a slight
shock; but the unfortunate corricolo was upset
with all its cargo. For a moment, the dust was
so thick that I could see nothing; but a gust of
wind blew the cloud away, and I beheld lying in the
road eleven persons, consisting of a monk, two nurses,
their two foster-infants, the husbands of the two
nurses, three lazzaroni, and the proprietor of the
vehicle. Besides these eleven unfortunate beings, two
boys were still in the net which swings between the
two wheels, where they remained like prisoners behind
a grating. The total number of passengers, therefore,
was thirteen. At first, everyone, except the two
infants and the prisoners in the net, ran to the monk.
They raised him up, condoled with him, and petted
him. He had nearly suffocated a nurse and two
lazzaroni; but fortunately he had not sustained a
scratch. From that moment, I knew I was safe; but,
if the monk had been killed or even wounded, I should
in all probability have been a dead man.

I ventured to get down from the carriage, and
offered to the party a piastre to drink the health of
the monk, which was gratefully accepted. I was thus
enabled to see the arrangement of the corricolo, and
to solve the problem how thirteen persons could be
placed in a carriage intended for only one.

The two boys remained where they were, in their
net. The monk got in first, and placed himself on
the seat, as on a throne; the nurses with their infants

sat one on each knee of the monk; the two husbands of these ladies placed themselves on the footboard; the driver got up behind the monk, over whose head he guided his horses; and the three lazzaroni were grouped round the coachman. The driver now bowed courteously to me, gave a little shout, touched the ears of the horses with his whip, and the equipage went off at a gallop, disappearing at about fifty paces in the cloud of dust which renders it invisible to mortal eyes. This was the first and last time I had an opportunity of penetrating the mysteries of the corricolo; and, but for the good fortune which attended the monk, I might have shared the fate of those who dared to invade the sanctity of the temple of Vesta.

But let us leave Naples, and its noisy streets and piazzas, and follow that beautiful road, stately with historical recollections, which, skirting the ever-verdant shores of the tideless sea, conducts us to the ancient city of Pompeii. It is there that the Italian traveller really feels the greatness of his forefathers—the conquerors of the world. It is there, amidst those still eloquent ruins, under those half-decayed arches and pillars, beneath the walls of the Necropolis and the shadow of the Forum columns, or on the threshold of the temple of Isidis, that the voice of ancient Rome is yet to be heard.

The last rays of the setting sun gild the gate leading to the Pretorium. We follow the loquacious guide, and penetrate into the narrow cells destined in former days for the criminals who were to pass the remainder of their lives in rowing the vessels of the great

Empire. Every building — though shattered by the progress of many centuries—tells of the power and genius of the Latin race. We tread the stone pavement of the road on which the wheels of the heavy Roman chariots have deeply impressed their marks. The peristylium and impluvium are silent; the shops are empty, the houses deserted; but our imagination is not at rest : it peoples all those dwellings with the phantoms of a by-gone race. We behold the senator and the matron of Rome making their entry into the city—their resting-place in the sweet autumn days—the magnificent sea-side town to which the legislators of the world, worn out by the cares of State, repaired to soothe their minds and restore their health. We almost expect to see the smoke rising from the golden censers of the Flamens—to hear the shouting of the jubilant people, the hymns of the priests, and the roaring of the lions restlessly awaiting the hour of the fight. And there, on the horizon, for ever and ever, rises the old grey column of smoke, sprinkled with numberless sparks of fire, as it rose on the terrible day when Pompeii and Herculaneum were buried beneath the showering cinders and the red-hot lava-torrents poured down from the thunder-shaken mountain. The thought of that tremendous calamity broods heavily over our minds. We hear—as if renewed by the power of an enchanter—the screams of a dismayed population struggling to escape from misery and death. Pliny the Elder, and the fleet anchored at Misenum, are for us like present facts. We see the aged man tottering along the shore whose pebbles are covered with myriads of sulphurous stones launched from the roaring crater—a rain of vivid fire amidst the obscurity of a starless night. And far off, by that lurid light, we behold the vessels tossed on the seething billows of the convulsed and quaking sea.

As, however, we proceed towards the northern end of the newly-discovered town, these gloomy thoughts give place to more cheerful ones, for we are now coming near the Forum—almost a heap of ruins, it is true, but ruins of exquisite Corinthian columns, of delicately sculptured chaptrels, of miracles of art, wrought out of Parian marble. Hard by are still to be seen the remains of buildings in which the merchants stored up the goods they had brought from eastern colonies—the *spolia opima* of the conquered nations.

But we must tear ourselves away from these glorious recollections of a day long past, and, following the road which runs along the foot of the mountains of Somma, must return to the life of our own days. What is that green and smiling spot which seems to rise from the blue waves of the Tyrrhene Sea, as if it were the dwelling of Armida? It is Castellammare, with its once strongly-built castle on the left, frowning over the town of gaiety and pleasure, amidst the old oaks which shroud it. Once there, we need not strain our imagination to animate the place. The sea-shore is peopled by an elegant crowd just returning from the mineral waters. The air is rent with the shouting of the ciuciari, who offer you their half-starved donkeys on which to gallop up the steep hill of Villa Qui si Sana. The speronare shoot swiftly by under the skilful hands of the rowers; whilst in the far distance the boats of Amalfi and Ischia glide on towards the looked-for harbour across the calm blue level of the sea. The sun-burnt lazzarone is going to and from the busy arsenal of the jetty, making a great deal of noise; and the lively naval officer is smoking his cigar, and flirting with the bright-eyed girls of the neighbouring café. Here is a company of Russians coming up from Villa Sabatelli; there, a batch of English travellers, with green veils on their "wide-awakes," escorting a party of ladies. Close at hand, amidst a merry group of Neapolitan gentlemen, you see the beauties of the watering-place—the Sant' Arpinos, the Melanos, the Camporeales, the Castellanas, all of whom will ere long return to their villas to receive the *beau monde*, and to dance and sing till dawn.

Evening is now coming on, and that busy hum, which in an Italian town precedes the stillness of night, seems to pervade the whole air. The bell of the Capuchin convent is tolling the Ave Maria—the hour of love and tender recollections, as the Italians say. The poor monk is hurrying up his tired donkey, laden with the somewhat heavy burden of corn and oil given by the charitable country people. The song of the returning fisherman falls upon the ear, and melts into the heart, like the notes of some mysterious harmony heard in a happy dream. All around is tranquillity: the air is balmy with the breath of flowers; and a myriad of fire-flies are glancing along the hedges of cactus and myrtle which separate the fields, and run up the distant hills.

By this time the moon has risen over the dark mountain tops of the Gulf of Salerno—a moon whose light is only conquered by the blazing stream of lava winding down the declivities of Vesuvius. At that hour, the unrivalled Bay of Naples stands in all its glory, Castellammare in all its beauty. Striking off from the sea, the road to Sorrento winds up in graceful convolutions towards the famous Piana. On the left is to be seen the Cathedral of Vico, its gothic fretwork glancing in the moon, as if carved in silver. Farther on, the eye takes in the sleeping village of Albero, the picturesque Martello tower, and the deep ravine which the colossal bridge spans with its marvellous arches. Then comes Sorrento, the beauty of which no pen can adequately portray.

How well I remember the first visit I paid to those enchanting places in 1861 ! I arrived at Castellammare on one of those delicious evenings of April which, in southern regions, fill the mind with so inexpressible a sense of the Divine beneficence. I hastened to the cemetery, that I might pay the tribute of a sincere grief over the graves of departed friends. The solemnity of night, the song of the homeward peasant, the sad but melodious notes of the nightingale, and the murmur of the waves, raised me into a state of rapture which I shall never forget.

On the following morning, I was ready for the guide when he knocked at the door of my room at the Britannia Hotel.

" Eccellenza," said he, " it is time for us to start if you would see the sunrise from the hills. The carrozzella is ready."

In half an hour I was driving along the road to Sorrento. Having arrived at the Sirena Hotel, the carriage was left behind, and up we went along the steep paths of the mountains amidst groves of orange and olive trees. I will not dwell on the scenery which, when the visitor has reached the top of Monte Sant' Angelo, spreads itself before him. As I said before, Sorrento, its sea and its hills, its vineyards and its gardens, cannot be described. I will therefore not attempt to depict the plain of Pæstum ; nor the gay Amalfi, with its red-tiled roofs peeping out from the green groves ; nor the gigantic, half-blue, half-grey rock of Capri in front ; nor the pretty costumes of the countrywomen of Massa Lubrenese, ascending the hills with their baskets on their heads—burdens which they carry with so much easy grace that they seem scarcely conscious of them.

One feature of the scene, however, I must not pass unnoticed....What is that small sailing vessel which has just left the creek of Capri, and is making its way towards Naples? It is a speronara—the gaily freighted speronara of olden times, now devoted to the humble duties of fishing, and carrying the wine of Capri to the metropolis. The speronara, like the corricolo, is fast disappearing before the steady advance of its natural enemy, the steamboat. Thirty years ago, the speronare abounded. They carried the mail-post, and were almost the only means of communication between Sicily and Naples. They were hired by tourists for six or eight ducats a day, and would often take eight days to go to Messina. Now, you can go to Messina for six or eight ducats in twelve hours. But this can hardly be called travelling : you start, and you arrive—that is all.

I will describe what a speronara is, or rather what
it was at that time. It was a little ship of twelve
metres long, with a small cabin, capable of holding
two mattresses and a table; more or less clean within,
more or less *coquet* without. Generally it was painted
green, with a red band. Its crew consisted of eight
or ten men and a boy, who were rarely in the pay of
the captain, the captain and crew being partners.
The captain, who owned the speronara, represented the capital; the sailors, who gave their
work, represented the labour. Labour and capital
made two equal shares; that is to say, the captain
took one half of the proceeds, the crew the other
half.

The speronara had over the land-post one considerable advantage, which I have not mentioned.
When the land-post had no horses, the traveller was
obliged to remain on the high road; but when the
speronara had no wind, it could use its oars. It is
true that it went but slowly; still, it made way,
and that kept one patient. It had also another advantage: it did not require to enter a port to enable it to
cast anchor; any shore was good enough, as it drew
scarcely four feet of water. You could land wherever
you wished, being carried ashore on the shoulders of
the sailors, who drew up the boat to await your
return. It was everywhere a home to you—far pre-
ferable to the miserable lodgings at the country inns.
Besides, you had dancing and music. It was seldom
that the sailors did not play the guitar—the Spaniards,
as one may easily believe, having left many of their
habits amongst the population of the two Sicilies;

and at the sound of that instrument the people near at hand flocked together. The young Calabrian or Sicilian girls were invited to come on deck ; and, though they might at first make some difficulty, their coyness would vanish as the musician redoubled his energy, till, like the fascinated bird which yields to the serpent, the young dancers would fall into the arms of their partners.

In the speronara you could make a voyage like that of Æneas, from Naples or Palermo to the Lybian shores ; you could land at Castellammare, at Sorrento, at Capri, at Salerno, at Pæstum, at the Piræus, at Scylla, at Reggio—anywhere, in fact. You could remain as long as you wished, and go when you liked ; you had not to be perpetually listening for the sound of the bell, giving note of departure ; you did not run till you were out of breath, fearing lest you should not reach the boat before it started. If you wished to walk along the coast, you said to your captain, " Follow me," and you could not lose sight of each other. Then, when you desired to get on board again, you made a sign, and instead of going to your boat, your boat came to you.

Such was the speronara ; and the friendly reader will sympathize, I hope, in these few praises devoted to its memory, and these passing regrets bestowed upon its loss.

CHAPTER XIV.

THE FUTURE OF ITALY.

Death of Count Cavour—Two original Letters of that Statesman
—His last Political Advice—Baron Ricasoli's Accession to
Power—His Plan for the Solution of the Roman Question—
Debate in the Italian Parliament on that Question—Difficul-
ties of the Situation—The *Commitati di Provvedimento*—
Rattazzi made Prime Minister—His previous Life—Recent
Journey of the Author into Italy—State of Public Opinion in
Italy with reference to the New Government—Interviews of
the Author with Rattazzi and Garibaldi last April—Tem-
poral Power of the Pope—The Venetian Question—Italy for
the Italians.

MY task is now drawing to its close, though, in
glancing over the subjects which I proposed to discuss, I find sufficient facts remaining to furnish matter
for another volume. Should the views I now put
forth meet with the sympathy of the English public,
I shall be encouraged to return to the various aspects
of the Italian question, and to narrate more fully the
progress of events since the death of Count Cavour.
For the present, however, I can only discuss them
very briefly.

At the commencement of June, 1861, I had made
up my mind to bid farewell to Naples, and return to
England. Whilst, however, on the 7th of that month,

I was directing my steps towards the Molo, to secure a place in the steam-boat which was to take me next day to Genoa, my attention was suddenly attracted by the news-boys who were announcing the death of Count Cavour. Although intelligence of the dangerous illness of the illustrious statesman had reached Naples a week before, I did not expect that the first of the Prime Ministers of Italy was so soon to be removed by death. Such, however, was the case. I hastened to the Royal Palace; for, knowing how easily false news is propagated at Naples, a gleam of hope still remained in my heart. But, alas! the statement was too true: Count San Martino dispelled all doubts—the great man had expired at seven o'clock on the previous morning. He who had had the principal share in the regeneration of my country had fallen suddenly and quietly, as a leaf falls in the stillness of an autumn day. From a world in which he had held so high a place he had passed away, just at the moment when Italy was most in need of his firm grasp at the helm. Which should be more pitied, the country or its Minister? There are deaths which induce us to mourn rather for the living than for the departed; and conspicuous among these was the death of Cavour. Subsequent events have impressed this sad conviction on every Italian heart; for, from the 6th of June, 1861, to this hour, not a day has passed in which thoughtful Italians have not had occasion to say to one another—"Had Cavour lived, public affairs would have progressed satisfactorily,—escaped this danger, or avoided that delay." And not one of my countrymen doubts that, were Cavour still with us, we should by this time have proclaimed the unity of Italy from the Capitol.

There may have been Italians whose plots Cavour "hated with the warmth of a brave and honest man," and who, in their turn, did not shrink from outraging his memory after his death; but these—to the honour of my country be it said—were few in number, a small class of rabid politicians who exercise no influence over public opinion. The memory of Count Cavour is honoured in Italy with a unanimity rarely manifested in any country or in any age; for Italians feel that a great sorrow has befallen the land from which Cavour has departed, after having rescued it from the slavery wherein it had been plunged for centuries. Italy can unquestionably boast of other men who, both by their moral influence and by the deeds they have performed, are entitled to the gratitude of their fellow-countrymen; and foremost among these, I need not say, stands the valiant conqueror of Naples and Sicily. Yet the services of Cavour exceed by far the achievements of all others. He it was who prepared and gave the first impulse to the great national struggle of 1859. He was the mind of Italy; the rest were but its arms. From the first assumption by Cavour of the duties of Prime Minister, in November, 1852, down to the 30th of May, 1861—the day on which he was taken ill—he was the very soul of the Italian movement. His prodigious activity was equal to any demand that might be made on it. He was not only the Minister of Foreign Affairs, but the *de facto* Minister of every department. He found time to attend to everything—to give the necessary impulse to all the branches of the public administration. Even the most trifling details of public affairs did not fail to attract his attention. On hearing one day that a former acquaintance of his had published a work on Socialism, he procured the book ; but, not having time to peruse it, he wrote to a friend the letter I here annex :—

"6th April, 1858.

"Dear ——,

"I have procured ——'s work, which you had described to me as a treatise on Socialism. I supposed it to be a small matter, and believed that a few hours would have sufficed for its perusal ; but, finding that it consisted of more than 600 pages, I had not the courage to undertake the search for those passages which you had indicated as being worthy the attention of the Government.

"I would therefore beg you to mark the pages containing them, as also the one in which an apocryphal passage of St. Augustine is referred to.

"Be good enough to offer to the Abbé Rosmini my respectful greetings, and to tell my brother that the health of his son progresses favourably, as also my own.

"Believe me, truly yours,

"C. Cavour."

Although trifling in itself, this letter shows the frankness of Cavour's high intellect, and his accessibility to truth, from whatever quarter it might come. Widely as his social views differed from those of the writer to whom he was referring, he did not disdain the antagonistic opinions ; but in this, as in every similar case, lent a willing and attentive ear to all his opponents had to say.

Engrossed with Neapolitan affairs at the period when he was stricken with mortal illness, the recollection of them haunted his fevered brain even a few hours before his death. " I will have no state of siege," he continually repeated whilst his last hour was approaching. It was by the beneficent influence of good laws and wise administrators that he hoped to bring the annexed provinces of the South to a steady and orderly condition. The mistakes he had been led into by the so-called *Consorteria* of political exiles, he willingly confessed ; and he had already set to work to have them repaired when his exertions were cut short by death. The sad experience of the previous six or eight months had convinced him of the necessity of sending to Naples men more competent to judge the difficulties of the situation, and to surmount them by an adequate policy. All patriotic and influential Neapolitans he urged to go back to their country, and do their best to help the National Government in the difficult task it had undertaken. With this view, a few months before his death, he addressed to a distinguished Neapolitan author the following letter :—

" DEAR ——,

" Thanks for the Biography. You will henceforth be entitled ' a Cavourite to the backbone.' I hope the day will never come when this title may be hurtful to you.

" As to your question, I lose no time in answering you, that I consider the Neapolitans incapable of effectively serving their country, unless it be at Naples itself.   There they may co-operate in the triumph of the great cause by hindering the municipal ideas from reawakening.

"Believe me, your affectionate

"C. Cavour."

As I have been compelled to speak of the untoward state of things existing in Southern Italy at the Count's death, I am happy to be able to add that this evil has been greatly diminished since the visit of Victor Emmanuel to Naples during last May.   This is, indeed, a fact deserving particular attention.   It is melancholy to find political men, both in this and in other countries of Europe, constantly citing the absence of order in the southern part of the Italian Peninsula to prove that the sway of Victor Emmanuel is opposed by the majority of the population, and that the unity of Italy is practically impossible.   Politicians who reason thus, overlook the important fact that there is no record in human history of a great constructive revolution being effected without a period of uneasy transition, from the old trammels which a few still hug, to the new freedom to which millions aspire.   "Principles," says Tennyson, "are rained in blood."   Parturition is ever a painful process; and only through a time of doubt, of conflict, of impassioned struggles, can that higher development of national life be reached, in which order and liberty will walk hand in hand, and the country be enabled to enjoy all those advantages which result from established institutions and traditions.   What— as Mr. Gladstone wisely asked in a recent debate in the House of Commons—what was the state of England

two years after the Revolution of 1688? Surely
there was less security in the streets of London in
those days than there is at present at Naples. The
people of Scotland and Ireland were then no less rebellious than those of the Abruzzi and of Terra di
Lavoro are now. And if the administration of Italy
under Victor Emmanuel be still imperfect, was not
the local and central government of England under
William III. also in need of the progressive improvement and consolidation which it has since received?
Let it be borne in mind, moreover, that there was not
in England at that time any foreign intervention
against the new Government, nor anything equivalent
to the continuous inroad of brigands, organized and
fostered in a neighbouring and independent State;
and I think it will be admitted that the condition of
Southern Italy is a settled one as compared with that
of this country even upwards of fifty years after the great
Revolution. I need not remind English readers that
so late as 1745-6 the second Pretender spread dismay
through the whole island, and very nearly succeeded in
upsetting the House of Hanover. Were the French intervention to cease at Rome — were the Eternal City
to become the capital of Italy — in less than a month
order would be restored in the Neapolitan provinces.
In spite of the errors committed by the new Government, the idea of Italian unity is as popular in those
provinces as it is in the other parts of the Peninsula.
The great majority of the educated classes among the
Neapolitans are almost to a man in favour of liberal
institutions, and of the unity of the country. There
may be an imperceptible minority still remaining

faithful to the Bourbons; but English politicians may be assured that the exiled Royal family will never be allowed to come back. As for the bulk of the population, they are able, notwithstanding their ignorance, to see that a Government which provides them with work and bread is better than one which made them alternately the instruments and victims of its inhuman tyranny.

Three days before his untimely end, Count Cavour, in a conversation with Commendatore Nigra, pointed out Baron Ricasoli as the best man to whom the King could apply to form an Administration. Although the Count's friendly relations with Commendatore Rattazzi had almost ceased since the month of April of the previous year, yet on his death-bed he did not fail to acknowledge that his political opponent could also render great services to the country. Cavour was a just man, and the consciousness of his approaching end made him forget the rancour which had for a time clouded the old friendship existing between himself and his former colleague.

A few days after the Count's death, Baron Ricasoli came into power. The task he inherited from his illustrious predecessor was an onerous one. Italy, as I have already more than once explained to the reader, is divided into two parties: the party which proclaims revolution as the only means of solving the two most important political questions of the day—the fixing of the capital of the kingdom at Rome, and the liberation of Venetia; and the party which proposes to itself the attainment of the same ends by diplomatic means, or at least by organizing the necessary force to carry out

a successful war, if war must be.   The representatives
of the first of these two parties sit at the extreme
Left of the Italian chamber; the members of the
second compose the great Liberal majority, and during
Ricasoli's rule upheld the policy of the Baron.   To
a certain extent, and under certain conditions, the
Moderates are now supporting the present Cabinet, as
the vote of the deputies on the 6th of June has
shown.

To encounter the difficulties which existed on his
accession to power, Baron Ricasoli summoned all the
strength of his mind, all the stern inflexibility of his
noble character.   With the straightforwardness of his
nature, he thought himself capable of settling the
Roman question at once; and he began to argue with
the Roman Court, or at least tried to do so, by writing
to Cardinal Antonelli and to the Pope the conciliatory
letters which will be found in the Appendix.   But
Ricasoli had to deal with a Power which, though
alleging Christianity as its basis, is constantly trampl-
ling on the pacific principles of that religion.   These
letters were sent through the French Government; but
they were scornfully refused by the Papal Court; and
the only answer the Prime Minister got was from M.
de Thouvenel, to the effect that the Pope "was not in
a humour" to entertain such proposals.   Ricasoli's
amicable appeal to the Pope was indeed a political
error on his part; for the mere fact of his arguing
with the Roman Court on the subject of the temporal
power, was liable to be construed, by the wily Catholic
diplomacy, as a virtual recognition of his Holiness's
sovereignty.   The plan of Baron Ricasoli, which was

based on the principle of "a free Church in a free State," would, in the long run, even if it had been accepted by the Pope, have fallen short of the desired result. Indeed, one of its provisions, leaving to the Roman Court the right of appointing Bishops, would have enabled the Papacy to lord it over Italy as it has done for so many centuries past. In the discussions which arose upon this question in the Italian Chamber of Deputies at the beginning of last December, these were the views put forth by the Opposition, and more especially by two of its most learned members—Professor Ferrari and Signor Petruccelli. They and their colleagues did not shrink from passing a severe judgment on the course which Baron Ricasoli had pursued in this matter.

"The Roman question," observed the last-named orator, " was created by the French Emperor in order to deprive Italy of the sympathy of Europe. The Catholic world opposed us because it deemed us foes to the Pope with regard to this question. The hatred which should have weighed upon France is turned into sympathy, because she is looked upon as the protectress of the Papacy and of Catholicism. But does this Roman question exist for us ? Is there a Roman question for the Italian people ? No : the Pope is a most holy Janus with two faces. One is serene and august—it is that of the Pontiff; the other is idiotic, ferocious, brutal—it is that of the King of Rome. Now, has Italy anything in common with the Pontiff, or with the King of Rome ? With the Pontiff, Yes. But the Italian Government is not a council. It does not discuss the Pope; it does not discuss whether the

Pope is or is not the head of Christendom,—whether he is the first of Bishops,—whether he is above the Councils,—whether he can fabricate dogmas, concordats, and so forth,—whether there could be a Catholicism without a Pope—the great solution of the Catholic question with which Henry VIII. of England busied himself. Italy does not discuss Christianity, though she knows that the scholars of a neighbouring nation, Strauss, Daub, Paulus, &c., look upon it as a myth, or a natural phenomenon. Italy does not enter into this question of the Lower Empire, well knowing that the Papacy is now like one of those Egyptian pyramids, grand outside, but having only a mummy within. Italy has the consciousness of the Revolution which it accomplishes—the complement of the French Revolution of 1789. What discussion can there be between the Pontiff and the Italian Government? The latter should have declared itself incompetent. They well knew that by combating the Pope they would give him life. If Pius IX., this Madame de Maintenon of the Papacy—" (Loud interruptions. The orator is called to order.) "So much for the Pontiff. As for the King, wherein does the question lie? It is simply a discord between the Prince and his subjects. The subjects of Parma, Modena, and Tuscany attack, overcome, and drive out their Princes. The Pope's subjects attack, endeavour to conquer, and have partly conquered, the King of Rome, as they before tried to do in 1831 and 1848. What business has the Italian Government in this matter? The Italian Government is called—and it comes; it is invited—and it accepts. And why does it come?

Why does it accept? To maintain public order; to maintain the balance of the social forces. And, if it ever goes to Rome, let us say in high tones that it will go there called by the Roman people, now oppressed by the French Government; but it will also go to save the lives of Locatelli's assassins. We go to Rome on that very principle proclaimed by Metternich when he interfered at Naples in 1821, and when he invaded Romagna in 1831—'that, when a neighbour's house is on fire, we have a right to break into it to put it out, lest the fire should spread to our own.'"

In spite, however, of this eloquent speech, and in spite of the censure passed by the Opposition, Ricasoli's policy was approved by the majority of the Chamber, after he had made a solemn promise that he would employ all those means which were likely to secure the speedy solution of the problem.

But the difficulties of the situation, both in regard to this question and to that of Venice, were daily increasing. Not long after Ricasoli came into power, a split occurred between the Italian Cabinet and that of the French Emperor. The stern dignity —nay, harshness—of the Florentine nobleman gave offence in high quarters, both at Turin and Paris. To these troubles, dissensions of another kind were soon added. Ricasoli and his colleagues were taxed by all parties, both in and out of Parliament, with having neglected the internal organization of the country. Since the resignation of Commendatore Minghetti— which was, indeed, a necessity, his project of law on the political and administrative reorganization of the country having been opposed by the *Ufficii*, or committees, of the Lower House—Ricasoli had been unable to find another statesman ready and qualified to fill up the vacant place. On the one hand, the Ministerial party was utterly disorganized ; on the other, the Left was becoming every day more and more determined in its opposition. The Left Centre, or Third Party, was anxiously awaiting its turn to assume the reins of power under its chief, Rattazzi. The old majority had not, indeed, as yet abandoned Ricasoli ; but it had broken loose from discipline, and the whims of an ill-disguised opposition became every day more apparent. On many divisions, the Baron's stanchest supporters went over to the camp of the enemy, although asserting that he was the only man who could govern the country ; and it grew more and more obvious that the Ricasoli Cabinet was doomed.

Matters thus went on till the middle of last February, when the democratic assembly, elected by the "Commitati di Provvedimento," was invited to meet at Genoa. The organization of this political society (whose avowed object, as its name indicates, is to provide means for hastening the solution of the Roman and Venetian questions) was the work of Mazzini and his friends, and, although presided over by Garibaldi, was looked upon by the Conservative party as a dangerous institution, which might lead the country into the perilous path of revolution, as the "Constituenti" of Tuscany and Rome had done in 1849. To avert this danger, the majority of the Chamber asked Ricasoli whether it was his intention to allow the assembly to take place, or to prevent its meeting. Ricasoli answered as any Minister desiring to remain within the bounds of the constitu-

tion would have done, and said, that as long as the deputies of the Commitati di Provvedimento respected the
law, he had neither the power nor the wish to prevent
their meeting. This declaration widened the existing
split between the Cabinet and majority; and, although
the former was supported by the Left, an order of the
day was passed which certainly contained by impli-
cation a censure on the Ministry.

Baron Ricasoli immediately resigned office, and
Rattazzi was charged by the King with the formation
of a new Cabinet. I need give nothing more than
a passing glance at the extra-parliamentary causes
which, according to the political friends of the late
Premier, placed his adversary at the head of affairs.
Calumnious attacks and unmerited reverses are
the lot of public men in all countries; and it
is not to be expected that those of Italy should
enjoy an exceptional immunity. Rattazzi is taxed
with having been a party to a courtly intrigue; and,
more than that, he is said to have been imposed on
the country by a foreign monarch. For my part, I
have too much confidence in the straightforwardness
of Victor Emmanuel to believe either one or the other
of these reports. Italy may not as yet be so strong as
she will be when more completely organized; but I am
certain that she would never endure the dictation of
a foreign sovereign, however great his power. It may
be that there was a growing estrangement between
the late Premier and the Crown; but this would not
have hastened the fall of Ricasoli's Government, had
the majority of the Chamber stood by the Minister's
side, and supported him, as they had done at the
beginning of the Parliamentary session.

Commendatore Rattazzi is a native of Alessandria, and was one of the most distinguished lawyers of Casale, when the Italian Revolution of 1848 broke out. Having been returned as a deputy to the Sardinian Parliament in its first session, he entered the Ministry of Gioberti a few months after the first unsuccessful campaign in Lombardy. Gioberti, who had proposed an armed intervention in Tuscany, with a view to putting down Guerrazzi's Government, and to restoring the Lorrainese Prince, was soon obliged to resign the premiership; for his project met with the opposition both of his colleagues and of Charles Albert. Rattazzi was then appointed First Minister of the Sardinian Crown; and it was under him that a second campaign against Austria was decided upon. The defeat of Novara led to the premiership of Massimo D'Azeglio, that honest and able statesman, to whom Italy owes a debt of gratitude for having saved the liberal institutions of Piedmont when, by the preponderance of Austria, they were thought to be in imminent danger. From the disastrous epoch of Novara to the end of D'Azeglio's Administration in 1854, Rattazzi fulfilled the functions, first of Vice-President, and afterwards of President of the Chamber. He had, in the meanwhile, contracted an intimate friendship with Count Cavour, who, after a short retirement from public affairs, succeeded D'Azeglio in the premiership of the Sardinian Administration. Cavour appointed him Minister of Justice—an office which was subsequently exchanged for that of Minister of the Interior. Though informed of the secret transactions of Compiégne, Rattazzi retained office till the départure from Genoa of the Mazzinian expedition, in which the unfortunate Pisacane lost his life. Assailed by his political adversaries—calumniated as to his private life—Rattazzi became the victim of misrepresentations which went so far as to embitter the friendly relations previously existing between him and Count Cavour. Nevertheless, he was recalled to power by Victor Emmanuel soon after the peace of Villafranca, but resigned office a few months later, when Cavour formed the Ministry which carried out the cession of Savoy and Nice, and proclaimed the necessity of having Rome as the capital of the Italian kingdom. A few months after the accession of Baron Ricasoli, Rattazzi went to Paris, and was received by the Emperor, who, it is stated, has always felt a great admiration for him, on account of his amiable character. This visit to the French metropolis, however, was seized upon by Rattazzi's adversaries as a means of still further aspersing his political reputation; motives being attributed to him which, although not justified by facts, gave renewed existence to all those suspicions that attended his first entry into power. It must, indeed, be admitted that these suspicions, though really unfounded, were apparently supported by the choice made by Rattazzi of Marquis Pepoli—a cousin of the French Emperor—as Minister for Agriculture and Commerce in the present Government of the Italian kingdom.

As a statesman, Rattazzi is a politician of the first order. A thoroughly practical man, fully acquainted with the laws of his country, initiated from his youth in the details of official life, he is undoubtedly the ablest Minister of the Interior Italy possesses. As a Premier, he has the great advantage over his pre-

decessor of being more calm and conciliatory.   These
qualities, coupled with simple and unpretending manners in his private life, make him a favourite with
Victor Emmanuel, who has always evinced the
warmest friendship for him.

The first act of Rattazzi, since his renewed accession
to power, was to make an appeal to Garibaldi, urging
him not to compromise the country by rash acts.   It
was, indeed, at Rattazzi's instance that the illustrious
General went into the provinces, and presided over
the opening of the *Tiro Nazionale*, of which the heir
of the Crown, Prince Umberto, is the active President.

At the beginning of last April, being in Turin, I had
an opportunity of judging by close observation the political situation of the country.   I found the opposition
to the new Ministers, and especially to Rattazzi, in full
swing.   The stories which people told each other
under the porticoes, and in other places of common
resort, though they would have been scarcely credited
by any reasonable man unblinded by prejudice, found
thousands of believers.   " Rattazzi," they said, " had
been imposed on the nation by the French Emperor ;
Ricasoli had been sacrificed to the jealousy which
actuates the French Government against England ;
Italy could no longer reckon upon the sympathy of
the latter, and her liberties would be undoubtedly
trampled upon to accommodate the exigencies of
the ruler of France ; the Roman question would
be indefinitely postponed, and Austria would be
allowed to tyrannize over the people of Venetia
as long as it pleased her."   Such were the views
entertained by the extreme parties.   The Conserva-

tives, too, indulged in equally gloomy forebodings. For them, Rattazzi was the man of the Revolution, inasmuch as he had come to terms with Garibaldi and his followers; and, according to their views, he might be expected to plunge the country into the miseries of a disastrous war with Austria, and of internal commotions, as fatal, they said, as those he stirred up in 1849.

Having had opportunities of talking over the political situation of our country both with Rattazzi and Garibaldi, I was not long in making out that the charges brought against the former, whether by Conservatives or Liberals, were utterly unfounded. The reader must not think I mean to imply that the Italian Premier has initiated me into all the secrets of his policy. Rattazzi is too prudent a statesman to unfold his designs to the first man he comes across. But I was, nevertheless, enabled to judge the general nature of his programme from what I heard. In the long conversations I had with him, he gave me a history of the incidents which brought him once more to the head of affairs, and an outline of the opinions he entertains on the two main questions of the day. As to Rome, he said, that, without the consent of the Emperor, it would be sheer madness to think of attempting to get possession of that city; and that the recent debates in the French Senate and Corps Legislatif were an undeniable proof that there is in France a strong party which supports the claims of the Roman Court. As to the second question, the views of the Italian Premier seem to differ but little from those of his predecessor. The acquisition of

Venice means war with Austria; and to be able to encounter such a war, Italy must organize herself, increase her armed forces, and permanently suppress Southern brigandage, against which the Government has at present to maintain an army of 80,000 men. When all this shall have been done, Italy may assume the attitude which becomes a powerful State. Alluding to the alliance with England, Commendatore Rattazzi said that, without her moral support, the Peninsula would probably never have been enabled to disprove that favourite saying of Metternich, that Italy was but a geographical expression. Rattazzi cordially recognised the twofold fact, that while France had shed her blood for the redemption of the country, England had powerfully aided her by maintaining the principle of non-intervention, and by giving her moral support to the several annexations.

As for Garibaldi, he was of course more explicit than the Minister. I found him always actuated by those noble aspirations which are natural to him; though perhaps he overrates the irregular forces of the country, and trusts too much in the practicability of developing them on an immense scale. Of war he did not say much; but, as the reader may imagine, he anticipated that it would come ere long. With regard to Rattazzi, he was neither satisfied nor dissatisfied with him; he only said that he would wait, and judge him by his acts. The affair of Sarnico, which led to the bloody scene at Brescia, and to the arrest of Colonel Nullo and Signor Ambiveri, seems, however, to have now placed Garibaldi in absolute opposition to Rattazzi. The French Emperor, as usual, he denounced with great energy, and all his sympathy was for the English people. "England," said the great warrior, "might save the liberties of Europe; and I hope that Italy may reckon upon her friendship in the coming struggle."

For that struggle Italy is now preparing; and when the hour strikes, she will be in arms to assert once more her incontestable right to regain what is her own.

So much has been said and written about Rome and Venice, that it would be useless to enter into any further discussion of the subject. The temporal power of the Pope, as Lord Palmerston rightly observed in his speech on the 11th of last April, cannot possibly endure: "sooner or later, the rule of the Pontiff will come to an end." When the French Emperor has persuaded himself that the occupation of the Eternal City by his troops is a constant violation of the principle of non-intervention, and when he has withdrawn the garrison he maintains there, the Romans will rise as one man, and get rid of their priestly rulers, as the people of Romagna, Umbria, and the Marches have already done. The catastrophe may be delayed, but not avoided; for the fall of the temporal power is but a question of time. Such is the conviction of all rational men throughout Europe. Nay, as far back as 1830, we find this opinion shared to a certain extent by the then Cardinal and Secretary of State, Bernetti, who, in a conversation he had with the French Ambassador, M. de Saint Aulaire, said :—

"My personal opinion is, that the secularization of the Legations is inevitable; it will take place a little

sooner or a little later; but the Pope will never pronounce it, and with good reason : first, because it is not
fit that he should draw upon himself the resentment of
the Cardinals ; secondly, because such a measure, if
proclaimed spontaneously by the Pope, would be
speedily followed by the complete destruction of the
ecclesiastical government. Now, it will be better that
the Pope should yield in this matter to the great
Powers than to his own subjects ; for then he will at
least not have given to the latter a proof of weakness. It is better for him to submit to the wish
of Europe, formally expressed, than to confess himself vanquished by his subjects, and suffer a concession to be extorted from him, which will lead to a
still more fatal consequence."

The opinion of a Cardinal on such a subject is
certainly of great weight ; and from these words of
Bernetti Italy may learn that the principle of the
Roman Court is, " Not to offer, not to accept, but to
undergo." Let Italy and England, therefore, work
so as to bring about a change of policy in the councils
of the French Emperor, and the Italians will then be
able to ascend once more the glorious steps of the
Capitol ; whilst the disastrous influence which Papal
Rome has so long exercised over Christianity will be
at an end for ever.

Venetia will of course only be obtained by arms ;
for the proud Hapsburgs will never be induced to sell
a province, even though it cost them more than it
produces. The German tendencies which, especially
since the cession of Savoy and Nice, have now and
then clouded the councils of England, encourage the

Viennese Cabinet in its determination not to come to terms with Italy. Austrian politicians are, besides, very clever in hinting the probability of imaginary dangers which, on the incorporation of Venetia with the rest of Italy, would threaten the predominance of England in the Adriatic, and even place in danger her protectorate of the Ionian Islands. But the time has gone by when the English people could be inspired with such illusive apprehensions. Even supposing the Italian kingdom to extend itself in the direction of the Julian Alps—for Istria and other provinces to the east of the Adriatic are essentially Italian, and belonged to the Republic of Venice from the thirteenth century down to 1797—England would have nothing to fear ; since, while the genius and hardihood of her sons remain, she will always retain her command of the ocean. It is true that this view is seemingly not shared by Earl Russell, whose famous despatch to Sir James Hudson, of the 31st of August, 1860, produced so painful an impression in Italy. The people of England, however, happily differ from the eminent statesman on this subject ; for they hold that the Italians have a right to embody in their country all populations of the same origin, and speaking the same language. When, therefore, the question of Venice shall be brought to an issue, Italy, which has suffered so bitterly from subjection, will not forget that, in the days of her distress, England was her constant friend.

In these, the final lines of my book, I would remind my readers that, when twenty-eight millions of human beings have made up their minds to attain national independence, they will at last succeed, whatever the obstacles in their way. This, I am certain, is the deeply-rooted purpose of all true Italians ; and it would be better for Europe to recognise at once the necessity of a fact which is on the eve of being fully accomplished, than to resist ineffectually, and submit unwillingly. Neither Imperial vacillation, nor Papal intrigues, nor Austrian bayonets, can prevail against the unalterable determination of the Italians. Founded in justice, and baptized with blood, the great idea of Italian Unity has become the abiding faith of millions—of millions with arms in their hands, and patient courage in their hearts. Till that Idea be realized in Fact, there will be no settlement of Italy—no peace for Europe. But realized it will be—must be! Trusting in Providence, and depending upon themselves, my countrymen will persevere in the struggle, deeply convinced that liberty and independence are always won by a people resolutely bent on attaining that end—a people with whom faith in the righteousness of their cause has become a second religion, and the earnest of a nobler life.

APPENDIX.

DUCHY OF PARMA.

Despatch found in the Archives of Parma, in October, 1859.

*Légation de S. A. R. le Duc de Parme à Vienne,
26 Mai, au soir, six heures et demie.* (Confidential.)

MONSIEUR LE MARQUIS,——Although I am not able to post this letter this evening, I write it in order to tell your Excellency things which are still impressed on my memory, reserving to myself to add a *post scriptum* to-morrow with the news I may have. This morning I went to see the Modenese Ambassador. He had not received any news, either from the Duke or his Ministers, since the last four or five days. Having read the telegraphic message (sent from Turin) published in the news-papers, by which he learned that his august master had left Modena, to retire to Brescello, with his troops, he waited upon Count Rechberg, to ask his Excellency whether the news was true or not. The Austrian Minister answered that he had received no information whatever about the matter. The Ambassador then telegraphed, not to Modena, but to Mautua, begging Field-Marshal Küloz to let him know some-thing about the Duke. This was done yesterday morning at six o'clock. At twelve o'clock I called on Count de Volo. He had not yet received an answer, but he expected it in the afternoon. M. de Volo having written to the Duke, accord-ing to the suggestion of Field-Marshal Hess, thinks that as, at the present moment, Austria could not send even a battalion to his (the Duke's) support, his Sovereign was, perhaps, under the necessity of withdrawing his troops from Massa and Carrara, and making them recross the Apennines before the Franco-Tuscan army had begun its forward movement. He thought, besides, that the retreat of these troops on Reggio and Brescello had, perhaps, led the Duke for a moment to leave Modena with the object of going to inspect them. This is the hypothesis offered by Monsieur de Volo; and God grant it may be true !

Count de Volo gave me the particulars about the visit that, according to the orders received from his Sovereign, he had paid to Monsieur de Rechberg, with the object of asking the help of Austria, foreseeing the imminent march of the Franco-Tuscan army on Modena. Monsieur de Rechberg answered that his Majesty the Emperor was extremely sorry (*désolé*) to be under the necessity of refusing the demand of the Duke, but that, his army being at present engaged in fighting against a superior enemy, he could not spare even a battalion; the more so as the reinforcements his Majesty had sent for could not arrive on the Po before the end of the present month. Monsieur de Volo then asked the Austrian Minister what would become of the Duke, adding that his Imperial Highness would be under the necessity of retiring from his State, for it was impossible that he could resist the forces which were on the point of coming from Tuscany. "*Que voulez-vous?*" answered M. de Rechberg. " I do not see what he can do except retire, but after awhile we shall retake his Duchy. Go and see Field-Marshal Hess; he will convince you that at present it is impossible for us to send any help to the Duke." The Count acted according to this advice ; and General Hess, referring to the map, and to the numerical condition of the Austrian army, showed that it was not practicable to withdraw any troops either from the fighting army, or from that which was garrisoning the places Austria was obliged to hold.

Your Excellency will therefore perceive how the help Austria can afford to give to the Duchies at present is reduced to the words, " We shall re-conquer the Duchies later," or to the other words which the Prime Minister addressed to me :—

" Everything shall be arranged at a later time, and her Highness will return into the possession of the States of her son,
which she will probably be obliged for a short time to abandon."
If this is all the protection which one can expect from Austria,
it is indeed a sad thing, and it was not worth our while to tie
ourselves to her by treaties (*ce n'était pas la peine de se lier
avec elle par des traités*).

I have the honour to be, Monsieur le Marquis, your Excellency's most humble servant,

J. THOMASIN.

To his Excellency the Marquis Pallavicini, Parma.

DUCHY OF MODENA.

Copy of the PETIZIONE, *or Citation, laid by the Inspector-General
of the State Appanages of the Duchy of Modena, against
Francis V. before the Modenese Tribunal.*

Protocol, No. 21432. 28 *Oct.* 1859. 1*st Head.* *Packet,* 1630.

Before Nardi, in his capacity of Inspector-General of the
State Appanages of the Modenese Provinces, and in pursuance
of the Dictatorial Decree of the 24th inst. (herewith attached), declares :—

That by order of Francis the Vth., ex-Duke of Modena,
there were borne away from the Public Library its choicest
codes and manuscripts, and from the Museum antique coins
and medals, in gold and silver, of the greatest value, viz. :

1. Illuminated Bible, in 3 vols.
2.   „   Roman Breviary.
3.   „   Office of the Blessed Virgin.
4. MSS., Provençal Poetry.   13th century.
5. Dante MS.   14th   „
6. Autographs of Tasso, 3 vols.
7.   „   „
8. Pauperum Bible.
9. Autograph Letters.   4 vols.

10. Oration of Aldo, anno 1501, in parchment.
11. Greek Gospel, 10th century.
12. Acts of the Apostles (11 c. 3).
13. Epistles of Hieronymus, MS., anno 1157.
14. Coins of Roman Consuls and Families. Packets 4.
15.   „   Roman Emperors.   „   6.
16.   „   Free Greece.   „   2.
17. D'Este Coins.   „   1.
18. Coins of the present and Middle Ages. „   5.
19. Duplicate Consular and Imperial Coins. „   1.
20. Silver Coins found at Rosola. „   1.

The which precious articles were, by order of the said ex-Duke, consigned to him, and transported out of the dominions, as per his receipt, dated April 13th, 1859, herewith produced.

These objects were and are the property of the State, and not by private right belonging to the Sovereign, who, in the opinion of all jurisconsults, has no right whatever to divert, dispense, or withdraw them from the place of their destination ; but, for the enhancement of the national splendour, dignity, and wealth, and for the study and progress of the Arts and Sciences, is even bound to the better and more careful custody of the same, in the places where they are deposited, and where they have been for ages preserved.

That the same Francis the Vth, before his departure, abstracted from the Treasury the sum of one hundred and fifty thousand Italian *lire*, alleged to be the allowance assigned from the Civil List for his maintenance during the months of June, July, and August. He likewise drew from the Exchequer another sum of six hundred thousand Italian *lire*, declared to be for military administration during the said three months : of which amount, on the 10th of June last, sixty thousand *lire* were restored by the said Administration ; so that the actual deficit——deducting from the original sum the amount returned——is six hundred and ninety thousand *lire*, as by certificate, authenticated by the Minister of Finance, herewith attached.

The subtraction of this great amount from the Public

Funds completely exhausted them, and was indubitably an illegal transaction.

A Sovereign who abandons the State and the Government, leading with him the armed force thereof to the ranks of the enemy, has no claim whatever on the Civil List, to enable him to live away from such State.

It would be an absurdity to expect that a military force, embodied, armed, and equipped at the expense of the State, should be kept up when no longer serving the purpose of its institution. Out of the dominions, it follows merely the will and caprice of its leader, who converts it into a personal escort, or Prætorian body-guard.

Such are the reasons, succinctly indicated, which support the Administrator of the State Appanages in demanding the recovery and restoration of the articles and sums above enumerated.

For the due execution, therefore, of such a right, the Plaintiff in this matter urges that, by means of a duplicate of the present document, and with the formalities prescribed by Article 155 of the Code of Procedure, Francis the Vth, ex-Duke of Modena, be summoned to pronounce and declare why he should not make restitution to the National Library and Museum of Modena all the herein-described objects, and repay to the National Treasury the above sum of six hundred and ninety thousand *lire ;* under penalty of being formally condemned for contumacy, and to refund all costs and expenses.

Save and except proceedings in the proper law courts, for the liquidation of the supposed value of the above-named precious articles, and for the prejudicial effect occasioned by their absence from the Public Library where they may not be efficiently substituted.

And save and except whatever other action may lie for other abstractions, and principally for arms and military effects.

Affirming all judicial expenses, in every instance, in short, that may be ordered by the Chancellery, for the special custody of Slip A.

Nardi, seconding the present demand, hereby cites his Royal Highness Francis the Vth of Austria and Este, now absent from these dominions (place unknown), at the end of thirty days (tripled) to respond to the present allegation ; and orders that a duplicate thereof be sent to the defendant, and publicly placarded ; and that an extract also be inserted in the official document as is ordered by Article 155 of the Code of Civil Procedure.

G. S. MANETTI.

November 7th, 1859.

DUCHY OF PARMA.

MURDER OF COLONEL ANVITI.

I.

FARINI'S PROCLAMATION.

PARMESANS !—Your city has been defiled by a hideous crime. A deep stain has been inflicted on our renown. The cause of freedom is disgraced. An insult has been cast upon Italy— that Italy which, by the generous behaviour of all her people hitherto, has been raised so high among civilized nations.

The public conscience demands a reparation ; it shall have it. The people charged me with the defence of all their rights— foremost of all with the vindication of public justice. Crime shall not be left unpunished. The name of Italy shall not be outraged in vain.

Citizens and National Guards ! Join me, and give me the strength of your compact opinion ; let us act together in the name of civilization and Italy ! Our Italian banner waves where men are lavish of life for its cause, not where a breach is made in its honour. Our good King is wounded to the soul. He is wont to rule over a people who shed their enemies' blood on the battle-field—a people who maintain freedom for themselves and win it for others, no less by their valour than by their allegiance to the law.

FARINI.

Parma, Oct. 11.

II.

GENERAL FANTI'S PROCLAMATION.

Order of the Day to the Troops of the Central Italian League.

OFFICERS, NON-COMMISSIONED OFFICERS, AND SOLDIERS!— A sense of the high mission with which I was trusted, not merely to fight the enemies of our independence, but also with equal resolution to maintain internal order, has moved me to appoint General Ribotti to the general command of the troops of the city and province of Parma.

You have all heard with the same indignation with which I am penetrated, the atrocious crime committed in Parma— a crime which reflects the greatest obloquy on the name of Italy, and which would neutralize all our warlike efforts were it suffered either to be repeated, or even to pass unpunished. The defence of the country is entrusted to hearts which beat under the soldier's garb. An Italian should give or receive death only on the battle-field. Your Generals have fought for freedom and independence. They spurn all cowardly deeds—all outrages against law and justice.

FANTI.

Modena, Oct. 11.

III.

FARINI'S PROCLAMATION, ORDERING THE GENERAL DISARMAMENT OF THE POPULATION OF PARMA.

REIGNING, HIS MAJESTY VICTOR EMMANUEL II.

The Dictator of the Provinces of Modena and Parma decrees :—

1st. In the city of Parma, all sorts of arms are to be given up to the military commander of the town, in the Palace of the Intendenza Generale, within forty-eight hours of the publication of the present ordinance.

The arms which belong to the National Guard are not included in this decree.

2nd. All the insidious arms described in Article 337 of the Penal Code will be at the same time given up to the above-mentioned authority.

3rd. Infringement of the above articles will be punished with six months' to a year's imprisonment, besides the other penalties applied by the penal code in the cases of insidious arms.

4th. For fire-arms and edged arms, which are not included in the dispositions of the 2nd article, a regular receipt will be given to the proprietors, in order that the arms may be restored in due time.

(Signed)   FARINI.

Parma, Oct. 12.

ROMAGNA.

I.

LETTER TO MONSIGNOR BEDINI, REFERRING TO THE DISTRIBUTION OF MEDALS, PRAYER-BOOKS, AND INDULGENCES.

To Monsignor Bedini, Commissioner Extraordinary of Bologna.

MOST REV. EXCELLENCY,—As you have been perhaps already informed, there are on the point of being struck at this mint 60,000 medals destined for the troops of the last foreign intervention.

Following the example of what was done in 1831, I have suggested this new distribution of medals, and have accordingly been authorized from Gaeta to have them struck.

The following are the numbers wanted :—

For the French . . . . . 32,000 ⎫
For the Spanish . . . . 10,000 ⎬ circiter.
For the Neapolitans . . . 16,000 ⎭

For the Austrians, your Excellency will send me as soon as possible the required number. Thirty thousand have already been struck, and at the end of the month the work will be, I hope, entirely accomplished. I notice here that the French want to send them as well to the families of the soldiers who fell on the battle-field. I have moreover been authorized to have printed 12,000 prayer-books, together with as many indulgences. They are eagerly asked for, and the great demand has obliged me to have them translated likewise into Spanish. I do not wish that the Austrians should also ask for them. I do not speak of this matter at Portici; but I pray you to consider the question in regard to political convenience. It might, perhaps, displease the Austrian Generals not to receive them when they see that they have been distributed to the French and Spanish soldiers. If there is a real necessity for having the book printed in German, we must do it with the usual type, for at Rome we have not the German. I have wished to inform your Excellency about this affair, for I should not like that one day you should say to me, " Why did you not inform me of it ?" In case your most reverend Excellency should approve it, and should consider my suggestion calculated to secure still more the sympathy of the Austrians, it is better you should write to Portici about it, without, however, mentioning my name. In case this work should be ordered, we shall do it in the printing-house of the Government, for several reasons, and especially for economy's sake.

Hoping for a prompt answer, I remain, with the greatest respect and veneration, your most reverend Excellency's most humble, obedient servant,

T. MORESCHI.

Rome, Jan. 7, 1850.

II.

EDICT OF THE HOLY INQUISITION.

(Issued from Pesaro in 1841.)

We, Brother Filippo Bertolotti, of the order of preachers, professor of theology in the towns of Pesaro, Rimini, Fano,

VOL. II.   E E

Pennabilli, and of the surrounding places, Inquisitor-General of the Holy Apostolic See, and especially appointed against heretical depravity.

According to the charge imposed upon us by this Holy Office, we desire to maintain the Catholic faith pure from every heretical contagion; but, it being manifest that many, from malice, disobedience, and ignorance, are slack in fulfilling their duty of denouncing such crimes to the Holy Office, thus causing great inconvenience and errors, and militating, not only against good morals, but expressly against the Catholic faith, we,—who are bound to take the glory of the Lord to heart, and to promulgate and preserve the holy faith, and to watch over the salvation of souls, command accordingly, under pain of excommunication and other penalties of the Pontiff, that all, no matter of what condition or dignity, ecclesiastical or laical, reveal and make known to us, and to the Holy Office anywhere and everywhere, within the period of a month, everything they have known or may know of offenders.

Whether they are heretics, or suspected or supposed to be heretics, or whether they adhere to Judaism, Mahometanism, or Gentilism, or whether they have become apostates from the holy Catholic faith.

Whether they have practised or are practising acts that may be ascribed " to an express or tacit compact with the devil," such as incantations, witchcraft, &c., prayers to discover treasures, or for other purposes of the kind, and all sorts of invocations where his name or his acts are concerned. Whether they exercise necromancy or any other magic, abusing the Sacrament, or holy and blessed things.

Whether, not being priests, they have usurped with sacrilegious daring the right to celebrate mass, or to administer to the penitent.

Whether they keep or have kept secret conventicles, or reunions likely to prejudice the holy Catholic religion. Whether they have been guilty of making use of oaths against the blessed Lord, the Holy Virgin, or the saints, or otherwise been guilty of any act against holy images.

Whether, in spite of their oaths, they have entered, or endeavoured to enter, into a contract of matrimony. Whether, with the first wife living, or the first husband, they have taken a second, or attempted to do so, or have in any way interfered with the Holy Office of the Inquisition, or with the Bull of his Holiness Pius V. Whether they have written satires or published writings against the Pope, the Sacred College, superiors, ecclesiastics, or religious orders; or composed and distributed writings likely to be detrimental to the holy word; or whether they possess writings or prints containing heresies, or books of heretics, speaking ex-professo against religion; or whether they read, print, or allow to be printed and distributed such things under any pretext. Whether they are persons who without a licence have eaten, or given to eat, meat, eggs, and the like, on a prohibited day; whether they have induced a Christian to become a Jew, or of any other religion; whether they have prevented a Jew or a Turk becoming baptized. We declare that those who do not denounce such acts cannot be absolved, and must be excommunicated. On purpose that this edict shall be generally known, we command its publication in every church and public place, so that nobody shall remain ignorant of it, and nobody evade its commands. We charge all publishers, librarians, shopkeepers, and hotel-keepers, to stick up the present edict in their respective places publicly, where everybody can see and read it.

The first, nay, the only object of the tribunal of the Holy Office being the glory of the Lord, the glorification of the holy faith, and the salvation of souls, we have commanded, and command as above, all those who consider themselves guilty, or who know others to be guilty, to present themselves before us or our substitutes voluntarily, before being denounced by others, and to confess sincerely and honestly their errors and failings, assuring them that, "unless accused by other legitimate ecclesiastical tribunals," they will be received with a charitable heart, and treated with particular mercy—a mercy very natural to the Holy Inquisition; and that they will be expedited and delivered without any expense, or any public penance.

According to the obligations imposed upon us concerning prints or books, we expressly command that no one dare to print, import, sell, or distribute books within or without our jurisdiction, unless such books have been previously submitted to the Holy Office. Adhering, besides, to the edicts of the supreme tribunal of the Holy Office at Rome, concerning any intercourse with Hebrews, viz., "cohabiting, associating, or living in familiar contact with them," we command that nobody dare to trangress such edicts, under the penalty therein expressed and promulgated.

Given at the Holy Office at Pesaro, on the 15th Sept., 1841.
Brother FILIPPO BERTOLOTTI, Inquisitor-General.
ANTONIO SEVERINI, Chancellor-General of the Holy Office.

SOUTHERN ITALY.

List of Neapolitan Nobles who have adhered to the Government of Victor Emmanuel.

Among the persons of distinction I am about to enumerate —all ex-subjects of Francis II.—some have returned to Naples after having quitted it in the first moments of the crisis, others have accepted appointments or retiring pensions, and all, whether as simple commoners or otherwise, have had abundant opportunities, official and non-official, of pronouncing in favour of the great programme, " Italy and Victor Emmanuel." The list to which I have alluded in the body of this work is as follows :—

1st. *Senators of the Kingdom of Italy.*—The Duke of Atri Acquaviva ; the Baron Alfonso Barracco ; the Duke of Cirella Catalano Gonzaga ; the Cavaliere Andrea Colonna, of the Princes of Stigliano ; the Cavaliere Gioachino Colonna, of the Princes of Stigliano ; the Marquis d'Afflitto of Montefalcone ; the Prince of Sangro Fondi ; the Marquis Louis Dragonetti ; the Marquis Gagliardi ; the Count Gallone of Nociglia, of the Princes of Tricase ; the Count Genoino ; the Prince Pignatelli Strongoli ; the Marquis of Salluzzo ; the Marquis Tupputi ; the Baron Bellelli ; the Count M. Amari ; the Marquis R. Bonelli ; the Count of Terranova

Correale; General Commander de Sauget; the Marquis of Gregorio; the Baron della Bruca; the Marquis of Riso Tancredi; the Prince of San Cataldo of Fiumesolato; the Marquis San Guiliano; the Marquis Sagarriga; the Count Lanza of Sommatino, of the Princes of Butera; the Marquis Torres; the Prince of San Guiseppe Pandolfini; the Prince of Fitalia Settimo; the Prince Torremozza; the Marquis Spitalieri of Mugghia; the Prince of St. Elia Trigona.   Total, 32.

2nd. Deputies to the National Parliament sitting at Turin.—The Duke of Terranova, P. Serra Montesantangelo; the Cavaliere Gerardo Bruzzano Carafa, of the Princes of Roccella; the Count Castellana Acquaviva Conversano, of the Dukes of Atri; the Marquis Caracciolo Bella, formerly Envoy Extraordinary from the King of Italy to Lisbon; the Baron Jean Barracco; the Count of Camaldoli Ricciardi; the Prince Vincent Spinelli of Scalea; the Cavaliere O. Lanza, of the Princes of Trabia; the Marquis Atenolfi of Castelnovo; the Cavaliere Mezzacapo, of the Marquises of Monterusso; the Baron Ch. Poerio; the Cavaliere Compagno; the Count Rendina di Campomaggiore; the Duke of Caballino Castromediano; the Baron Stocco; the Baron Mazziotti; the Marquis Bonaccorsi of Casolotto; the Baron Majorano Cucuzzella; the Baron d'Ondes Reggio; the Baron Schinina of San Filippo; the Marquis of Torrearsa; the Baron Turrisi Colonna; the Baron Pisani; the Baron Nicotera.   Total, 24.

3rd. Dignitaries or Functionaries nominated by the Italian Government (positions at Court, in Diplomacy, Army and Navy, Staff, and Chief Magistracy).—The Duke of Sant Arpino Caracciolo; the Cavaliere Somma, of the Princes of Colle; the Duke de Grisolia Gonzaga Cirella; the Cavaliere Gerardo Quarto, of the Dukes of Belgioioso; the Baron Riso, of Colobria; the Prince O. Gaetani of Piedimonte Lamenzana; the Count Constantino Ludolf, diplomatist under the fallen régime; the Cavaliere Caraffa di Traetto, idem; the Cavaliere Curtopassi, idem; the General Filippo Colonna, of the Princes of Stigliano; Admiral the Marquis Garofalo; the Baron Broceletti; the Count de Montfort; the Cavaliere de Renzis, of the Barons of Montanaro; the Cavaliere A. Dentice of Frasso; the young

Marquis Tupputi; the Cavaliere San Felice, of the Dukes of Bagnoli; the Cavaliere Giacomo Winspeare (brother of a diplomatist, and of an officer faithful to the fallen monarchy); the Cavaliere de Sangro of Sansevero; the Duke of Noja de Gregorio, of the Princes of Sant Elia.   Total, 20.

4th. *Adherents to the New Régime.*——The Prince d'Avellino; the Duke of Fragnito; Montalto, Prince of Lequile; the Duke of Bovino; the Marquis del Vasto Pescara; the Prince of Sansevero; the Marquis of Genzano Sangro; the Duke of Forli Carafa, Count of Policastro; the Baron S. Borracco; the Baron M. Barracco; the Marquis Salsa; the Prince Hector Pignatelli Monteleone; the Duke Laurito Montfort; the Duke of Marigliano; the Prince of San Lorenzo; the Duke of Castagneto; the Duke Gaetano Caracciolo of Castagneto; the Duke del Vasto of Santa Lucia; the Marquis of Bugnano; the Cavaliere Piccolellis; the Duke of Castrovillari-Friozzi; the Count Balsorano Lefébvre; the Prince of Villafranca; the Prince Niscemi; the Marquis Ugo; the Cavaliere Gravina, of the Princes of Valdisavoia; the Duke of Arinella; the Prince Giardinelli; the Marquis of San Giovanni; the Prince of Carini La Grua, the Younger; the Marquis Cimino di Valenzano; the Cavaliere M. Cimino di Valenzano; the Cavaliere F. Cimino di Valenzano; the Marquis Paolo Ulloa; the Count N. Gabrielli; the Baron de Blasio of Palizzi; the Marquis Trentola; the Duke of Accadia; the Baron Savarese; the Baron Guglielmo Acton; Count Capece Latro; Baron Drammis; the Baron Francesco Zezza of Zapponeto; the Marquis of Rivadebro Serra Cassano; the Marquis de Santasilia; the Marquis Casanova; the Duke Cardinale Serra; the Cavaliere Trigona Sant' Elia; the Prince of Sant' Elia de Gregorio; the Cavaliere Pisicelli; the Marquis of Rodio; the Cavaliere Mario Tufo, of the Marquises of Matino; Prince Cesarò Colonna; Prince of Ottajano.   Total, 54.   Total of the four classes, 130.

THE ROMAN QUESTION.

BARON RICASOLI'S LETTER TO CARDINAL ANTONELLI.

Turin, August, 1861.

EMINENCE,—The Government of his Majesty King Victor Emmanuel, seriously concerned at the disastrous consequences which may be caused, both in religious and in political order, by the attitude of the Court of Rome towards the Italian nation and its Government, is desirous of making one more appeal to the mind and heart of the Holy Father, in order that in his wisdom and goodness he may consent to an agreement which, while leaving intact the rights of the nation, may effectually provide for the dignity and greatness of the Church. I have the honour to transmit to your Eminence the letter which, by the express order of his Majesty the King, I have humbly addressed to his Holiness. Your Eminence, by the high dignity with which you are invested in the Church, by the important place which you occupy in the administration of the State, not less than by the confidence which his Holiness places in you, may, under these circumstances, give, better than any one else, useful and acceptable counsels. Your Eminence can scarcely fail to add to an appreciation of the true interests of the Church a sentiment favourable to the prosperity of the nation to which you belong my birth. I hope, therefore, your Eminence will apply yourself to the achievement of a task by which you will have deserved well, not only of the Holy See and of Italy, but of the whole Catholic world.

RICASOLI.

BARON RICASOLI'S LETTER TO THE POPE.

To His Holiness Pope Pius IX.

Turin, August, 1861.

MOST HOLY FATHER,—Twelve years have elapsed since Italy, moved by words of gentleness and pardon which came from your lips, conceived the hope of closing the series of its secular misfortunes, and beginning the era of its regeneration. But, as the Powers of the earth had divided the land among different masters, and kept it under patronage and subjection, the work of regeneration could not peaceably develope itself within our frontiers, and it was necessary to resort to arms to free ourselves from the foreign domination encamped in our midst, in order that civil reforms might not be impeded, or stifled and annihilated, in their birth.

You, then, Most Holy Father, remembering that you are upon earth the representative of a God of peace and mercy and the Father of all the faithful, refused your co-operation to the Italians in their sacred cause of independence. But, as you are also an Italian Prince, this determination filled them with great bitterness. Men's minds were irritated, and the tie of concord which had rendered so happy and effectual the beginning of our revival was broken; the national disasters which almost immediately followed still further inflamed the excited passions of the people, and, after a fatal succession of deplorable events which we all desire to forget, there commenced between the Italian nation and the Apostolic See a fatal conflict, which is but too active now, and which is equally prejudicial to both.

Every contest must end either by the defeat or death of one of the combatants, or by their reconciliation. The rights of nationality are imperishable, and the See of Holy Peter, by virtue of a Divine promise, is imperishable also. Since neither of the two adversaries can disappear from the field of battle, they must become reconciled, so that the world may not be thrown into terrible and endless perturbations. As a Catholic and as an Italian, I have deemed it my duty, most Holy

Father, to meditate long and profoundly on the difficult problem which the times have given us to solve. As a Minister of the Italian Kingdom, I have judged it my duty to submit to your Holiness the considerations according to which a reconciliation between the Holy See and the Italian nation may be regarded, not only as possible, but as extremely useful, the necessity being more evident than ever. In thus acting, I follow not only the impulse of my own inner sentiment and the duties of my office; I obey the express wish of his Majesty the King, who, faithful to the glorious and pious traditions of his House, is animated by an equal love for the greatness of Italy and the greatness of the Catholic Church. This reconciliation would be impossible, and the Italians, eminently Catholic, would dare neither to ask nor to hope for it, if, in order to obtain it, the Church would have to abandon one of those principles and rights which belong to the treasury of the faith, or which are part of the immortal institution of the God-Man. What we ask is, that the Church, which, as the interpreter and guardian of the Gospel, has brought into human society a principle of supernatural legislation, and has become the initiator of social progress, should pursue its Divine mission, and demonstrate still more the necessity of its existence, by the inexhaustible fruitfulness of its relations with the work already commenced and inspired by it. If, at every step in society's progress, the Church were not capable of creating new forms upon which the successive stages of social life may be founded, the Church would not be a universal and perpetual institution, but a temporary and perishable thing. God is immutable in His essence, and nevertheless displays an infinite fertility in the creation of new substances and in the production of new forms.

The Church has hitherto given striking evidence of this fruitfulness by wisely accommodating itself to the civil world at every new development of society. Will those who in the present times contend that it should remain immovable dare to affirm that it has never changed externally, in that which relates to its forms? Will they dare to assert that the forms of the Church have been from Leo X. until now what they were from Gregory VII. to Leo X., and that since Gre-

gory VII. they have been what they were between Holy
Peter and that Pontiff?   It was a great spectacle in the early
times to see the Church in the catacombs, poor and ignored by
the world, gathered together for the contemplation of eternal
truths.   But, when the faithful became free,—when they left
their concealment, and contracted new ties with each other,—
the altar passed from the obscurity of the catacombs to the
splendour of the temples.   The worship and the ministers of
the worship participated in this new state of things, and the
Church, no longer restricted to secret prayers, publicly and
solemnly spread its doctrine in the world, over which it began
to exert its sublime mission.   In the medley and contest of
different and often contrary elements by which the modern
era was preparing itself in the midst of the Middle Ages, the
Christian idea, thanks to the Church, penetrated into the orders
of the family, the city, and the State; it created in men's
consciences the dogma of a public law; it was able in its
legislation to determine the application, and to cause to be felt
the advantages, of that law; and then the Church became a
civil power, and made itself the judge of princes and peoples.
When, however, society had attained a more perfect degree of
education,—when its reason had been exercised and enlightened,—the necessity for this clerical tutelage ceased, and consequently the tie of that tutelage was broken.   The traditions
of an ancient civilization were sought and recovered; and a
Pontiff associating himself with this work deserved to give
his name to the century in which he lived.

   If, then, the Church, imitating God, its supreme model,
who, in His almightiness and infallibility, controls with infinite wisdom the exercise of His power, so as not to injure
human liberty; if the Church has hitherto known how to
accommodate itself, while preserving intact the purity of its
dogmas, to the necessities imposed by social transformations;
are not those who injure and prejudice it the men who would
wish to make it immovable, to isolate it from civil society, and
to render it the enemy of the spirit of modern times, rather
than we, who ask but one thing—namely, that it preserve its
supreme spiritual functions, and that it may be in the moral
order the moderator of that liberty which gives to peoples

arrived at the maturity of their reason the right to obey neither laws nor governments to which they have not legitimately consented? As the Church, by its constitution, cannot be the enemy of a proper civil liberty, neither can it be opposed to the development of the nationalities. It is by virtue of a providential design that the human species is found distributed in groups distinct by race and language, and established in certain definite territories, where each has contracted a certain unity of tendencies and institutions, so that it does not trouble the habitation of another, and suffers no interference with its own. God has shown what value man ought to attach to his nationality when, wishing to punish the Hebrew people, rebellious against warnings and chastisements, He inflicted foreign domination upon them as the most terrible punishment of all. You yourself have well shown it, Holy Father, when, writing to the Emperor of Austria in 1848, you exhorted him "to put an end to a war which cannot conquer for the Empire the spirit of the Lombards and the Venetians, rightfully jealous of their nationality." The Christian idea does not permit that the social power should issue in the oppression of one individual by another; it does not permit the oppression of one nation by another. Conquest cannot legalize the domination of one nation over another; for force is powerless to constitute right.

Thus, the Italians, in recovering their rights as a nation, and forming a kingdom with free institutions, have attacked no principle of religious or of civil order. They have not found in their faith as Christians and Catholics any precept which condemns their work. The proof that, in entering on the paths which Providence has opened to them, they have not entertained the idea of disregarding religion or injuring the Church, is to be found in the joy and veneration with which they encircled you in the early days of your Pontificate; and in the profound grief and unutterable concern with which they received the encyclic of the 29th of April, 1848. They had to deplore the conflict which unhappily took place in your soul between the duties of the Pontiff and those of the Prince; they desired that an agreement might be effected between the two eminent characters united in your sacred person. But, unfortunately, repeated protests and significant acts convinced them that this agreement was not possible. Then, not being able to renounce their own existence, their indefeasible rights as a nation, any more than they could give up the faith of their fathers, they deemed it necessary that the Prince should cede to the Pontiff. The Italians could not but observe the contradictions into which the meeting of these two attributes frequently caused the Apostolic See to fall. These contradictions, in embittering men's minds against the Prince, added nothing certainly to their respect for the Pontiff. They began, then, to examine the origin of this power, the manner of its existence, the use which has been made of it; and it must be avowed that in several respects this examination was not favourable to it. They inquired as to its necessity, as to its usefulness relatively to the Church. From this point of view, also, public opinion did not pronounce favourably. The Gospel contains numerous words and examples of contempt and condemnation of terrestrial wealth, and Jesus Christ himself often warned His disciples not to dream of possession and domination; and we do not find one of the doctors or theologians of the Church who affirm that political sovereignty is indispensable to the exercise of the holy ministry. There was a time, perhaps, when all rights were uncertain, and a prey to force, during which the prestige of a temporal sovereignty contributed to the independence of the Church. But since modern States have left the chaos of the Middle Ages—since they have become consolidated by the association of their natural elements, and the public European law is founded upon a just and reasonable basis—what advantage can the Church find in the possession of a little kingdom which throws it into the agitations, contradictions, and embarrassments of politics; in which it is distracted by the care of its mundane interests from the pursuit of its celestial good, and is enslaved to the jealousies, cupidities, and intrigues of the Powers of the earth? I would, Holy Father, that the rectitude of your conscience and the goodness of your heart would alone judge if this be just, useful, or expedient for the Holy See and the Church. This deplorable conflict has the saddest consequences for Italy as well as for the Church.

The clergy are already divided; the flock is separated from its pastors. There are prelates, bishops, and priests who openly refuse to take part in the war which is being waged from Rome against the Kingdom of Italy: a much greater number loathe that war in secret. The multitude see with indignation ministers of the sanctuary mixing in conspiracies against the State, and refusing to the public voice the prayers which are asked of them by the authorities. They groan with impatience when they hear the Divine Word abused from the pulpit, so as to make it an instrument of censure and malediction against all that the Italians have learnt to admire and bless. The multitude, little accustomed to subtle distinctions, may in the end be led to impute to religion that which is but the act of men who are its ministers, and to separate from that communion to which for eighteen centuries the Italians have had the glory and happiness to belong.

Do not, Holy Father, cast into the abyss of doubt an entire people who sincerely desire to be able to believe and to venerate you. The Church needs to be free; we will give it its entire liberty. More than any one we wish that the Church may be free; for its liberty is the guarantee of ours. But to be free it must disentangle itself from the ties of politics, which have hitherto made it an instrument of war against us in the hands of this or that Power. The Church has the eternal truth to teach, with the authority of its Divine Founder, whose assistance is never wanting to it. It should be the mediator between combatants, the protectress of the feeble and the oppressed. But how much more reverently will its voice be listened to when not open to the suspicion that worldly interests inspire it!

You can, Holy Father, once more change the face of the world; you can raise the Apostolic See to a height unknown to the Church during past ages. If you wish to be greater than the Kings of the earth, free yourself from the miseries of this Royalty which makes you only their equal. Italy will give you a secure see, an entire liberty, a new grandeur. She venerates the Pontiff, but she cannot arrest her march before the Prince; she wishes to remain Catholic, but she wishes to be a nation free and independent. If you listen to the prayer of this favourite daughter, you will gain in souls more power than you have lost as a Prince; and from the height of the Vatican, when stretching your hand over Rome and the world to bless them, you will see the nations, re-established in their rights, bending before you, their defender and their protector.

ARTICLES PROPOSED FOR THE ACCEPTANCE OF THE POPE.

Article 1. The Sovereign Pontiff preserves the dignity, the inviolability, and all the other prerogatives of the sovereignty, and, in addition, the precedence established by custom over the King and other Sovereigns. The Cardinals of the Holy Church shall retain the title of Prince, and the honours which are attached to it.

Art. 2. The Government of his Majesty the King of Italy pledges itself not to interpose an obstacle on any occasion to the acts performed by the Sovereign Pontiff in virtue of his Divine right as Chief of the Church, and of the canonical law as Patriarch of the West and Primate of Italy.

Art. 3. The same Government recognises the right of the Sovereign Pontiff to send nuncios abroad, and undertakes to protect them so long as they shall be in the territory of the State.

Art. 4. The Sovereign Pontiff shall have full liberty of communication with the Bishops and all the faithful, and, reciprocally, without interference on the part of the Government. He shall also be able to convoke, in the places and in the forms that he shall judge expedient, the councils and the ecclesiastical synods.

Art. 5. The Bishops in their dioceses, and the curates in their parishes, shall be exempt from all Governmental interference in the exercise of their ministry.

Art. 6. They shall live, notwithstanding, in subjection to the common law in regard to offences punished by the laws of the kingdom.

Art. 7. His Majesty renounces entirely the right of patronage as respects ecclesiastical benefices.

Art. 8. The Italian Government renounces all interference in the nomination of Bishops.

Art. 9. The same Government undertakes to furnish to the Holy See a fixed and irrevocable dotation, the amount of which shall be regulated by mutual consent.

Art. 10. The Government of his Majesty the King of Italy, in order that all the Powers and all the Catholic nations may contribute to the maintenance of the Holy See, will open with those Powers the proper negotiations for determining the quota of each of them in the dotation spoken of in the preceding article.

Art. 11. The negotiations shall also be directed towards obtaining guarantees for what is established in the preceding articles.

Art. 12. In accordance with these conditions, the Sovereign Pontiff and the Government of his Majesty the King of Italy shall come to an agreement by means of commissioners delegated for that purpose.

THE END.

VOL. I.—SAM SLICK'S NATURE AND HUMAN NATURE.

Messrs Hurst and Blackett have very fitly inaugurated their Standard Library of Popular Modern Works with this admirable volume.   With regard to this we can truly say :—Who can tire of the genuine sallies, the deep wisdom wrapped up in merry guise, and the side-splitting outbursts of genuine wit, in the pages of Haliburton? 'Nature and Human Nature' is particularly full of all these qualities; and to those who love a good laugh, when they can enjoy it accompanied by good matter for reflection, and who have not yet read this production of Sam Slick, we can heartily recommend this elegant Edition."—*Critic.*

" The first volume of Messrs Hurst and Blackett's Standard Library of Cheap Editions forms a very good beginning to what will doubtless be a very successful undertaking. 'Nature and Human Nature' is one of the best of Sam Slick's witty and humorous productions, and well entitled to the large circulation which it cannot fail to obtain in its present convenient and cheap shape.   The volume combines with the great recommendations of a clear, bold type, and good paper, the lesser, but attractive merits, of being well illustrated and elegantly bound."—*Post.*

VOL. II.—JOHN HALIFAX, GENTLEMAN.

" This is a very good and a very interesting work.   It is designed to trace the career from boyhood to age of a perfect man—a Christian gentleman, and it abounds in incident both well and highly wrought.   Throughout it is conceived in a high spirit, and written with great ability.   This cheap and handsome new edition is worthy to pass freely from hand to hand as a gift book in many households."—*Examiner.*

" The new and cheaper edition of this interesting work will doubtless meet with great success.   John Halifax, the hero of this most beautiful story, is no ordinary hero, and this his history is no ordinary book.   It is a full-length portrait of a true gentleman, one of nature's own nobility.   It is also the history of a home, and a thoroughly English one. The work abounds in incident, and many of the scenes are full of graphic power and true pathos.   It is a book that few will read without becoming wiser and better.—*Scotsman.*

" 'John Halifax' is more than worthy of the author's reputation.   We consider, indeed, that it is her best work.   There are in it many passages of beautiful writing. The closing scenes are deeply pathetic, and few will lay down the book without tearful eyes.   'John Halifax' is a picture, drawn with a masterly hand, of one of nature's gentlemen.   Everybody who ever reads a novel should read this one."—*Critic.*

" The story is very interesting.   The attachment between John Halifax and his wife is beautifully painted, as are the pictures of their domestic life, and the growing up of their children; and the conclusion of the book is beautiful and touching."—*Athenæum.*

VOL. III.—THE CRESCENT AND THE CROSS.
BY ELIOT WARBURTON.

" Independent of its value as an original narrative, and its useful and interesting information, this work is remarkable for the colouring power and play of fancy with which its descriptions are enlivened.   Among its greatest and most lasting charms is its reverent and serious spirit."—*Quarterly Review.*

" A book calculated to prove more practically useful was never penned than 'The Crescent and the Cross'—a work which surpasses all others in its homage for the sublime and its love for the beautiful in those famous regions consecrated to everlasting immortality in the annals of the prophets, and which no other writer has ever depicted with a pencil at once so reverent and so picturesque."—*Sun.*

[CONTINUED ON THE FOLLOWING PAGES.]

HURST AND BLACKETT'S STANDARD LIBRARY
(CONTINUED).

VOL. IV.—NATHALIE. BY JULIA KAVANAGH.

" ' Nathalie' is Miss Kavanagh's best imaginative effort. Its manner is gracious and attractive. Its matter is good. A sentiment, a tenderness, are commanded by her which are as individual as they are elegant. We should not soon come to an end were we to specify all the delicate touches and attractive pictures which place 'Nathalie' high among books of its class."—*Athenæum*.

" A more judicious selection than Nathalie could not have been made for Messrs Hurst and Blackett's Standard Library. The series as it advances realises our first impression, that it will be one of lasting celebrity."—*Literary Gazette*.

VOL. V.—A WOMAN'S THOUGHTS ABOUT WOMEN.
BY THE AUTHOR OF "JOHN HALIFAX, GENTLEMAN."

" A book of sound counsel. It is one of the most sensible works of its kind, well-written, true-hearted, and altogether practical. Whoever wishes to give advice to a young lady may thank the author for means of doing so."—*Examiner*.

" These thoughts are good and humane. They are thoughts we would wish women to think: they are much more to the purpose than the treatises upon the women and daughters of England, which were fashionable some years ago, and these thoughts mark the progress of opinion, and indicate a higher tone of character, and a juster estimate of woman's position."—*Athenæum*.

" This really valuable volume ought to be in every young woman's hand. It will teach her how to think and how to act. We are glad to see it in this Standard Library."—*Literary Gazette*.

" These thoughts are worthy of the earnest and enlightened mind, the all-embracing charity, and the well-earned reputation of the author of 'John Halifax.' "—*Herald*.

VOL. VI.—ADAM GRAEME OF MOSSGRAY.
BY THE AUTHOR OF "MRS MARGARET MAITLAND."

" 'Adam Graeme' is a story awakening genuine emotions of interest and delight by its admirable pictures of Scottish life and scenery. The plot is cleverly complicated, and there is great vitality in the dialogue, and remarkable brilliancy in the descriptive passages, as who that has read 'Margaret Maitland' would not be prepared to expect? But the story has a 'mightier magnet still,' in the healthy tone which pervades it, in its feminine delicacy of thought and diction, and in the truly womanly tenderness of its sentiments. The eloquent author sets before us the essential attributes of Christian virtue, their deep and silent workings in the heart, and their beautiful manifestations in the life, with a delicacy, a power, and a truth which can hardly be surpassed."
—*Morning Post*.

VOL. VII.—SAM SLICK'S WISE SAWS
AND MODERN INSTANCES.

" We have not the slightest intention to criticise this book. Its reputation is made, and will stand as long as that of Scott's or Bulwer's Novels. The remarkable originality of its purpose, and the happy description it affords of American life and manners, still continue the subject of universal admiration. To say thus much is to say enough, though we must just mention that the new edition forms a part of the Publishers' Cheap Standard Library, which has included some of the very best specimens of light literature that ever have been written."—*Messenger*.

VOL. VIII.—CARDINAL WISEMAN'S RECOLLECTIONS
OF THE LAST FOUR POPES.

" A picturesque book on Rome and its ecclesiastical sovereigns, by an eloquent Roman Catholic. Cardinal Wiseman has here treated a special subject with so much generality and geniality, that his recollections will excite no ill-feeling in those who are most conscientiously opposed to every idea of human infallibility represented in Papal domination."—*Athenæum*.

CPSIA information can be obtained
at www.ICGtesting.com
Printed in the USA
BVHW081615220819
556561BV00018B/3937/P